Taxation at the European Court of Human Rights

Taxation at the European Court of Human Rights

Robert Attard
Paulo Pinto de Albuquerque

Wolters Kluwer

Published by:
Kluwer Law International B.V.
PO Box 316
2400 AH Alphen aan den Rijn
The Netherlands
E-mail: lrs-sales@wolterskluwer.com
Website: www.wolterskluwer.com/en/solutions/kluwerlawinternational

Sold and distributed by:
Wolters Kluwer Legal & Regulatory U.S.
920 Links Avenue
Landisville, PA 17538
United States of America
E-mail: customer.service@wolterskluwer.com

ISBN 978-94-035-1896-1

e-Book: ISBN 978-94-035-2006-3
web-PDF: ISBN 978-94-035-2016-2

Table of Contents

Acknowledgement

We feel we must acknowledge the assistance of the following persons who helped us in different stages in the publication of this book: Alida Mizzi, Ben Kiekebeld, Claire Chouzenoux, Ivan Mifsud, Jack Attard, Lisa Zoltowska, Mariah Sapiano, Marthea Grech, Miriam Haidara, Pasquale Pistone, Philip Baker, Piers Gardner, Roberta Attard, Yana Marie Busuttil, the Chartered Institute of Taxation, the Faculty of Law of the Portuguese Catholic University (Lisbon), the Faculty of Law at the University of Malta, the Malta Institute of Management, Society Education and EY Malta.

Prologue

AN UNINVITED GUEST

The tax judgments of the European Court of Human Rights (ECtHR) are characterised by an element of hesitation. The Judges of the ECtHR are wary of 'giving the devil the benefit of the law'.[1] Upon reading the tax jurisprudence of the ECtHR one tends to form the view that the ECtHR is reluctant to interfere in matters that are perceived as not quite pertinent to its domain. Pronouncements on matters of fiscal policy are perceived as being intrusions, and the ECtHR threads carefully an approach which, when viewed in the broader history of the European Convention on Human Rights (ECHR),[2] is entirely understandable.

The ECHR was signed at Rome in November 1950 at a time when Rome was still scarred by the ravages of the Second World War. The smouldering city had been liberated from the Nazis less than six years earlier, and its drafters were coming to terms with the moral post-traumatic stress disorder caused by a war that had been characterised by unprecedented brutality and depravity.

Europe was recovering from the horrors of the Nazi concentration Camps, and the ECHR was Europe's response to the Universal Declaration of Human Rights proclaimed by the General Assembly of the United Nations on 10 December 1948.[3] The Universal Declaration had not mentioned tax with its main concern being 'to secure freedom from torture, unjustified imprisonment, summary execution, enforced disappearance, persecution and unjust discrimination, as well as fair access to education, economic opportunities, and adequate resources and health-care'. Taxation crept into the jurisprudence of the ECtHR by stealth.

1. This expression was first by Robert Bolt in *A Man for All Seasons*.
2. Viewed at https://www.echr.coe.int/Documents/Convention_ENG.pdf in May 2022.
3. Viewed at https://www.un.org/en/udhrbook/pdf/udhr_booklet_en_web.pdf in May 2022.

A LEAGUE OF EXTRAORDINARY GENTLEMEN

The ECHR was the masterwork of some of the finest military and legal veterans of the Second World War, a league of extraordinary gentlemen. In their debates leading to the creation of the ECHR they spoke of the mammoth task of securing 'the foundation of justice and peace in the world', but they were avant-garde enough to anticipate that even tax had the potential of becoming an instrument of oppression. Thus, the dangerous phenomenon of unfair taxation was put up for discussion. Nazism had been vanquished, but the world was aware that predatory Communist regimes were as dangerous.

The first to mention taxation was M. Edberg, the Swedish rapporteur who, in August 1949, raised the point 'as to how far the taxation of property should go'.[4] M. Tiegen, the French rapporteur, asked the question 'whether fiscal charges ... could be brought before the Court'.[5] Mr M. Azara, the Italian rapporteur pointed out to the principle of subsidiarity underpinning the ECHR, 'each State may decide, through its legislative power, in what form and to what extent the right of the individual should be conformable to the general interest'.[6]

Sir David Maxwell-Fyfe of Nuremburg-trial fame remarked that 'As far as taxation is concerned ... we distinguish between arbitrary confiscation and legislation to ensure that possessions are used in accordance with the general interest.'[7]

In September 1951, the Assembly concluded that the text dealing with the Article on the Right to Property would be 'expanded to make it clear that this article does not prevent the State from collecting taxes, or other penalties such as fines, even though they might constitute the whole of the property of the individual in question'.[8] Taxation would be allowed as a necessary derogation to the sacred right to property, but Hettier de Boislambert, a veteran of the French resistance and an aristocrat descending from French property owning gentry, warned that 'We cannot go into details of the idea of property, to the extent of mentioning legal action on fiscal matters, without ever clearly stating that property acquired or inherited or coming from any other source mentioned a moment ago by M. Tiegen, must be protected and defended.'[9]

The die was cast; the very same matters identified by the ECHR's rapporteurs would return to haunt the Judges of the ECtHR, taking pride of place in some of their most intriguing tax judgments.

AN HONOURABLE MENTION

The subject of taxation barely features in the text of ECHR at all. Taxation is mentioned only once and in a context that, rather than conferring rights, limits their application.

4. Council of Europe, Travaux Preparatoires de l' Article 1er du premier Protocole additional à la Convention Européenne des Droits de l' Homme (Strasbourg 1976) p. 19.
5. *Ibid.*, p. 40.
6. *Ibid.*, p. 68.
7. *Ibid.*, p. 95.
8. *Ibid.*, p. 158.
9. *Ibid.*, p. 167.

Taxation is specifically mentioned in the proviso to Article 1 of Protocol 1 ECHR, and its role there will be discussed in Chapter 1. Nonetheless, references to public prerogatives pertinent to taxation are present in several articles in the ECHR, and such references create an implied normative framework that has heavily influenced the tax jurisprudence of the ECtHR.

The preamble to the ECHR establishes that in assuming the responsibility to secure the rights and freedoms defined in the ECHR, State Signatories 'enjoy a margin of appreciation, subject to the supervisory jurisdiction of the European Court of Human Rights established by this Convention'. The extant of such margin of appreciation and the ECtHR's appetite to exercise supervisory jurisdiction over States' margin of appreciation in taxation matters is a core theme of this book. In addition, several articles concede that certain fundamental human rights must, in certain circumstances, be sacrificed in the name of 'the public interest'. The public interest exception is present in the right to property,[10] as well as in the freedom of movement.[11]

Taxation is levied in the public interest, and the public interest exception is another concept that has influenced the development of the ECtHR's tax jurisprudence. Other ECHR articles provide for exceptions to certain Fundamental Human Rights for the sake of 'public order', an exception that is mentioned in the right to a fair (public) hearing,[12] freedom of thought, conscience and religion.[13] Another tool that is used by the ECHR to allow digressions from fundamental human rights is the tool of 'national security', a concept found in the context of freedom of expression,[14] freedom of assembly and association,[15] freedom of movement[16] and the right to respect for private and family life[17] which combines the restriction with a limitation with a tax flavour: 'the economic well-being of the country'.

Without taxation, States cannot raise the finances necessary to fund national security, and a threat to State finances posed by tax evasion may be viewed as an indirect threat to national security. Naturally, taxation and the economic well-being of

10. Article 1 of Protocol 1 ECHR speaks of 'No one shall be deprived of his possessions except in the public interest.'
11. Article 2 of Protocol 4 ECHR says that 'The rights set forth ... may also be subject, in particular areas, to restrictions imposed in accordance with law and justified by the public interest in a democratic society.'
12. Article 6 ECHR provides that 'Judgment shall be pronounced publicly but the press and public may be excluded from all or part of the trial in the interests of morals, public order or national security in a democratic society'.
13. Article 9 ECHR provides of 'Freedom to manifest one's religion or beliefs shall be subject only to such limitations as are prescribed by law and are necessary in a democratic society in the interests of public safety, for the protection of public order, health or morals, or for the protection of the rights and freedoms of others'.
14. Article 10 ECHR.
15. Article 11 ECHR.
16. Article 2 of Protocol 4 ECHR.
17. Article 8 ECHR speaks of 'There shall be no interference by a public authority with the exercise of this right except such as is in accordance with the law and is necessary in a democratic society in the interests of national security, public safety or the economic well-being of the country, for the prevention of disorder or crime, for the protection of health or morals, or for the protection of the rights and freedoms of others.'

a State go hand in hand, implying that the text of the ECHR itself creates a number of lines of defence hampering judicial activism in the tax arena.

One of the leading texts on the ECHR acknowledges that the only Article of the ECHR to speak of tax 'concedes a practically unlimited power to a state' and that 'powers of the State under the provision are very wide'.[18] The legal concept of margin of appreciation is omnipresent in the tax jurisprudence of the ECtHR and is mentioned without fail in all attempts to impugn tax measures on the basis of Article 1 of Protocol 1. In this day and age, taxation is perceived as a matter which is grave enough to be relevant to matters relating to 'public interest', 'public order', 'national security' and, certainly, 'the economic well-being of the country'.

Lastly, Article 15 ECHR contemplates a nuclear option allowing a general suspension of 'most'[19] fundamental human rights in perceived highly exceptional circumstances. Article 15 prescribes that in times of war or other public emergency threatening the life of the nation, any High Contracting Party may take measures derogating from its obligations under this Convention to the extent strictly required by the exigencies of the situation, provided that such measures are not inconsistent with its other obligations under international law. The authors are not aware of any tax judgment based purely on Article 15, but experience has shown that the ECtHR was quite indulgent with tax measures which came as a response to emergency.[20] Therefore, the concept of 'emergency' is another calamity that the student of the tax judgments of the ECtHR must factor in.

FROM THE PERIPHERY TO THE CORE

Over sixty years after Hettier de Boislambert and Tiegen expressed their fears of the spectre of predatory taxation by totalitarian regimes, the ECtHR delivered a suite of tax cases that hit the international headlines.[21] A multinational owned partly by a dissident Russian businessman was subjected to a series of tax investigations which led to the collapse of an enormous financial empire, the ruin and imprisonment of its ultimate beneficial owner. During the tax trials, the officers of the company were kept in a metal cage. The company's lawyers took their Russian 'tax cases' to the ECtHR, and the ECtHR's response was decisive and unprecedented. One of the ECtHR's four judgments

18. David Harris, Michael O'Boyle, Ed Bates and Carla Buckley, *Harris, O'Boyle, and Warbrick: Law of the European Convention on Human Rights* (3rd ed.), Oxford, OUP, 2018, pp. 901–903.
19. Such an exception is not allowed in the case of Article 2 ECHR (except in respect of deaths resulting from lawful acts of war) or from Articles 3, 4 (paragraph 1) and 7. In any case, any High Contracting Party availing itself of this right of derogation shall keep the Secretary General of the Council of Europe fully informed of the measures which it has taken and the reasons therefor. It shall also inform the Secretary General of the Council of Europe when such measures have ceased to operate and the provisions of the Convention are again being fully executed.
20. Robert Attard, 'Not a Pleasure to the Eye; The ECtHR's Judgment in P. Plaisier B.V. Against the Netherlands', EC Tax Review, Volume 27, Issue 3 (2018) pp. 177–179.
21. Megan Davies, Vladimir Soldatkin and Gilbert Reilhac, 'European Court Rules Russia Must Pay Yukos Shareholders 1.9 Billion Euros', in *Reuters Business News*, 31 July 2014 viewed at https://www.reuters.com/article/uk-russia-yukos-echr-idUKKBN0G00QO20140731 in May 2022.

on the matter made the history of the ECtHR becoming the 'ECtHR's Largest Ever Award for Just Satisfaction'.[22] Jan Kleinheisterkamp noted that a financial award of '1.9 billion euros is humongous in terms of compensation granted by the ECHR'.[23] The ECtHR had shown its teeth, and it had done so in what was essentially a case over international tax avoidance with an element of transfer pricing. The suite of cases[24] that became known as the '*Yukos* cases' had made history. When it comes to taxation and human rights, there is so much more than meets the eye and the future tends to be full of surprises and unpredictable.

While litigators were fighting their landmark cases 'on the front' in Strasbourg, academics were making their inroads in the thought leadership sphere. In 2000, Philip Baker QC published his seminal article on taxation and human rights.[25] Besides charting all known cases to date of publication, his article created awareness of what was previously dismissed as a peripherical and theoretical subject. Baker's article identified salient issues that would acquire a great deal of practical significance going forward; issues arising from the classification of tax penalties, the special nature of tax proceedings, retrospectivity, *non bis in idem*, *nemo tenetur se ipse accusare* and other matters. Baker's leading study encouraged the publication of further studies on the subject, and regular updates on taxation on human rights began to appear in leading tax journals.[26] Taxation and the ECHR became the subject of academic publications and began to be included in the syllabi of several tax courses, and its added value began to be appreciated.

The past few years have witnessed a flurry of publications on taxation and human rights. The Observatory on the Protection of Taxpayers' Rights tends to benchmark developments by reference to conclusions reached by the ECtHR. Eventually, even the Press Unit of the ECtHR itself released a detailed fact sheet on the matter which it updates regularly.[27] Not surprisingly, the past twenty years have witnessed a surge in cases.

Although the ECHR mentions taxation only once, it has become abundantly clear that tax policies of State Signatories must be regularly stress-tested against the requirements of the ECHR for the same reason why all public prerogatives must pass the human rights test. This book will examine important cases which create a human rights code of conduct for State Signatories.

---

22. Conor McCarthy, 'The ECtHR's Largest Ever Award for Just Satisfaction Rendered in the Yukos Case', EJIL:Talk! Blog of the European Journal of International Law viewed at https://www.ejiltalk.org/the-ecthrs-largest-ever-award-for-just-satisfaction-rendered-in-the-yukos-case/ in May 2022.
23. *Supra* note 21, Reuters 2014.
24. Including especially the cases *OAO Neftyanaya Kompaniya Yukos v. Russia*, Application 14902/04, *Mikhail Borisovich Khodorkovskiy v. Russia*, Application no. 11082/06, and *Khodorkovskiy and Lebedev v. Russia*, Applications nos. 51111/07 and 42757/07.
25. Philip Baker, 'Taxation and the European Convention on Human Rights', European Taxation, Volume 40, Issue 8 (2000).
26. Baker's own updates in European Taxation must be singled out. Updates by other authors appeared in EC Tax Review and Intertax.
27. Press Unit ECtHR, 'Taxation and the European Convention on Human Rights', updated on April 2022 and viewed on May 2022 at https://www.echr.coe.int/documents/fs_taxation_eng.pdf.

CHAPTER 1
Right to Property

Article 1 Protocol 1
Protection of property

> Every natural or legal person is entitled to the peaceful enjoyment of his possessions. No one shall be deprived of his possessions except in the public interest and subject to the conditions provided for by law and by the general principles of international law.
>
> The preceding provisions shall not, however, in any way impair the right of a State to enforce such laws as it deems necessary to control the use of property in accordance with the general interest or to secure the payment of taxes or other contributions or penalties.

Understandably, the wording of the law acknowledges that the right to property applies both to natural and legal persons and some of the most interesting tax cases have been submitted to the ECtHR by companies. More importantly, the right to property applies to some form of 'res' falling under the ECHR's definition of 'possession'. The ECtHR's tax judgments have delivered some extremely interesting explanations of the meaning of 'possession' taken in a tax context.

The law itself mentions that all interferences with the right to property, taxation included, must occur 'in the public interest', and the drafters of the ECHR wanted to emphasise that the right to property does not impair the State's Signatory's right 'to secure the payment of taxes or other contributions or penalties', but that is not where the story ends.

As is often the case with the tax judgments of the ECtHR, there is always more than meets the eye, and the ECtHR's pronouncements have not only fleshed out the meaning of the right to property in a tax context but developed what can be described as the essential requisites of a tax policy compatible with the ECtHR.

The words 'except in the public interest' bind States to levy taxes only if such taxes are raised for the common good, implying the maintenance of a fair balance between the private good and public interest. The terms 'subject to the conditions provided for by law and by the general principles of international law' create further constraints on State Signatories imposing standards of legality and fairness. Furthermore, the phrase 'laws as it deems necessary' implies an element of proportionality. The ECtHR was left with room for manoeuvring its supervisory function, and there were times when the ECtHR exercised it bravely.

1.1 AN 'INTERFERENCE' WITH A 'POSSESSION'

First of all, for the right to property to apply, there must be a 'possession'. The right to 'peaceful enjoyment' and the protection from deprivation are linked to the holding of a 'possession'. Interestingly, the French text uses slightly different terminology. Peaceful enjoyment is linked to 'biens', and deprivation of property is linked to 'propriété' which could lead to the wrong conclusion that for there to be a 'possession' within the meaning of the ECHR, there should be ownership.[1] Both in a tax and in a non-tax context, the ECtHR had adopted quite a liberal interpretation of the term 'possessions', conceding that the right does not apply solely to rights of pure ownership but to other economic entitlements too.[2] The ECtHR has held that a 'claim' can only fall within the scope of that Article 1 of Protocol 1 if it is sufficiently established to be enforceable.[3] In its Guidance Note, the Registry of the ECtHR explains that:

> The concept of 'possessions' in the first part of Article 1 of Protocol No. 1 is an autonomous one, covering both 'existing possessions' and assets, including claims, in respect of which the applicant can argue that he or she has at least a 'legitimate expectation'. 'Possessions' include rights 'in rem' and 'in personam'. The term encompasses immovable and movable property and other proprietary interests.[4]

---

1. The French text is being reproduced hereunder, 'Toute personne physique ou morale a droit au respect de ses biens. Nul ne peut être privé de sa propriété que pour cause d'utilité publique et dans les conditions prévues par la loi et les principes généraux du droit international.'
2. The leading case on the subject of 'possession' is a non-tax case, the 1976 case of *Handyside v. The United Kingdom*, Application no. 5493/72, a case involving obscenity law. The ECtHR concluded that:

   > Admittedly the expression 'deprived of his possessions', in the English text, could lead one to think otherwise but the structure of Article 1 (P1-1) shows that that sentence, which originated moreover in a Belgian amendment drafted in French (Collected Edition of the 'travaux préparatoires', document H (61) 4, pp. 1083, 1084, 1086, 1090, 1099, 1105, 1110-1111 and 1113-1114), applies only to someone who is 'deprived of ownership' ('privé de sa propriété') … .

3. *OAO Plodovaya Kompaniya v. Russia*, Application no. 1641/02, § 27; *Zhigalev v. Russia*, Application no. 54891/00, § 146; *Uskova v. Russia (dec.)*, Application no. 20116/02; and *Grishchenko v. Russia (dec.)*, Application no. 75907/01.
4. Registry ECtHR, 'Guide on Article 1 of Protocol No. 1 to the European Convention on Human Rights Protection of Property', updated on 31 December 2021.

Typically, tax cases involve situations where the taxpayer is a debtor of the State Signatory,[5] with the State Signatory asserting ownership rights over the taxpayer's assets based on claims to 'raw tax', tax penalties and punitive interest (interferences with possessions based on a pure confiscation), but there could also be inverse situations where taxpayers would be asserting rights over the State Signatory.

Taxpayers could hold 'tax assets' in the form of vested rights to tax credits, tax refund claims, claims over compensatory interest for late payment of tax refunds, tax deductions, tax exemptions, right to set-off, legitimate expectations[6] granted by tax rulings and similar instruments. The ECtHR has had the opportunity to adjudicate both cases over tax liabilities and cases involving tax assets delivering some strong judgments.

The 1994 case *Guido Ferretti v. Italy*[7] was one of the first cases involving a right that was not a straightforward property right. The *Ferretti* case involved the late payment of a tax refund and a complaint that interest on late payment of refunds was not set at market rates. Ferretti wanted to claim compound interest running in terms of rules applicable on the market, but the law provided for lower rates. While the Commission was receptive to his argument that he had some form of 'possession' recognised by the ECHR, his claim was dismissed on the basis that the regime of interest payment was judged to be fair nonetheless:

> Cependant, la Commission note que les sommes perçues par le requérant à titre d'intérêt sont supérieures aux taux d'inflation pour la période concernée. Dans ces circonstances, la Commission considère que les retards dont le requérant se plaint paraissent compensés par le versement d'intérêts au moment du remboursement. En conséquence, la Commission estime que le paiement de ces intérêts ménage un 'juste équilibre' entre l'intérêt de la collectivité et les impératifs de la protection des droits fondamentaux de l'individu, en réalisant de façon raisonnable un rapport de proportionnalité entre les moyens employés et le but visé.

In the 2002 case *S.A. Dangeville v. France*,[8] a case involving the Community Right to claim reimbursement of value-added tax (VAT), a right assimilated to a 'definite, immediately payable debt', the ECtHR was initially hesitant to treat the case as a case over a 'possession' preferring to first deal with the case as a case over 'control of property':[9]

> However, as regards the payment of a tax, a more natural approach might be to examine the complaints from the angle of a control of the use of property in the

5. For a typical case involving tax intended as expropriation, *see Wasa Liv Ömsesidigt, Försäkrings-bolaget Valands Pensionsstiftelse and a group of approximately 15,000 individuals v. Sweden*, Application no. 13013/87, when the Commission observed that, 'The Commission is of the opinion that any legislation which introduces some sort of fiscal obligation will as such deprive the involved of a possession.'
6. On the point of legitimate expectations, *see Plalam S.P.A. v. Italy*, Application no. 16021/02.
7. Application no. 25083/94.
8. Application no. 36677/97.
9. The same approach was adopted in *Nicola Colazzo and Others v. Italy*, Application no. 36944/06.

> general interest 'to secure the payment of taxes', which falls within the rule in the second paragraph of Article 1 (see Building Societies, cited above, p. 2353, § 79).

Nonetheless, it later reached the conclusion that the applicant company had a valid claim against the State when it lodged its appeals for VAT paid in error, a claim that 'constituted an asset' and therefore amounted to a 'possession' within the meaning of the ECHR. The ECtHR considered that the applicant company had at least a legitimate expectation of being able to obtain the reimbursement of the disputed sum concluding that:

> 61. The Court finds that in the instant case the interference with the applicant company's right to the peaceful enjoyment of its 'possessions' was disproportionate. Both the negation of the applicant company's claim against the State and the absence of domestic procedures affording a sufficient remedy to ensure the protection of the applicant company's right to the peaceful enjoyment of its possessions upset the fair balance that must be maintained between the demands of the general interest of the community and the requirements of the protection of the individual's fundamental rights.

The fact that the ECtHR's tax judgment was endorsing principles of interpretation established in the non-tax judgment in the case of *Van Marle and Others v. the Netherlands*[10] indicated a clear direction of travel.

The 2003 Judgment in the case *Buffalo srl (in liquidation) v. Italy,*[11] involving the late payment of a refund of overpaid tax, consolidated the application of the Van Marle principle in the field of taxation.

In *Buffalo srl,* the ECtHR acknowledged that a claim for a tax refund amounted to a 'possession' within the scope of the right to property:

> 27. La requérante dénonce les retards dans le remboursement de crédits d'impôts et soutient que cette situation relève de l'article 1 du Protocole no 1 ...
>
> 29. En conclusion, la Cour estime que la requérante était titulaire d'un intérêt patrimonial reconnu en droit italien, bien que modifiable dans certaines conditions, depuis la réception par l'administration fiscale de la déclaration de revenus et jusqu'au moment où le remboursement a été effectué. L'intérêt de la requérante constituait dès lors un 'bien', au sens de l'article 1 du Protocole no 1.

A similar approach was adopted in 2006 in *Eko-Elda Avee v. Greece*[12] when the ECtHR added that the complainant was entitled to interest on late payment of a tax refund:

> 30. With particular regard to the payment of taxes, the Court reiterates that the financial obligation arising out of the levying of taxes or contributions may infringe the rights guaranteed in Article 1 of Protocol No. 1 if the conditions for a refund impose an excessive burden on the person or entity concerned or fundamentally interfere with their financial security (see, to that effect, Buffalo S.r.l. in

10. Applications nos. 8543/79, 8674/79, 8675/79 and 8685/79.
11. Application no. 38746/97.
12. Application no. 10162/02.

> liquidation, cited above, § 32). In that case the Court, examining a question similar to the one under consideration here, held that there had been a breach of Article 1 of Protocol No. 1 on the sole ground that the prolonged unavailability of the tax that had been unduly paid by the applicant company had had a definite and considerable impact on its financial situation (*ibid.*, § 37).
>
> 31. In the instant case the Court observes that the tax unduly paid was refunded ... five years and approximately five months after ... the Court considers that the authorities' refusal to pay late-payment interest for such a long period upset the fair balance that has to be struck between the general interest and the individual interest. Accordingly, there has been a violation of Article 1 of Protocol No. 1.

The classification of tax credits was once more carefully examined in the 2007 case *Intersplav v. Ukraine*,[13] a case over a VAT Refund Claim. In *Intersplav*, the ECtHR had the opportunity to explain[14] that:

> Even though a particular claim for a VAT refund may be subject to checks and objections from the competent State authorities, the relevant provisions of the Law on Value-Added Tax do not require the prior judicial review of a claim to validate a company's eligibility for a refund ...
>
> 32. While the Court does not find it necessary to determine the precise content and scope of the legal interest in question, it is nevertheless satisfied that the factors outlined above show that the applicant had a proprietary interest recognised by Ukrainian law, and protected by Article 1 of Protocol No. 1 (see, mutatis mutandis, Buffalo S.r.l. en liquidation v. Italy, no. 38746/97, § 29, 3 July 2003).

The principle established in *Intersplav v. Ukraine* was followed in some subsequent tax judgments, including especially the 2009 case of *Bulves AD v. Bulgaria*,[15] another case involving a VAT refund claim. In *Bulves*, the ECtHR confirmed *Intersplav* elaborating and reinforcing conclusions reached:

> 'Possessions' can be either 'existing possessions' or assets, including claims, in respect of which the applicant can argue that he or she has at least a 'legitimate expectation' of obtaining effective enjoyment of a property right. By way of contrast, the hope of recognition of a property right which it has been impossible to exercise effectively cannot be considered a 'possession' ...
>
> 57. In the light of the foregoing, the Court considers that, in so far as the applicant company had complied fully and in time with the VAT rules set by the State, had no means of enforcing compliance by its supplier and had no knowledge of the latter's failure to do so, it could justifiably expect to be allowed to benefit from one of the principal rules of the VAT system of taxation by being allowed to deduct the input VAT it had paid to its supplier. Moreover, only once a claim for such a deduction had been made and a cross-check of the supplier had been conducted by the tax authorities could it be ascertained whether the latter had fully complied with its own VAT reporting obligations. Thus, the Court considers that the

13. Application no. 803/02.
14. Arguably, an analogous conclusion had been reached by the Commission in the 1997 case *Guido Ferretti v. Italy*, Application no. 25083/94.
15. Application no. 3991/03.

> applicant company's right to claim a deduction of the input VAT amounted to at least a 'legitimate expectation' of obtaining effective enjoyment of a property right amounting to a 'possession' within the meaning of the first sentence of Article 1 of Protocol No. 1 … .

The case in *Bulves* was interesting because the State sought to justify its non-issuance of the VAT refund on the basis of non-compliance by one of Bulves' suppliers.

The conclusions reached in *Intersplav* and *Bulves* created an element of *jurisprudence constante* and were followed in a number of subsequent judgments that included the 2018 case of *Euromak Metal DOO v. the Former Yugoslav Republic of Macedonia*[16] when the ECtHR confirmed that the right to a tax refund is protected as a right to a 'possession' safeguarded in Article 1 adding that a taxpayer's right to claim a deduction amounted to at least a 'legitimate expectation'. Failures by third parties did not weaken taxpayer's case for the tax credit. Given that Euromak Metal DOO was fully compliant, the fact that its suppliers had failed to declare or pay tax to the State of which Euromak Metal DOO had no knowledge of did not impair its rightful claim to receive its credit.

The ECtHR's avant-guard 2013 judgment in the case of *R.Sz. v. Hungary*[17] stands out because it expressly referred to a legitimate expectation to a particular tax treatment as a vested right falling within the scope of the right to property:

> In this connection the Court recalls that taxation at a considerably higher tax rate than that in force when the revenue in question was generated could arguably be regarded as an unreasonable interference with expectations protected by Article 1 of Protocol No. 1 (see M.A. and 34 Others, cited above). The tax complained of was not intended to remedy technical deficiencies of the pre-existing law, nor had the applicant enjoyed the benefit of a windfall in a changeover to a new tax-payment regime (compare and contrast, National etc., cited above, §§ 75 to 83).

The 2015 case of *Robert Huitson v. the United Kingdom*[18] involved a tax right of a much less straightforward nature than a simple tax credit. The *Huitson* case involved a claim for income tax relief, but, surprisingly, the ECtHR declined the offer to express itself on the important issue of Tax Treaty Recognition and Double Tax Relief. Disappointingly, the ECtHR failed to express itself on the matter, dismissing the case on the basis of the 'control of property' and 'margin of appreciation' arguments:[19]

> 23. The first question which therefore arises in this case is whether the applicant's claim for income tax relief, relying on section 3(2) of the DTA, constituted an 'asset' attracting the guarantees of Article 1 of Protocol No. 1 … .
>
> However, the Court does not consider it necessary to determine that issue as it finds that the applicant's complaint is in any event inadmissible for the reasons set out below …

16. Application no. 68039/14.
17. Application no. 41838/11.
18. Application no. 50131/12.
19. Vide *infra*.

> 26. It would appear to the Court to be the most natural approach to examine the applicant's complaint from the angle of a control of the use of property in the general interest 'to secure the payment of tax'.

From an interpretational perspective, the concept of 'interference' inherent in the concepts of deprivation and control of property contemplated in Article 1 of Protocol 1 was far less controversial and, in most tax cases, parties took the fact that there had been an interference for granted.

1.2 'CONTROL OF THE USE OF PROPERTY ... TO SECURE PAYMENT OF TAXES OR OTHER CONTRIBUTIONS OR PENALTIES'

The concurring opinion in the case of *Könyv-tár KFT and Others v. Hungary*[20] and a Council of Europe Report[21] offer major insights relating to the meanings of the terms 'control of use of property ... to secure payment of taxes or other contributions or penalties'.

In the concurring opinion in *Könyv-tár KFT*, it was explained that Article 1 of Protocol No. 1 ECHR provides for two forms of interference with possessions: control and deprivation. Deprivation is the transfer de jure or de facto of the possession away from its owner to the State or a third party, or its destruction. Control involves no transfer: the owner retains his possession, but is restricted in his use of it. *Sporrong and Lönnroth* acknowledged a third type of interference: 'interference with the substance of ownership', based on the first sentence of Article 1 of the Protocol ECHR; a form of interference, said to be of a general nature, allowing the ECtHR to review all situations not falling under the other two forms (deprivation or control of use). Nonetheless, what qualifies a measure as incompatible with the substance of the right to the peaceful enjoyment of property remains fairly unclear.

The concept of deprivation of property implies a transfer of ownership, like expropriation or nationalisation. Case law of the ECtHR has not yet precisely defined what constitutes regulation of the use of a possession but refers to cases where there was no transfer of ownership and in which the national authorities sought to limit or control the use of the possession:

> The Council of Europe Report cited above seeks to establish the meaning of 'tax' for the purposes of the ECHR and it begins to delve into the core topic of national tax sovereignty versus the fundamental human rights of the taxpayer: 'The concepts of taxation, contributions and penalties have been clarified in the case-law. Taxes usually apply over a period of time, whereas contributions tend to be more specific. The Commission has singled out two further characteristics of taxes, making the point that the purpose for which a tax is raised "does not alter the nature of the tax as such", and emphasising that taxation inevitably differentiates between different groups of taxpayers, and varies with the state's social and economic objectives.'

---

20. Application no. 21623/13.
21. Laurent Sermet, The European Convention on Human Rights and Property Rights (Council of Europe Publishing Human Rights Files, no. 11 rev.), 1992, pp. 25–27.

1.3 THE ECtHR'S SUPERVISORY FUNCTION

Although the wording of the law empowers States to levy taxation acknowledging their wide powers, case law of the ECtHR has confirmed that these wide sweeping powers remain subject to the ECtHR's supervision.

The ECtHR's power of supervision was acknowledged in some of the earlier cases. The ECtHR's supervisory function was taken as read in the 1995 Decision *Riccardo Travers and 27 others v. Italy*[22] when the Commission observed:

> The Commission recalls the principle that taxation is an interference with the rights guaranteed in Article 1 para 1 of Protocol No. 1, but that this interference is justified under the second paragraph of that Article which provides expressly for an exception in respect of taxes or other contributions (see No. 11089/84, DfC 11.11.86, D.R. 49 p. 181).
>
> The Commission observes, however, that despite this, an issue of this nature does not escape the Commission's power of review, since the Convention organs must ensure that Article 1 of Protocol No 1 has been correctly applied.

Similarly, in the 1997 case *Guido Ferretti v. Italy*,[23] the Commission pointed out that:

> La Commission rappelle d'abord que l'imposition fiscale est en principe une ingérence dans le droit garanti par le premier alinéa de l'article 1 du Protocole N° 1 (P1-1) et que cette ingérence se justifie, conformément au deuxième alinéa de cet article, qui prévoit expressément une exception pour ce qui est du paiement des impôts ou d'autres contributions (cf. N° 11089/84, déc. 11.11.86, D.R. 49, p. 200).

In the 1998 case *Helene Musa v. Austria*,[24] the Commission continued to describe its supervisory function as a power of review:

> The Commission recalls the principle that taxation is an interference with the rights guaranteed in Article 1 para. 1 of Protocol No. 1, but that this interference is justified under the second paragraph of that Article which provides expressly for an exception in respect of taxes or other contributions (see No. 11089/84, Dec. 11.11.86).
>
> The Commission observes, however, that despite this, an issue of this nature does not escape the Commission's power of review, since the Convention organs must ensure that Article 1 of Protocol No. 1 has been correctly applied.

Nonetheless, history has shown that the ECtHR and the Commission were reluctant to exercise its power of review on the assumption that States must be allowed a margin of appreciation in designing their own tax policies with French judgments such as the case of *Dominique Rheims and others v. France*[25] speaking of 'une compétence limitée pour vérifier le respect du droit interne'.

22. Application no. 15117/89.
23. Application no. 25083/94.
24. Application no. 40477/98.
25. Application no. 32492/08.

1.4 'FAIR BALANCE' WITHIN A MARGIN OF APPRECIATION AND PUBLIC INTEREST EXCEPTION

The ECtHR has consistently acknowledged that a wide margin of appreciation is allowed to States over general measures of economic or social strategy[26] and implementing policy in the area of taxation.[27] Several tax judgments of the ECtHR reiterate that due to their direct knowledge of their society and its needs, national authorities are in principle better placed than the international judge to decide what is 'in the public interest',[28] an approach that was critically analysed in the dissenting opinion in *Correia De Matos v. Portugal.*[29] The aforesaid dissenting opinion explained that if a margin of appreciation is to be recognised, there should be a specific reason for doing so, which the mantra of 'better placed' does not provide. There has to be a specific reason why the ECtHR considers that domestic authorities will perform some kind of assessment better than the ECtHR itself.

The ECtHR has consistently held that when framing and implementing policies in the area of taxation, States enjoy a wide margin of appreciation, and the ECtHR has held that it will respect the legislature's assessment in such matters unless it is devoid of reasonable foundation.[30] In the 1994 case *Hentrich v. France,*[31] the ECtHR observed that:

> The Court reiterates that the notion of 'public interest' is necessarily extensive and that the States have a certain margin of appreciation to frame and organise their fiscal policies and make arrangements – such as the right of pre-emption – to ensure that taxes are paid.

In *WASA Ömsesidigt, Försäkringsbolaget Valands Pensionsstiftelse, a group of approximately 15,000 individuals v. Sweden,*[32] the Commission described the margin of appreciation as being 'wide'. Even in the seminal decision in *Travers*, a decision which is perceived as the decision that paved the way for the (few) successful applications, the Commission had been clear:

> The Commission further recalls that it is in the first instance for the national authorities to decide on the type of tax or contributions they wish to levy. Decisions in this area normally involve, in addition, an assessment of political, economic and social problems which the Convention leaves to the competence of the member States, for the domestic authorities are clearly better placed than the Commission to assess such problems (see No 11089/84, aforementioned Dec, p. 202) The member States therefore have a wide margin of appreciation in this area.

26. *Wallishauser v. Austria* (no. 2), Application no. 14497/06.
27. *Gasus Dosier- und Fördertechnik GmbH v. the Netherlands,* Application no. 15375/89.
28. *Maggio and Others v. Italy,* Applications nos. 46286/09, 52851/08 and 53727/08.
29. Application no. 56402/12.
30. *Imbert de Trémiolles v. France (dec.),* Applications nos. 25834/05 and 27815/05 joined; and *Arnaud and Others v. France,* Applications nos. 36918/11 and 5 others.
31. Application no. 13616/88.
32. Application no. 13013/87.

The same point was made in *Kaira v. Finland*[33] when the Commission concluded:

> ... It is in the first place for the national authorities to decide what kind of taxes or contributions are to be collected. Furthermore, the decisions in this area will commonly involve the appreciation of political, economic and social questions, which the Convention leaves within the competence of the Contracting States. The power of appreciation of the Contracting States is therefore a wide one ... .

The application of the 'margin of appreciation' principle has resulted in the dismissal of the vast majority of tax cases shielding State Signatories from interference. Unfortunately, in the jurisprudence of the ECtHR, the concept per se has evolved very little, but recent developments relating to the way it is to be procedurally applied in the context of tax discrimination are welcome.

Predictably, the margin of appreciation defence was keenly accepted in the earlier, more conservative judgments. The levying of taxation is a deprivation of possessions falling under the public interest exception, and States are allowed wide discretion in formulating policies in the public interest.

Margin of tolerance and appreciation is high, especially when measures aimed at combatting suspected and actual fiscal conduct are concerned. In the 2005 judgment, in the case of *Rosenzweig and Bonded Warehouses Ltd. v. Poland*,[34] the Court ruled that interferences with the right to property such as the revocation of a licence are justified on the grounds of suspected fiscal misconduct and tax evasion:

> ... company had ever disclosed any misconduct which would cast doubt on its lawfulness. Neither has it been argued or shown that there had been any suspicions on the part of the domestic authorities that the applicants' operations were in any way dishonest, or that they had been involved in any attempts of customs tax evasion. Such arguments would have been capable of lending credibility to the Government's view that the revoking of licences served the public interest, but they had not been advanced. In the Court's opinion this absence of any wrongdoing on the part of the applicants established by the domestic authorities cannot but have incidence on the overall assessment whether the measures complained of met the requirements of the standards laid down by Article 1 of Protocol No. 1.

The ECtHR tends to be more prudent in accepting the margin of appreciation defence in cases with penal repercussions. Thus, in the 2011 case of *OAO Neftyanaya Kompaniya Yukos v. Russia*,[35] a case that will be discussed in more detail hereunder, the ECtHR held that:

> 574. Overall, notwithstanding the State's margin of appreciation in this sphere, the Court finds that there has been a violation of Article 1 of Protocol No. 1 on account of the change in interpretation of the rules on the statutory time-bar resulting from the Constitutional Court's decision of 14 July 2005 and the effect of this decision on the outcome of the Tax Assessment 2000 proceedings.

33. Application no. 27109/95.
34. Application no. 51728/99.
35. Application no. 14902/04.

Nonetheless, even 'modern' judgments continue to treat state margin of appreciation in designing tax policies as being 'wide'.[36] Even in the (rare) successful case *R.Sz. v. Hungary*[37] impugning a high Hungarian tax, the ECtHR conceded that:

> For the Court, given the margin of appreciation granted to States in matters of taxation, the applicable tax rate cannot be decisive in itself, especially in circumstances like those of the present case.

In the 2018 judgment *Concetta Cacciato and Michele Cacciato v. Italy*,[38] the ECtHR went even a step further describing margin of appreciation in tax matters as being 'particularly' wide:

> 25. Turning to whether a fair balance has been struck in the case at hand, the Court considers at the outset that it was well within the area of discretionary judgment for the Italian legislature to develop substantive tax rules providing for taxation of expropriation compensation. ... The same can be said as regards the choice as to the concrete means of enforcement, namely deduction at source, with the option left to the taxpayer to choose the regular taxation route (see paragraph 12 above). In view of the foregoing, the Court considers that the respondent State should be afforded a particularly wide margin of appreciation in the present case.

In describing the margin of appreciation, the 2022 case of *Bežanić and Baškarad v. Croatia*,[39] a case involving the claw-back of an exemption of a 5% real estate tax, the ECtHR possibly even went a step further using dangerous adjectives like 'deference':

> 64. Furthermore, in so far as the tax sphere is concerned, the Court's well-established position is that States may be afforded some degree of additional deference and latitude in the exercise of their fiscal functions under the lawfulness test ... .

The 2016 judgment in *Guberina v. Croatia*[40] was a breath of fresh air indicating an innovative and fairer approach in managing the margin of appreciation defence. In *Guberina*, the ECtHR spoke of a 'varying' margin of appreciation that can be narrowed down when the need arises. In certain cases, the onus of proving that the margin of appreciation was exercised correctly could be shifted onto the State:

> 73. On the one hand, a wide margin is usually allowed to the State under the Convention when it comes to general measures of economic or social strategy, for example (see Hämäläinen v. Finland [GC], no. 37359/09, § 109, ECHR 2014). This also includes measures in the area of taxation.
>
> However, any such measures must be implemented in a non-discriminatory manner and comply with the requirements of proportionality (see R.Sz. v. Hungary, no. 41838/11, § 54, 2 July 2013). On the other hand, if a restriction on fundamental rights applies to a particularly vulnerable group

36. *Azienda Agricola Silverfunghi s.a.s. and Others v. Italy*, Applications nos. 48357/07, 52677/07, 52687/07 and 52701/07.
37. Application no. 41838/11.
38. Application no. 60633/16.
39. Applications nos. 16140/15 and 13322/16.
40. Application no. 23682/13.

> in society that has suffered considerable discrimination in the past, then the State's margin of appreciation is substantially narrower and it must have very weighty reasons for the restrictions in question.
>
> 74. Lastly, as regards the burden of proof in relation to Article 14 of the Convention, the Court has held that once the applicant has shown a difference in treatment, it is for the Government to show that it was justified (see D.H. and Others v. the Czech Republic, cited above, § 177; Kurić and Others, cited above, § 389; and Vallianatos and Others v. Greece [GC], nos. 29381/09 and 32684/09, § 85, ECHR 2013).

In this context, it must be emphasised that *Guberina* was a case involving a complaint based on the right to property combined with a complaint based on discrimination, a factor that influenced the ECtHR's particular approach in this case. The application of the margin of appreciation principle in discrimination cases will be discussed in more detail in the analysis of Article 14 ECHR.

1.5 LAWFULNESS

States have a margin of appreciation in designing their tax policy, but the wording of the law implies that, for a law to be compatible with the ECHR, it must respect the principle of lawfulness. Tax laws of State Signatories must fulfil certain minimum qualitative standards.

Fortunately, the right to property tax judgments of the ECtHR have been influenced by the dictum of a case which was neither a tax case nor an Article 1 Protocol 1 Case.

In 1996, the ECtHR delivered an important judgment on the correct interpretation of Article 7 ECHR (No punishment without law), the case of *Cantoni v. France*,[41] a case when the ECtHR developed the following rules:

(a) The concept of 'law' comprises statutory law as well as case law.
(b) The concept of law implies qualitative requirements, notably those of accessibility and foreseeability.
(c) The text of a law must be read in the light of the accompanying interpretive case law.
(d) It is not for the ECtHR to express a view on the appropriateness of methods chosen by the legislature of a Contracting State; its task is confined to determining whether they are in conformity with the Convention.
(e) The scope of the notion of foreseeability depends to a considerable degree on the content of the text in issue, the field it is designed to cover and the number and status of those to whom it is addressed.
(f) A law may still satisfy the requirement of foreseeability even if the person concerned has to take appropriate legal advice to assess, to a degree that is reasonable in the circumstances, the consequences which a given action may entail.

41. Application no. 17862/91.

Years later, the ECtHR would draw from the principles enunciated in *Cantoni* in tax judgments applying Article 7 ECHR 'criminal law type principles' to tax cases based on Article 1 of Protocol 1.

The writing on the wall was in the unsuccessful 1995 case of *Spacek sro v. Czech Republic*,[42] a case involving a challenge to a tax law that was criticised on qualitative grounds. Spacek sro questioned the validity of a Czech law providing for a certain form of tax accounting on the basis that the law had not been published in the Official Gazette. Spacek complained that the tax compliance law framework imposed upon him was unforeseeable and unpredictable. The ECtHR dismissed his case on the merits but seemed prepared to accept arguments drawn from the world of criminal law.

The 2010 case of *Shchokin v. Ukraine*[43] was a turning point. Contrary to the spirit and letter of several tax judgments of the ECtHR, the Ukrainian tax authorities had arbitrarily and abusively increased a withholding tax rate without following the mandatory procedure contemplated in domestic law. Predictably, the ECtHR found for Shchokin. The ECtHR reminded that tax measures should be based on principles of legality enshrined in domestic law and that tax measures must be accessible to the persons concerned, precise and foreseeable in their application. Although the ECtHR acknowledged a margin of appreciation in tax policy, the ECtHR referred to its inherent residual power to stress-test such policies against the core values of the ECHR. It was clear that the Ukrainian tax authorities had arbitrarily elected to disregard a withholding tax prescribed by law in favour of a more onerous rate of withholding tax that did not have a sound legal basis. The ECtHR observed that:

> In this regard the Court notes that the Income Tax Decree had a legal force of the law of Parliament and provided special rules for the taxation of specific types of citizens' income. It is remarkable that, in contrast to the rates fixed in the Presidential Decree, the tax authorities continued to apply, for example, the special rule of Article 7 § 2 of the Income Tax Decree (see paragraph 40 above). In these circumstances it is unclear why the Presidential Decree had to be understood as prevailing over Article 7 § 3 of the Income Tax Decree.

The ECtHR held that the discrepancy between the legitimate rate of withholding tax established by law and the arbitrary rate unilaterally applied by the authorities created a violation because the impugned measure failed the 'qualitative requirement' standard set by the ECHR:

> 57 ... However, in the present case the authorities opted for the less favourable interpretation of the domestic law which resulted in the increase in the applicant's income tax liability.
>
> 58. The foregoing considerations are sufficient to enable the Court to conclude that the interference with the applicant's property rights was not lawful for the purpose of Article 1 of Protocol No. 1. It holds for this reason that there has been a violation of that provision.

42. Application no. 26449/95.
43. Applications nos. 23759/03 and 37943/06.

The ECtHR reiterated that any interference by a public authority with the peaceful enjoyment of possessions should be lawful because the law uses the terms 'subject to the conditions provided for by law' and recognises that the States have the right to control the use of property by enforcing 'laws':

> In the Court's opinion the lack of the required clarity and precision of the domestic law, offering divergent interpretations on such an important fiscal issue, upset the requirement of the 'quality of law' under the Convention and did not provide adequate protection against arbitrary interference by the public authorities with the applicant's property rights.

The ECtHR cited *Scordino v. Italy*,[44] acknowledging that it is primarily for the national authorities to interpret and apply domestic law, but it highlighted that the ECtHR retained a supervisory function to verify whether the way in which the domestic law is interpreted and applied produces consequences that are consistent with the principles of the ECHR as interpreted by the ECtHR's case law.

The qualitative requirements of tax law returned on the ECtHR's agenda in three of the four cases involving the decline and fall of the Russian multinational oil company Neftyanaya Kompaniya Yukos. This chapter will discuss the complaint under Article 1 of Protocol 1; complaints under Article 7 will be discussed in the relevant chapter.

The 168-page judgment in *Oao Neftyanaya Kompaniya Yukos ('Yukos') v. Russia*[45] addressed multiple aspects of the right to property with some complaints being specific to the qualitative requirement. Among others, Yukos complained that tax assessment for the years 2000–2003 had not been based on a reasonable and foreseeable interpretation of domestic law. The ECtHR observed that it is not its task to take the place of domestic courts. It referred to the merits of the case and discussed some topical issues in international tax law. For the first time, the ECtHR discussed in detail issues relating to transfer pricing and the use of letter-box companies:

> 591. From the findings of the domestic courts and the parties' explanations, the Court notes that the company's 'tax optimisation techniques' applied with slight variations throughout 2000-2003 consisted of switching the tax burden from the applicant company and its production and service units to letter-box companies in domestic tax havens in Russia. These companies, with no assets, employees or operations of their own, were nominally owned and managed by third parties, although in reality they were set up and run by the applicant company itself ... The applicant company used the method of transfer pricing, which consisted of selling the goods from its production division to its marketing companies at intentionally lowered prices and the use of sham entities registered in the domestic regions with low taxation levels and nominally owned and run by third persons (see paragraphs 14-18, 48, 62-63 for a more detailed description).
>
> 592. The domestic courts found that such an arrangement was at face value clearly unlawful domestically, as it involved the fraudulent registration of trading entities by the applicant company in the name of third persons and its corresponding failure to declare to the tax authorities its true relation to these companies (see paragraphs 311, 349-353, 374-380) ... .

44. Application no. 36813/97.
45. Application no. 14902/04.

The ECtHR found nothing wrong in the anti-abuse measures directed against tax avoidance schemes. On this ground, the ECtHR decided in favour of Russia, concluding that Russia's anti-avoidance rules contained a sufficiently clear legal basis:

> 594 ... Thus, the Court cannot agree with the applicant company's allegation that its particular way of 'optimising tax' had been previously examined by the domestic courts and upheld as valid or that it had used lawful 'tax optimisation techniques' which were only subsequently condemned by the domestic courts. The above considerations are sufficient for the Court to conclude that the findings of the domestic courts that applicant company's tax arrangements were unlawful at the time when the company had used them, were neither arbitrary nor manifestly unreasonable.

Another complaint referred to the fact that the Russian Courts had failed to apply statutory time-bars established by law, implying that one of the tax assessments raised against it had been unlawful, unforeseeable and retroactive. Drawing from the Cantoni principles, the ECtHR admitted the complaint pointing out that:

> 568. Furthermore, the term 'law' implies qualitative requirements, including those of accessibility and foreseeability (see, among other authorities, Cantoni v. France, 15 November 1996) ... . These qualitative requirements must be satisfied as regards both the definition of an offence and the penalty the offence in question carries ...
>
> 573 ... the Court finds that there has been a violation of Article 1 of Protocol No. 1 on account of the change in interpretation of the rules on the statutory time-bar resulting from the Constitutional Court's decision of 14 July 2005 and the effect of this decision on the outcome of the Tax Assessment 2000 proceedings.

In the innovative 2013 judgment *Gáll v. Hungary*,[46] one of the best tax judgments of the ECtHR, the ECtHR seemed to extend the application of the values of foreseeability and predictability to unexpected sudden legislative changes creating unanticipated hardship:

> For the Court, it is quite plausible that the element that she was subjected to the impugned measure while unemployed, together with the unexpected and swift nature of the change of the tax regime which made any preparation virtually impossible for those concerned, exposed the applicant to substantial personal hardships ... Moreover, the Court observes that the legislature did not afford the applicant a transitional period within which to adjust herself to the new scheme.

In 2019, the ECtHR delivered a low-profile customs duty judgment which creates an interesting precedent on the qualitative requirements of law taken in a tax treaty context. In the case of *Lopac and Others v. Croatia*,[47] the complaint referred to an incorrect application of an international convention, the Istanbul Convention. The applicant complained that Croatian law contravened an international treaty binding Croatia. The ECtHR criticised Croatia for its inconsistent application of the Istanbul Convention, creating uncertainty and ambiguity as to who could benefit from an

46. Application no. 49570/11.
47. Application no. 7834/12.

exemption from duty.[48] The ECtHR drew heavily from Article 7 'criminal law' jurisprudence finding a violation:

> 57. However, the Court further reiterates that the existence of a legal basis is not in itself sufficient to satisfy the principle of lawfulness. When speaking of 'law', Article 1 of Protocol No. 1 alludes to a concept which comprises statutory law as well as case-law and implies qualitative requirements, notably those of accessibility and foreseeability … . In particular, the law is 'foreseeable' when an individual is able – if need be with appropriate advice – to foresee, to a degree that is reasonable in the circumstances, the consequences which a given action may entail and when it affords a measure of protection against arbitrary interferences by the public authorities …
>
> 60. Having examined all the material submitted to it, the Court considers that the Government have not put forward any fact or argument capable of persuading it to reach a different conclusion in the present case. Since, as noted above (see paragraphs 57-58), Article 1 of Protocol No. 1 to the Convention requires that any interference with the right to the peaceful enjoyment of one's possessions must be lawful, which implies the qualitative requirement of foreseeability, the Court's findings in Žaja apply with equal force in the present case.

Interestingly, in the 2020 judgment in *Gospodăria Ţărănească Chiper Terenti Grigore v. the Republic of Moldova*,[49] ECtHR acknowledged statutory clarity as a requirement contemplated in the principle of lawfulness:

> 39. In the light of the above, the Court comes to the conclusion that the interference with the applicant's possessions which followed as a result of non-compliance with those unclear warning letters cannot be considered lawful and that no fair balance was struck between the demands of the public interest on the one hand and the applicant's right to the peaceful enjoyment of its possessions on the other.
>
> 40. There has therefore been a violation of Article 1 of Protocol No. 1.

1.6 PROPORTIONALITY

The use of the terms 'general principles of international law' in Article 1 of Protocol 1 and the concept of 'fair balance' imply that all tax measures must respect the value of proportionality, a value that is part and parcel of the European legal system.[50] The value of proportionality entails that taxation must not create an excessive burden, that tax collection procedures must fulfil certain standards relating to due process and that punitive measures must not go beyond what is strictly necessary.

Even the Commission's tax cases of the 1980s have acknowledged that the second paragraph of Article 1 of Protocol No. 1 has to be construed in the light of the

48. Eligibility to the exemption was based on domicile/residence.
49. Application no. 71130/13.
50. Joanna Dlugosz, 'The Principle of Proportionality in European Law as a Prerequisite for Penalization', in Jonas Christoffersen (ed.), *Fair Balance: Proportionality, Subsidiarity and Primarity in the European Convention on Human Rights* viewed at https://brill.com/view/book/9789004180819/Bej.9789004170285.i-670_003.xml.

general principle set out in the first sentence of the article implying that any interference with the right to property should strike a fair balance between 'the demands of the general interest of the community and the requirements of the protection of the individual's fundamental rights ... the concern to achieve this balance is reflected in the structure of Article 1 as a whole ... and hence also in the second paragraph'. There must be a reasonable relationship of proportionality between the means employed and the aims sought to be realised.[51] Consequently, 'the financial liability arising out of the raising of tax or contributions may adversely affect the guarantee secured under this provision if it places an excessive burden on the person or the entity concerned or fundamentally interferes with his or its financial position'.

The 2003 decision *Vincent Baláž v. Slovakia*[52] acknowledged that the concept of 'excessive burden' entails a subjective test; it is the impact of the tax measure on the financial position of the particular taxpayer that must be considered:

> The Court further recalls that a financial liability arising out of the raising of taxes or contributions may adversely affect the guarantee secured under Article 1 of Protocol No. 1 if it places an excessive burden on the person or entity concerned or fundamentally interferes with his or its financial position.

The same approach was taken in the case of *Gáll v. Hungary*,[53] repeating that the test of proportionality entails an analysis of the personal situation of the complainant, an approach that turned out to be very effective in cases involving penalties:

> Nevertheless, the Court cannot abdicate its power of review and must therefore determine whether the requisite balance was maintained in a manner consonant with the applicant's right to the peaceful enjoyment of possessions, within the meaning of the first sentence of Article 1 of Protocol No. 1 (see Jahn and Others v. Germany [GC], nos. 46720/99, 72203/01 and 72552/01, § 93, ECHR 2005-VI). In the determination of the proportionality of the measure, the Court did in the past also consider the personal situation of the applicants, including their good faith (see Vistiņš and Perepjolkins, cited above, § 120).

The individual excessive burden test was applied extremely strictly in the case of *Azienda Agricola Silverfunghi s.a.s. and Others v. Italy*[54] when the fact that the taxpayer could afford to pay the contested tax and had actually paid it was taken as evidence that the contested tax did not create an excessive burden on complainant:

> 106. As to the effects of the interference on the applicant companies' financial position, the Court notes that the companies uninterruptedly paid the relevant contributions without the concession being applied to them.

It is submitted that the latter argument is extremely dangerous because it basically states that taxation is a fait accompli.

---

51. *Tre Traktörer Ab v. Sweden*, Application no. 10873/84, *James and Others v. the United Kingdom*, Application no. 8793/79 and *Sporrong and Lönnroth v. Sweden*, Application no. 7151/75.
52. Application no. 60243/00.
53. Application no. 49570/11.
54. Applications nos. 48357/07, 52677/07, 52687/07 and 52701/07.

The strongest as well as the weakest judgments tend to involve the proportionality test when the ECtHR may be criticised for not always being entirely coherent.

The concept of proportionality must be examined under three heads reflecting the ECtHR's activism in the respective areas. Judgments of the ECtHR suggest that the ECtHR's appetite for intrusion depends on whether the notion of proportionality is examined in the contexts of:

(a) Raw Tax.
(b) Tax Collection Procedures.
(c) Punitive Measures.

It is submitted that while the ECtHR has been ultra-conservative in actions to impugn 'raw' taxes, the ECtHR has been more liberal in judgments involving tax collection procedures, and even more magnanimous in cases involving punitive measures.

1.7 RAW TAX

The vast majority of cases challenging 'raw' tax systems on the basis of Article 1 of Protocol 1 were dismissed, but there have been random exceptions that have raised expectations.

The 2008 decision in *Imbert de Tremiolles v. France*[55] reflects the ECtHR's traditional approach to the matter. Spouses Imbert de Tremiolles contested the French wealth tax on the basis that the tax exceeded their earnings from the base assets, but their complaint was rejected:

> Accordingly, in view of the margin of appreciation which the States were afforded in this sphere, the payment of the tax in question had not affected the applicants' financial situation seriously enough for the measure to be considered disproportionate or an abuse of a State's right, acknowledged in Article 1 of Protocol No. 1, to secure the payment of taxes and other contributions: manifestly ill-founded.[56]

The ECtHR adopted a bolder stance in the oft-quoted case of *N.K.M. v. Hungary*[57] when the ECtHR forcefully struck down a Hungarian tax that was blatantly disproportionate.[58]

55. Application no. 25834/05.
56. Drawn from the ECtHR's Press Release Information Note on the Court's case law no. 104 January 2008 viewed at https://hudoc.echr.coe.int/eng#{%22itemid%22:[%22002-2323%22] in May 2022.
57. Application no. 66529/11.
58. The judgment followed the progressive jurisprudential line set out in *Demir and Baykara v. Turkey*, Application no. 34503/97, which had a decisive impact on a number of cases, where it can be witnessed that a social rights-friendly and relevant international and comparative law approaches were effectively used to progress the Court's case law. *See* Paulo Pinto de Albuquerque, 'The Rights of Workers, Migrant Workers and Trade Unions under the European Convention on Human Rights', European Human Rights Law Review, Issue 1 (2020) pp. 24–37, and 'Plaidoyer for the European Court of Human Rights', European Human Rights Law Review, Issue 2 (2018) pp. 119–133.

The *N.K.M.* case originated in an application lodged by a Hungarian national, Ms N.K.M complaining that the imposition of a 98% tax on the upper bracket of her severance constituted an unjustified deprivation of property, or else taxation at an excessively disproportionate rate, with no remedy available.

The ECtHR held that a measure to secure payment of taxes must strike a 'fair balance' between the demands of the general interest of the community and the requirements of the protection of the individual's fundamental rights. The Court held that there must be a reasonable relationship of proportionality between the means employed and the aims pursued. The Court held that the question that had to be answered was whether, in the applicant's specific circumstances, the application of the tax law imposed an unreasonable burden on her or fundamentally undermined her financial situation - and thereby failed to strike a fair balance between the various interests involved.

The ECtHR observed that the applicant, who was entitled to statutory severance on the basis of the law in force and whose acting in good faith was never called into question, was subjected to a tax whose rate exceeded about three times the general personal income tax rate of 16%. In the ECtHR's view, the applicant, together with a group of dismissed civil servants, was made to bear an excessive and disproportionate burden, while other civil servants with comparable statutory and other benefits were apparently not required to contribute to a comparable extent to the public burden, even if they were in the position of leadership that enabled them to define certain contractual benefits potentially disapproved by the public. Furthermore, the Court observed that the legislature did not afford the applicant a transitional period within which to adjust herself to the new scheme. Against this background, the Court found that the measure complained of entailed an excessive and individual burden on the applicant's side. In this connection, the Court recalled that taxation at a considerably higher tax rate than that in force when the revenue in question was generated could be regarded as an unreasonable interference with expectations protected by Article 1 of Protocol No. 1. The Court found for Mrs NKM awarding financial compensation.

The 2013 case of *Gáll v. Hungary*,[59] quoted previously, followed closely the conclusions in *N.K.M. v. Hungary*[60] delivered earlier on in the same year sharing similar merits. Interestingly, the scholarly judgment of *Gáll* gave an added perspective to the concept of proportionality. The ECtHR pointed out that selective and arbitrary tax policies are not even allowed in times of recession:

> 71. Against this background, the Court finds that the measure complained of entailed an excessive and individual burden on the applicant's side. This is all the more evident when considering the fact that the measure targeted only a certain group of individuals, who were apparently singled out by the public administration in its capacity as employer. Assuming that the impugned measure served the interest of the State budget at a time of economic hardship, the Court notes that the majority of citizens were not obliged to contribute, to a comparable extent, to the public burden ...

59. Application no. 49570/11.
60. Application no. 66529/11.

> 74. The Court concludes that the specific measure in question, as applied to the applicant, even if meant to serve social justice, cannot be justified by the legitimate public interest relied on by the Government. It affected the applicant (and other dismissed civil servants in a similar situation) being in good-faith standing and deprived her of the larger part of a statutorily guaranteed, acquired right serving the special social interest of reintegration ... .

Returning to the point of good faith, the ECtHR concluded:

> In the Court's opinion, those who act in good faith on the basis of law should not be frustrated in their statute based expectations without specific and compelling reasons. Therefore the measure cannot be held reasonably proportionate to the aim sought to be realised.

The ECtHR has consistently pointed out that, for the purposes of the proportionality test, high rates of tax are per se not decisive but are given some weighting nonetheless. Tax rate amount was duly considered in *Concetta Cacciato and Michele Cacciato v. Italy*[61] when the ECtHR observed that:

> 27. The Court considers at the outset that the tax rate applied in the present case, which amounted to 20% of the total expropriation compensation awarded, cannot be considered, from a quantitative standpoint, as prohibitive ... .

The ECtHR adopted a similar approach in the 2019 judgments *Nicola Colazzo and Others v. Italy*[62] and *Stefano Guiso-Gallisai and Others v. Italy*,[63] another two Italian cases involving taxation on expropriation awards.

Due consideration to tax rates and individual impact of same was given in most cases. A detailed analysis of tax rates was conducted in the leading cases. In the judgments delivered in *R.Sz. v. Hungary*[64] previously cited and in *Gáll v. Hungary*,[65] the ECtHR made the following observation:

> ... tax rates exceeding 50% have been found unconstitutional in Germany, a Member State of the Council of Europe (see paragraph 20 above). However, in several European countries – such as Sweden, Belgium, the Netherlands, Portugal and Italy – personal income tax rates reached about 75% in the past – although those rates were usually applicable only to the highest income brackets, related to revenues clearly exceeding the amount that is contemplated in the context of the Hungarian statutory severance. It is also to be noted that the OECD average of top combined statutory personal income tax rates was 65.7% in 1981, 50.6% in 1990, 46.5% in 2000 and 41.7% in 2001 ...
>
> 66 ... For the Court, given the margin of appreciation granted to States in matters of taxation, the applicable tax rate cannot be decisive in itself, especially in circumstances like those of the present case.

The proportionality point articulated in the Hungarian cases discussed above created an expectation that the ECtHR would become more intrusive by becoming

61. Application no. 60633/16.
62. Application no. 36944/06.
63. Application no. 95/06.
64. Application no. 41838/11.
65. Application no. 49570/11.

more detailed on the point of proportionality. There was a hope that the ECtHR would endorse a principle analogous to the German concept of 'Halbteilungsgrundsatz' or 'fifty per cent rule'[66] according to which the overall tax load on assets must be limited to 50%–60% of the yield on those assets.

Sadly, all these hopes were dashed in the 2017 judgment in the case of *Plaisier B.V v. the Netherlands* and two other applications,[67] a case involving the draconian 2012 Dutch Emergency Tax, an austerity levy set at a crippling high wages tax surcharge of 16% on wages in excess of EUR 150,000 paid in 2012, 2013 and 2014.

Unfortunately, the ECtHR's conclusions were heavily influenced by the fact that the austerity tax had been projected as a temporary crisis levy. Consequently, the ECtHR based its judgment on case law allowing austerity measures including a Romanian emergency measure allowing a temporary reduction of income for certain segments of the population,[68] a Portuguese emergency measure cutting holiday and Christmas allowances payable to certain categories of public-section pensioners[69] and a Greek austerity measure known as 'haircut' resulting in the compulsory exchange of Greek Government bonds held by investors.[70]

Thus, the ECtHR promptly dismissed the case on the basis of the State margin of appreciation:

> 82. There can be no doubt that the Netherlands were entitled in principle to take far-reaching measures to bring its economy back into line with its international obligation. This entitlement is however subject to the proviso that no 'individual and excessive burden' be imposed on any person ...
>
> 97. Finally and more generally, the Court cannot accept the applicant's argument that the legislative interference in issue affected so few taxpayers that its impact on the State budget was minimal, and that other measures would have resulted in more meaningful revenue. In this connection it reiterates that, provided that the legislature chose a method that could be regarded as reasonable and suited to achieving the legitimate aim being pursued, it is not for the Court to say whether the legislation represented the best solution for dealing with the problem or whether the legislative discretion should have been exercised in another way (see James and Others, cited above, § 51).

The subject of emergency tax measures returned on the ECtHR's agenda in 2019 in the case of *Alexandru-Mihai Pop and Others v. Romania*,[71] a case involving a

66. Paragraph 11 in Application no. 66529/11. *See also* Oliver Lepsius, 'Constitutional Review of Tax Laws and the Unconstitutionality of the German Inheritance Tax', German Law Journal, Volume 16, Issue 5 (October 2015) pp. 1191–1226, and also available in https://www.cambridge.org/core/journals/german-law-journal/article/constitutional-review-of-tax-laws-and-the-unconstitutionality-of-the-german-inheritance-tax/3E5224175054B22DFC9B35A229E95E80.
67. Application no. 46184/16.
68. *Mihăieş and Senteş v. Romania (dec.)*, Applications nos. 44232/11 and 44605/11, § 8.
69. *Da Conceição Mateus and Santos Januário v. Portugal (dec.)*, Applications nos. 62235/12 and 57725/12, passim. *See also Da Silva Carvalho Rico v. Portugal (dec.)*, Application no. 13341/14, § 12.
70. *Mamatas and Others v. Greece*, Applications nos. 63066/14 and 2 others, §§ 22 and 48–51.
71. Applications nos. 54494/11, 67699/11 and 21251/12.

pollution tax that was held to be incompatible with European Union (EU) law.[72] The ECtHR declared the case inadmissible because of non-exhaustion of domestic remedies and thus it will be discussed in the chapter dealing with Article 35.

The ECtHR retained a conservative stance in the 2021 judgment in the case of *Iofil AE v. Greece*,[73] a case involving a Greek capital gains tax on the sale and repurchase of securities held in a subsidiary. In the case of IOFIL, the sale and buy-back had been executed within only two days. IOFIL AE complained that the imposition of the tax had violated its right to the peaceful enjoyment of its possessions, as the transaction in its listed subsidiary had merely served as a means of revaluing its assets to comply with its obligation under regulatory law. The ECtHR noted that the fact that the tax imposed on it in respect of the disputed transaction amounted to two-thirds of corporate tax IOFIL AE had paid for a whole financial year was not sufficient to prove that the tax had been disproportionate. The ECtHR added that it had not seen any evidence in the case file that the levying of the tax fundamentally undermined the applicant company's financial situation dismissing the application.

1.8 PUNITIVE MEASURES

Whereas the ECtHR has been criticised for its hesitant stance in cases involving proportionality of taxes, the ECtHR is praised for taking a firm stand against oppressive tax penalty regimes.

The ECtHR's leading case on tax penalties is the 2007 judgment in *Mamidakis v. Greece*,[74] a case involving an administrative sanction of EUR 3,008,216 for contraband of goods of a commercial value of EUR 4,946,145. While acknowledging the State's Signatory's wide margins and discretions in laying down their tax penalty regimes, the ECtHR unanimously held that, in this particular case, the penalty was exorbitant[75] to such an extent that it created an excessive burden that was incompatible with the right to property:

> 48. Dans ces circonstances, même en tenant compte de la marge d'appréciation dont disposent les Etats contractants en cette matière (voir, Baláž c. Slovaquie (déc.), no 60243/00, 16 septembre 2003; Valico S.r.l. c. Italie (déc.), no 70074/01, 21 mars 2006), la Cour estime que l'imposition de l'amende en question a porté une telle atteinte à la situation financière du requérant qu'il s'agissait d'une mesure disproportionnée par rapport au but légitime qu'elle poursuivait. Partant, 8l y a eu violation de l'article 1 du Protocole no 1.

The 168-page judgment in *Oao Neftyanaya Kompaniya Yukos ('Yukos') v. Russia*[76] incorporated a complaint relating to the proportionality of penalties too. The ECtHR declared that it was satisfied that, subject to its findings in respect of the

72. The issue of incompatibility between a domestic measure and EU Law was also raised in the 2019 Application no. 68475/10, *Heinrich Josef Bley v. Germany*, but the case failed on the merits.
73. Application no. 50598/13.
74. Application no. 35533/04.
75. The penalties were of EUR 3,008,216 and EUR 4,946,145.
76. Application no. 14902/04.

lawfulness of the fines, penalties imposed constituted a proportionate measure in pursuance of a legitimate aim. The ECtHR found that the fines as such were not particularly high, and given the gravity of the tax fraud, there was nothing to suggest that the rates of the fines or interest payments can be viewed as having imposed an individual and disproportionate burden, as such, on Yukos.

In 2022, the ECtHR delivered another interesting case involving a penalty, but that lacked an element of proportionality with the evaded tax nonetheless. In the case of *Krayeva v. Ukraine*,[77] the Court highlighted the fact that the penalty in issue created an individual excessive burden. The case involved a young customs clearance officer who, because of a petty oversight caused by erroneous documents provided by a supplier, committed an error that rendered her liable to a penalty that was equivalent to the tax in danger amounting to EUR 48,661. The system did not provide for an abatement of the penalty because the penalty was set by statute. Ms Krayeva brought evidence proving that the penalty caused her significant financial hardship.

While acknowledging that the impugned measure was a measure imposed in a compelling public interest, the ECtHR reminded that penalties should never create an excessive individual burden. The ECtHR found that an assessment of the proportionality of the penalty was not incorporated in domestic judgments leading to the imposition of the penalty. No assessment of the relevant circumstances, including the diligence and behaviour of the delinquent, the relationship between her conduct and the offence or her financial situation, had been exercised. The law did not allow for the abatement of the penalty, and scope for judicial review was too narrow to satisfy the requirement of seeking a fair balance contemplated in the ECHR. Consequently, the ECtHR found a violation of Article 1 of Protocol No. 1.

1.9 TAX COLLECTION MEASURES

Early cases involving powers relating to the seizure of assets and retention of same were decided *pro auctoritate*. The 1989 case of *Gasus Dosier- und Fördertechnik Gmbh v. the Netherlands*[78] cited previously involved the seizure of industrial equipment by the tax authorities. Gasus complained that it had been deprived of its property in payment of a tax debt owed by a third party; a purchaser ended up being deprived of its rightful property because of failings committed by the seller. The ECtHR did not find a violation because:

> 66 … The power of recovery against goods which are in fact in a debtor's possession although nominally owned by a third party is a not uncommon device to strengthen a creditor's position in enforcement proceedings; it cannot be held incompatible per se with the requirements of Article 1 of Protocol No. 1 (P1-1). Consequently, a legislature may in principle resort to that device to ensure, in the general interest, that taxation yields as much as possible and that tax debts are recovered as expeditiously as possible. Nonetheless, it cannot be overlooked that, quite apart from the dangers of abuse, the character of legislation by which the

77. Application no. 72858/13.
78. Application no. 15375/89.

State creates such powers for itself is not the same as that of legislation granting similar powers to narrowly defined categories of private creditors. … .'

In more recent cases, the ECtHR has taken a more balanced approach. The ECtHR's landmark 2011 judgment in *Oao Neftyanaya Kompaniya Yukos ('Yukos') v. Russia*[79] left an impact on this area too.

The ECtHR held that the manner Russia enforced the debt resulting from the 2003 tax assessment proceedings violated Yukos' right to property. According to the ECtHR, the 7% enforcement fee by Russia pendente lite was by its very nature unrelated to litigation costs. The ECtHR observed that there is nothing wrong as a matter of principle with requiring a debtor to pay for the expenses relating to the enforcement of a debt or to threaten a debtor with a sanction to incite his or her voluntary compliance with enforcement writs, but in the circumstances of the case the resulting sum was completely out of proportion to the amount of the enforcement expenses which could have possibly been expected to be borne or had actually been borne by the bailiffs. Because of its rigid application, instead of inciting voluntary compliance, it contributed very seriously to the applicant company's demise. The Court concluded that:

> 656. Lastly, the Court would again emphasise that the authorities were unyieldingly inflexible as to the pace of the enforcement proceedings, acting very swiftly and constantly refusing to concede to the applicant company's demands for additional time … Nevertheless, the Court finds that in the circumstances of the case such lack of flexibility had a negative overall effect on the conduct of the enforcement proceedings against the applicant company.
>
> 658. To sum up, the Court concludes that there has been a violation of the applicant company's rights under Article 1 of Protocol No. 1 on account of the State's failure to strike a fair balance between the aims sought and the measures employed in the enforcement proceedings against the applicant company.

In the case of *Dominique Rheims and others v. France*,[80] the Commission held that a bailiff's fee charged by the Government in tax litigation procedures did not constitute a violation of the right to property because, unlike the case with the charge in Yukos, the French system met all requirements relating to lawfulness.

The 2013 case of *Rousk v. Sweden*[81] involved a taxpayer who had accumulated a debt with the Swedish tax authorities. The applicant's total enforceable debts amounted to SEK 255,329, but the tax authorities seized the taxpayer's home which was worth over SEK 1,372,000. As a consequence, the taxpayer ended homeless. The ECtHR held that it accepted that it would sometimes be necessary for the State to attach and sell property, including an individual's home, in order to secure the payment of taxes due to the State through enforceable debts, but it emphasised that these measures must be enforced in a manner which ensures that the individual's right to his or her home is properly considered and protected. Having regard to the lack of effective procedural safeguards for the applicant to protect his interests, the ECtHR found violations both of Article 8 and Article 1 of the First Protocol. The part of the complaint

79. Application no. 14902/04.
80. Application no. 32492/08.
81. Application no. 27183/04.

dealing with Article 8 will be discussed in more detail in the chapter discussing Article 8.

The ECtHR built a strong line of judgments condemning arbitrary policies relating to the seizure of assets.

In the 2015 case of *Dimitrovi v. Bulgaria*,[82] the ECtHR saw through an oppressive Bulgarian tax collection regime. This case involved a challenge to a Bulgarian law providing for the forfeiture of property believed to have originated from tax evasion. The ECtHR found that the relative Bulgarian law was incompatible with the right to property because the Bulgarian regime was too arbitrary. The law was too general and vague. It was neither foreseeable nor precise. It did not incorporate safeguards against arbitrariness. Therefore, it was not in line with the minimum standards set by the ECHR.

Similarly, in 2017 the ECtHR did not mince its words in the case of *Polimerkonteyner, TOV v. Ukraine*[83] when the applicant company alleged a violation of its right to property caused by the fact that it had been forced to pay the wrong customs tariff. The customs office had adopted an irregular practice of assigning the wrong classification code to its goods contrary to numerous final judicial decisions in that regard. The ECtHR attached a lot of weight to statements of the domestic courts condemning the tax authorities' practice that undermined both the finality of their judgments and the courts' authority in general. The ECtHR held that the customs authorities acted in an arbitrary manner and that, effectively, the applicant company had been left without mechanisms for putting an end to that practice. The ECtHR noted that it examined a somewhat comparable situation in the case of *Intersplav v. Ukraine*, where the applicant company had been obliged to institute judicial proceedings in respect of numerous instances of the authorities' failure to confirm the VAT refund amounts payable to it. The Court had found that the systematic nature of the failings of the State authorities had resulted in an excessive burden being imposed on the applicant company. The ECtHR held that the same criticism held true for the present case. Like in the cited case, the applicant company had to go through rounds of judicial proceedings to recover the overpaid customs duty. Furthermore, during those proceedings, it could not use the imported goods belonging to it, which had been impounded and were held until a resolution in the case. The Court held that there had been an interference with the peaceful enjoyment of the applicant company's possessions, which, as confirmed by the domestic courts on several occasions, was unlawful. The ECtHR concluded that there had been a violation of Article 1 of Protocol No. 1.

In the 2021 case of *Trafik Oil – 1 Eood v. Bulgaria*,[84] the ECtHR found that refusal to release impounded fuel after proceedings of judicial review had ordered the release of the fuel amounted to a violation. Although there was no question as to the foreseeability and predictability of the impugned measure, and it was abundantly clear that the impugned interference pursued a legitimate aim (the unauthorised sale of excise goods), Bulgaria's failure to effectively allow Trafik Oil to challenge the

82. Application no. 12655/09.
83. Application no. 23620/05.
84. Application no. 67437/17.

confiscation of its property, deprived it of an assessment of the proportionality of the measure and the requisite safeguards against arbitrariness and was thus not necessary in a democratic society. Consequently, the ECtHR found a violation of Article 1 of Protocol No. 1.

A similar balanced approach was adopted in the 2022 case of *Fu Quan, S.R.O. v. the Czech Republic*[85] involving retention of the applicant company's merchandise for almost a year and a half after the acquittal of its officers in criminal proceedings involving tax evasion. The fact that the tax authorities had retained the goods after the case was closed was held to amount to a violation.

1.10 OTHER MATTERS PERTINENT TO THE RIGHT TO PROPERTY

1.10.1 Payment of Tax as a Consolidation of a Right Creating a 'Possession'

Interestingly, in several judgments, the ECtHR has ruled that the payment of tax due over an asset consolidates a right over such asset. Paying tax over an asset creates a vested right over such an asset. The implication is that when a State Signatory accepts payment of tax over an asset, such State seems to be recognising that taxpayer has some form of right over it, a principle that has been confirmed in a number of judgments of the ECtHR. In the 2005 case of *Hamer v. Belgium*,[86] the ECtHR observed that:

> Since then, the applicant had been paying an annual property tax and second-residence tax ... It is therefore clear that the authorities knew or should have known of the existence of the applicant's house for a long time. However, notwithstanding the provisions of the relevant legislation, they failed to take the appropriate action to ensure compliance. They thus contributed to the continuation of a situation which could only be detrimental to the protection of the forested area which that legislation sought to protect.

The ECtHR took the same view in the 2020 case of *Elif Kizil v. Turkey*[87] where it equated the payment of tax on an asset as a 'possession' of such an asset:

> la Cour a conclu à l'existence d'un bien en se fondant sur plusieurs circonstances: la requérante était titulaire d'un titre formel de propriété, notarié et inscrit dans les registres immobiliers; elle pouvait fonder son espérance légitime sur une pratique remontant au XVe siècle, consistant à reconnaître à des particuliers des titres de propriété sur les vallées de pêche et à tolérer de leur part une possession et une exploitation continue de ces biens; elle payait les impôts fonciers sur ladite vallée, occupait le lieu et s'y comportait en propriétaire sans avoir jamais suscité de réactions de la part des autorités.

In the 2005 case of *Aminat Madarovna Elsanova v. Russia*,[88] the ECtHR referred to the payment of tax on an asset as prima facie evidence of ownership of an asset:

85. Application no. 24827/14.
86. Application no. 21861/03.
87. Application no. 4601/06.
88. Application no. 57952/00.

> The applicant submitted no documents relevant to her claims of ownership of property in the village of Nizhaloy, such as land or property titles, extracts from land or tax registers, documents from the local administration, plans, photographs or any other relevant evidence.

In the 2017 case of *Maharramov v. Azerbaijan*,[89] the ECtHR concluded that the payment of land tax created a proprietary right analogous to a possession. Paying tax is not only an obligation but it creates vested rights too. Thus, in the 2005 Grand Chamber judgment *STEC and Others v. the United Kingdom*,[90] a Social Security case, the ECtHR observed that:

> Given the variety of funding methods, and the interlocking nature of benefits under most welfare systems, it appears increasingly artificial to hold that only benefits financed by contributions to a specific fund fall within the scope of Article 1 of Protocol No. 1. Moreover, to exclude benefits paid for out of general taxation would be to disregard the fact that many claimants under this latter type of system also contribute to its financing, through the payment of tax.

1.10.2 Positive, Preventive and Remedial Action

Regrettably, the ECtHR has never had the opportunity to express itself on State Signatory's positive obligations to take preventive measures to defend citizens from unlawful interferences into their possessions caused by oppressive taxation. Hopefully, the day will come when the ECtHR's tax jurisprudence borrows from non-tax judgments when the ECtHR will be called to establish principles applicable in a tax arena too.

The ECtHR's conclusion reached in the 2004 case of *Öneryildiz v. Turkey*[91] binding State Signatories to take positive, preventive, and remedial action against human rights infringements should apply equally to cases over arbitrary taxation and failure to recognise vested tax rights in a timely manner.

In 2013 in the case of *Zolotas v. Greece*,[92] a case involving the confiscation of a bank account that had been dormant for twenty years by the Greek State made reflections that are entirely applicable in the tax sphere:

> The principle of legal certainty being implicit in all the Articles of the Convention, the State had an obligation to protect the right of its citizens to the enjoyment of their possessions. The banks should thus have been obliged to inform the holder of a dormant account of the risks incurred in the run-up to the end of the limitation period. The failure to provide such information had placed an excessive and disproportionate burden on Mr Zolotas that could not be justified by the need to

89. Application no. 5046/07.
90. Applications nos. 65731/01 and 65900/01.
91. Application no. 48939/99.
92. Application no. 66610/09.

> terminate legal relationships whose existence had become uncertain or to ensure the proper functioning of the banking system.[93]

The non-tax judgment in *Zolatas* suggests that Tax Authorities should be pro-active in settling tax refunds, managing tax credits and paying interest on late payment of the same.

1.10.3 The Issues of Retrospectivity and Retroactivity

In previously quoted judgments including especially the 2013 judgments *Gáll v. Hungary, R.Sz. v. Hungary*[94] and *OAO Neftyanaya Kompaniya Yukos v. Russia*,[95] the ECtHR effectively struck down what may be described as retroactive tax measures, but the jurisprudence of the ECtHR does not contain an absolute prohibition of retroactive taxation, far from it.

The issue of retrospective taxation arose in some early cases including decisions of the 1970s such as *ABC&D v. United Kingdom*[96] and cases of the 1990s like the *Building Societies* case,[97] *Voggenberger Transport GmbH v. Austria*[98] and *Nap Holdings UK Ltd v. United Kingdom.*[99] None of the decisions excluded the legality of retrospective taxation measures. More recently, the 2011 judgment *Maggio and Others v. Italy*[100] acknowledged that the ECtHR's jurisprudence established that laws with retrospective effect which were found to constitute legislative interference still conformed to the lawfulness requirement of Article 1 of Protocol No. 1.

The leading decision on the matter is the 2003 decision *M.A. and 34 Others v. Finland*[101] involving a complaint under Article 1 of Protocol No. 1 that the applying of a retrospective tax law, leading to a considerably higher tax liability than the previous law, violated the right to the peaceful enjoyment of possessions. Complainants cleverly contested the measure on the basis of the 'lawfulness' criterion, providing that laws must be foreseeable and predictable. The ECtHR dismissed the argument:

> In the Court's view the changes in the tax legislation which took effect on 1 January 1995 as such certainly fall within this margin despite the fact that they applied, as from the above-mentioned date, even to existing stock option arrangements ... .
>
> As to the impact of the measure, the Court considers that the legislation was not such as to amount to confiscatory taxation or of such a nature as could deprive the legislation of its character as a tax law. Despite its important financial consequences for the applicants, the measure cannot be said to have imposed an

93. Taken from ECtHR Press Release issued by the Registrar of the Court ECHR 031 (2013) 29.01.2013.
94. For an identical case, *see also* the case of *T.K. v. Hungary*, Application no. 64321/13.
95. Application no. 14902/04.
96. Application no. 8531/1979.
97. Applications nos. 21319/1993, 21449/1993 and 21675/1993.
98. Application no. 21294/1993.
99. Application no. 27721/1995.
100. Applications nos. 46286/09, 52851/08 and 53727/08.
101. Application no. 27793/95.

> excessive burden on them, taking into account the maximum percentage of the tax levy. It follows that this complaint is manifestly ill-founded.

The ludicrous facts in issue in the more clear-cut 2010 case of *di Belmonte v. Italy*[102] gave the ECtHR a splendid opportunity to come up with some mild prohibition of retrospective taxation, but the ECtHR steered clear of sweeping statements. In the *di Belmonte* case, Italy's violation of taxpayer's rights was glaring, but the ECtHR bit its tongue nonetheless. Belmonte owned a plot of building land that had been expropriated. Years after the expropriation, a retrospective tax law came into force, and di Belmonte discovered that he had a tax debt of which he could not have been aware of at the time when his property was expropriated.

The ECtHR began its assessment by reminding that States have a wide discretion in determining the types of taxes to be levied and that they have sole competence on the matter. The ECtHR added that the possibility of retrospective application of the law does not per se raise an issue under the ECHR, since Article 1 of Protocol No. 1 did not prohibit as such the retrospective application of a law on taxation.

Returning to the facts of the case, the Court noted that the retrospective tax law had come into force months after the final amount of compensation for the expropriation had been finally determined by the Courts. Accordingly, the delay by the authorities had a decisive impact on the application of the new tax system, since the compensation awarded to the applicant would not have been subject to the tax provided for by the new tax legislation if the judgment had been executed properly and punctually. The Court concluded unanimously that there had been a violation of Article 1 of Protocol No. 1. The Court awarded Belmonte EUR 1,100,000 for the pecuniary damage sustained (reimbursement of the sum deducted in tax, adjustment of that amount to offset the effects of inflation, and interest).

The ECtHR was particularly conservative in the 2015 judgment *Huitson v. the United Kingdom.*[103] The way the BBC reported the case said it all. In an interview to the BBC, Professor Anne Redston of King's College, London described the case as '... nevertheless worrying ... allowing HMRC to get its own way without bothering to argue its case in the courts ... What is certain is that backdating legislation is a cheap, quick and certain way of closing a tax loophole, and it may be irresistibly tempting for the government to use the same method again'.[104]

The *Huitson* case involved international tax avoidance and tax treaty shopping. Huitson had used the UK's double tax treaty with the Isle of Man in a way that had been judged artificial and fictitious. The UK relied on a retroactive specific anti-avoidance provision cancelling Huitson's tax treaty rights. Huitson argued that the provision breached his right to property.

The ECtHR noted that the applicant entered into what the domestic courts described as a marketed and wholly artificial tax avoidance scheme with the effect that the general rule that United Kingdom taxpayers should pay United Kingdom income tax on the profits of their trade or profession was contravened. By the time the challenged

102. Application no. 72638/01.
103. Application no. 50131/12.
104. http://news.bbc.co.uk/2/mobile/business/8496921.stm.

legislation, with its retrospective amendments, was enacted, there were about 2,500 taxpayers exploiting similar arrangements, and the amount of income tax at stake for the respondent Government had risen to GBP 100 million. As a result of the scheme, the applicant claimed that he was able to reduce his effective income tax rate to 3.5%, thereby ensuring a considerable competitive advantage in comparison to other IT consultants.

The ECtHR noted that the object of the legislative amendments in issue was to prevent the Double Tax Agreement Tax relief provisions from being misused for a purpose different from their originally intended use, that is relieving tax payers from double taxation. The ECtHR considered that it is a legitimate and important aim of public policy in fiscal affairs that a Double Tax Agreement should do no more than relieve double taxation and should not be permitted to become an instrument by which persons residing in the United Kingdom avoid, or substantially reduce, the income tax that they would ordinarily pay on their income. Moreover, it is in the general interest of the community to prevent taxpayers resident in the United Kingdom from exploiting the Double Tax Agreement in a way which would enable them to substantially reduce their income tax and secure a competitive advantage over those who chose not to use such a scheme.

As to the reasonable relationship of proportionality between the means employed and the aims pursued, the ECtHR considered that it was within the area of discretionary judgment for the British Parliament to legislate with retrospective effect to ensure a fair balance between the general body of resident taxpayers and the individuals who sought to benefit from the scheme, in particular taking into account the number of taxpayers relying on the scheme and the potential financial loss at stake for the Respondent Government.

The ECtHR accepted the domestic courts' finding that there was no legal requirement on the respondent Government to carry out either a formal or informal impact assessment before enacting retrospective legislation, nor was there any legal obligation to bring legal proceedings in respect of the scheme before enacting retrospective legislation. Given the highly artificial nature of the tax avoidance scheme, the ECtHR held that the absence of such an assessment, as well as test litigation, does not affect the proportionality of the impugned measure.

Taking into account the wide margin of appreciation which the States have in taxation matters, the ECtHR held that the actions taken by the respondent State, in legislating retrospectively, did not upset the balance which must be struck between the protection of the applicant's rights and the public interest in securing the payment of taxes. It held that the complaint was manifestly ill-founded.

The 2016 judgment *Arnaud and Others v. France*[105] gave the ECtHR the opportunity to return to the subject of retrospectivity in international anti-tax avoidance environment. The case involved a retrospective tax law that forced French nationals who had settled in the Principality of Monaco liable, retroactively with effect from

105. Applications nos. 36918/11, 36963/11, 36967/11, 36969/11, 36969/11, 36970/11 and 36971/11.

2005, to pay a solidarity tax on wealth on the same basis as if they were domiciled or residents in France.

The ECtHR did not find a violation because it held that the retrospective law had been enacted in the context of a foreseeable longstanding and close relationship between France and Monaco in tax matters. The ECtHR concluded that the taxpayers had received advanced notice of the retrospective tax law, enabling them to comply with their obligations to the best of their abilities, noting that measures to mitigate the severity of retroactivity were in place. In view of the above, the ECtHR concluded that the retrospective tax charge had not upset the fair balance which was to be struck between the applicants' interests and the general interest.

Against this background, in the 2017 case of *Plaisier B.V v. the Netherlands* and two other applications, quoted previously, the ECtHR expeditiously despatched issues relating retrospectivity as follows:

> 84. The Court accepts that the surcharge had retrospective effects. It observes, however, that retrospective tax legislation is not as such prohibited by Article 1 of Protocol No. 1. It has accepted that the public interest may override the interest of the individual in knowing his or her tax liabilities in advance, provided that there are specific and compelling reasons for this.

The issue of retrospective tax measures returned on the ECtHR's agenda in the 2021 case of *HI Tech Corporation DOO v. North Macedonia.*[106] HI Tech Corporation DOO complained under Article 1 of Protocol No. 1 to the Convention that administrative tax proceedings instituted against it had been reopened after the statutory limitation period had expired and that it had been unjustifiably reassessed for income tax purposes.

The issue in front of the Macedonian authorities involved an incorrect application of a tax depreciation rate, a matter which had been picked up by the Macedonian tax authorities after they had closed their investigation for the relevant years and were examining later years.

Noting that the company should have anticipated the issue relating to incorrect tax accounting fell under its responsibility, the ECtHR dismissed the complaint. The ECtHR's judgment was not very detailed in its dismissal of the retrospectivity argument concluding that the company had neither presented any arguments nor submitted any examples of domestic practice militating against the consistency of the tax authorities' approach. Referring to the wide margin of appreciation given to States in taxation, the ECtHR held that the application was manifestly ill-founded. In November 2022, the Grand Chamber reached a similar conclusion in the Article 6 judgment in *Vegotex International S.A. v. Belgium.*[107]

106. Application no. 69776/17.
107. Application no. 49812/09.

1.10.4 Vicarious, Joint and Several Liability

Tax regimes providing for personal liability of officers of corporations for the tax liabilities and omissions of the corporations they serve in have come under the scrutiny of the ECtHR. Regimes providing for vicarious, joint and several liability have been held to be per se compatible with the ECHR. In the 2019 case *Mate Matić v. Croatia*[108] the ECtHR ruled that:

> 54. That being so, the Court, having regard to the domestic authorities' wide margin of appreciation in tax matters, also finds that it cannot be said that the rule imposing joint and several liability for customs debt on those who knew or must have known that the goods they had acquired had been imported illegally is at odds with the principle of proportionality inherent in Article 1 of Protocol No. 1 to the Convention (see paragraph 45 above).

The same matter returned on the ECtHR's agenda in 2020 in the case of *Agapov v. Russia*[109] when the ECtHR found a violation but only because the Russian regime provided for automatic vicarious, personal, joint and several liability within a system that did not allow the complainant a hearing to contest:

> 60 ... Nevertheless, the national courts granted the tax authorities' claims and considered it sufficient to conclude that the applicant was liable for the damage resulting from the LLC's failure to pay taxes merely by referring to the investigator's finding that the applicant had evaded payment of VAT, without examining any evidence or making independent findings of their own under the applicable provisions of civil law that the applicant was in fact responsible for non-payment of taxes. Furthermore, none of the facts cited by the investigator in the relevant decision and relied upon by the civil courts was scrutinised or validated in any adversarial manner either in the criminal or civil proceedings ...
>
> 63. Regard being had to the above, the Court considers that the order for the applicant to pay damages to the tax authorities was made in an arbitrary fashion and was therefore contrary to the requirement of lawfulness under Article 1 of Protocol No. 1.

The leading ECtHR judgment on the matter is the 2018 non-tax judgment in *Lekić v. Slovenia*,[110] a case in which the author had the opportunity to submit arguments relating to the piercing of the corporate veil in a tax environment. The ECtHR returned to this point in 2021 in the case of *Busuttil v. Malta*,[111] a case involving Article 6 ECHR which will be discussed in the chapter dealing with Article 6.

1.11 CONCLUSIONS

The judgments above imply the following rules:

---

108. Application no. 1962/12.
109. Application no. 52464/15.
110. Application no. 36480/07.
111. Application no. 48431/18.

(a) Taxation is *ex natura rerum* an interference with 'possessions', but certain forms of interference are allowed.
(b) Nonetheless, the ECtHR retains a right of review.
(c) It is in the first instance for the national authorities to decide on the type of tax or contributions they wish to levy. Decisions in this area normally involve, in addition, an assessment of political, economic and social problems which the ECHR leaves to the competence of the Member States, for the domestic authorities are clearly better placed than the ECtHR to assess such problems. The Member States therefore have a wide margin of appreciation in this area.[112]
(d) The ECtHR will respect the national authorities' assessment in such matters unless it is devoid of reasonable foundation by failing the following minimum standards:[113]
    (i) 'Fair balance' between the demands of the general interest of the community and the requirements of the protection of the individual's fundamental rights.
    (ii) 'Lawfulness' implying qualitative requirements comprising accessibility, predictability and foreseeability.[114] Reasonable relationship of proportionality between the means employed and the aims sought to be realised. The financial liability arising out of the raising of tax or contributions may adversely affect the guarantee secured under Article 1 if it places an excessive burden on the person or the entity concerned or fundamentally interferes with his or its financial position.[115]

The margin of appreciation doctrine is applied differently in Western and Eastern European, Northern and Southern European cases, most notably on taxation and tax policy-related cases (compare and contrast, for example, *Huitson v. UK* and *Yukos v. Russia*). The sovereign debt crisis increased the use of the margin of appreciation doctrine. The Court was sensitive to the proposal made by the Portuguese Constitutional Court in the case *Rico v. Portugal*, following similar jurisprudence of the German Federal Constitutional Court on the concept of the *proviso of the possible, Vorbehalt des Möglichen*, as a convincing justification for extraordinary taxation. According to the *proviso of the possible* constitutional law doctrine, States are only obliged to provide social allowances in so far as economic circumstances permit and can tax, diminish or even cut these allowances as an emergency budgetary measure during times of severe economic and financial crisis if this measure is temporary and proportionate:

112. Drawn from *Travers v. Italy*, Application no. 15117/89.
113. *Gasus Dosier-und Fördertechnik GmbH v. the Netherlands*, Application no. 15375/89.
114. *Špaček sro v. Czech Republic*, Application no. 26449/95.
115. Drawn from *Travers v. Italy*, Application no. 15117/89.

> Progressive taxation of higher-income households is more likely to comply with the principle of proportionality whereas socially 'blind' measures, which effectively target all citizens as if they were all in the same financial situation, will not be accepted as falling within the margin of appreciation of a state.[116]

The rules above create a tight filter explaining why the majority of tax cases based on the right to property have been dismissed as inadmissible and manifestly ill-founded. Nowadays, drawing up statistics speculating on rates of success has become next to impossible because, after the introduction of the single-judge system, cases that are summarily dismissed are not even published.

In Baker's analysis of the judgments delivered before 2000, there is a reference to over sixty cases which have considered Article 1 of the First Protocol. Most of these cases were dismissed for the following reasons:

(a) The tax measure complained of was in accordance with law.[117]
(b) The tax measure under scrutiny fell within the State's wide margin of appreciation.[118]
(c) The tax measure under scrutiny was justified serving a legitimate purpose.[119]
(d) The Tax measure under scrutiny was reasonable and proportionate.[120]

The ECtHR's approach to the interpretation of what constitutes a 'possession' is highly praiseworthy. Even in the earliest judgments, the ECtHR was prepared to recognise 'latent' rights existing in the tax world. In some cases, the ECtHR has exercised its supervisory functions, in many cases less so, shielding State Signatories with an impenetrable margin of appreciation. Inroads were made in the sphere of discriminatory taxation where the ECtHR held that the onus of proof of a correct exercise of margin of appreciation should revert on the State Signatory, but it still needs to be seen whether such a balanced approach will be applied in complaints that do not combine Article 1 of Protocol 1 with Article 14. The ECtHR has created a strong line of judgments dealing with the concept of 'lawfulness' of tax measures, and such

116. Paulo Pinto de Albuquerque, 'The Rights of Workers, Migrant Workers and Trade Unions under the European Convention on Human Rights', European Human Rights Law Review, Volume 2020, Issue 1 (2020), p. 37.
117. *Špaček Sro v. Czech Republic*, Application no. 26449/95.
118. *X v. Germany*, Applications no. 8724/79, *Svenska Managementgruppen AB v. Sweden*, no. 11036/84, *Hugo Hanzmann v. Austria*, no. 12560/86, *Antonino Amitrano and 159 others v. Italy*, no. 17154/90, *Voggenberger Transport GmbH v. Austria*, no. 21294/93, *Pietrantonio Gianquitto v. Italy*, no. 26779/95, *Giuliana Galeotti Ottieri Della Ciaja and others v. Italy*, no. 46757/99, *X v. Germany*, no. 8724/79, *Tre Traktörer AB v. Sweden*, no. 10873/84, *Svenska Management gruppen AB v. Sweden*, no. 11036/84, *Wasa Liv v. Sweden*, no. 13013/87, *Antonino Amitrano and 159 others v. Italy*, no. 17154/90, *Matti & Eliina Försti v. Finland*, no. 22588/93.
119. *ABC&D v. UK*, Application no. 8531/79.
120. *Riccardo Travers v. Italy*, Applications no. 15117/89, *Gasus Dosier und Fördertechnik GmbH v. Netherlands*, no. 15375/89, *Schneider Austria GmbH v. Austria*, no. 21354/93, *X v. Austria*, no. 7287/75, *Gasus Dosier und Fördertechnik GmbH v. Netherlands*, no. 15375/89.

judgments do not always reconcile with conclusions reached over matters of retroactivity and retrospectivity.[121] Some of the Hungarian and Italian judgments dealing with the subject of proportionality are very scholarly creating a clear code of conduct with respect to the exercise of margin of appreciation.

Cases over the proportionality of tax penalties are extremely encouraging, creating hope for the introduction of some form 'ultra duplum' rule. In the 'Pillar 2 Age' with its mandatory Minimum Taxation regime, the time is ripe for the introduction of rules governing 'Maximum Taxation' regulating the combined effect of raw tax, penalties and punitive interest. More granularity is advised in the regulation of punitive regimes. The core value of subsidiarity cannot be applied selectively and arbitrarily.

121. It is submitted that the ECtHR should distinguish clearly between retroactive and retrospective tax legislation. Retroactive legislation taxes a past act or activity, i.e., an act or activity that occurred in the past and no longer occurs at the time of the approval of the new legislation. Retrospective legislation taxes a still pending act or activity, i.e., an act or activity that is still occurring at the time of the approval of the new legislation. For example, a new law approved in December 2022 to tax the professional activity of the year 2021 would be retroactive. A new law approved in December 2022 to tax professional activity of the year of 2022 would be retrospective. Retroactive tax legislation should require much stricter conditions than retrospective tax legislation.

Chapter 2

Right to Life & Prohibition of Inhuman and Degrading Treatment

ARTICLE 2
Right to life

1. Everyone's right to life shall be protected by law. No one shall be deprived of his life intentionally save in the execution of a sentence of a court following his conviction of a crime for which this penalty is provided by law.

2. Deprivation of life shall not be regarded as inflicted in contravention of this Article when it results from the use of force which is no more than absolutely necessary:

(a) in defence of any person from unlawful violence;

(b) in order to effect a lawful arrest or to prevent the escape of a person lawfully detained;

(c) in action lawfully taken for the purpose of quelling a riot or insurrection.

ARTICLE 3
No one shall be subjected to torture or to inhuman or degrading treatment or punishment.

2.1 FROM THE FRINGES OF TAX LAW

Experiences at the ECtHR demonstrate that tax enforcement procedures may cause significant distress and hardship, and, curiously, the ECHR's case law has even entertained complaints based on the right to life and protection from inhuman and degrading treatment.

Article 2 is almost irrelevant to tax matters, with only one known case with a tax element being declared admissible. Even Article 3 ECHR remains only of marginal importance, and picturing inhuman and degrading in a tax context requires a stretch of the imagination. Nonetheless, the ECtHR recorded three successful 'mixed' cases that were an eye-opener and could pave the way for further challenges.

Degrading treatment may take many forms, and it cannot be excluded that heavy-handed investigative pressures could lead to implications under Article 3 too. Torture and inhuman and degrading treatment represent two of the ECHR's red-zones, and the ECtHR adopts a zero-tolerance role in this area regardless of whether the treatment occurs in a tax environment shielded by the margin of appreciation. In fact, considerations based on the margin of appreciation do not find a place in Article 3 ECHR cases and, to the contrary, are replaced with commitments that the ECtHR must apply a particularly thorough scrutiny even if certain domestic proceedings and investigations have already taken place.[1]

2.2 THE ONLY KNOWN TAX CASE UNDER ARTICLE 2

The only known case to deal with taxation and the right to life is the 1999 case *Józef Lewandowski v. Poland.*[2] Lewandowski complained under Articles 1 and 2 ECHR about actions of tax bailiffs which allegedly resulted in the death of his wife, and the subsequent refusal of the authorities to prosecute the bailiffs. With respect to the complaint under Article 2, the ECtHR found no evidence in the case file of a causal link between the death and the action of the bailiffs. With regard to the applicant's complaint about the refusal of the authorities to prosecute the bailiffs, the ECtHR acknowledged that the obligation to protect the right to life under Article 2, read in conjunction with the State's general duty under Article 1 ECHR to 'secure to everyone within their jurisdiction the rights and freedoms in Convention', requires by implication that there should be some form of effective official investigation when individuals have been killed as a result of the use of force by, *inter alia*, agents of the State.

The ECtHR noted that, although the case before it did not involve the killing resulting from the use of force, but the death of an individual which occurred twenty-seven days after the actions of the agents of the State had taken place, the national authorities conducted an official investigation of the circumstances relating to the death of the applicant's wife. The evidence collected in the course of the two aforesaid investigations, including the depositions of the applicant and his children, who had witnessed the incident, as well as an expert medical opinion, did not show the existence of a causal link between the actions of the bailiffs and the death of the applicant's wife. This finding obliged the prosecution to refuse to lay charges against the bailiffs. Consequently, the ECtHR held that there was no appearance of a violation

1. *See* the non-tax 1995 judgment in *Ribitsch v. Austria*, Application no. 18896/91, § 32, and *Avşar v. Turkey*, Application no. 25657/94, § 283.
2. Application no. 43457/98.

of either Article 2 or Article 2 in conjunction with Article 1 ECHR. The case was dismissed.

2.3 THE THREE CASES UNDER ARTICLE 3

The 2007 judgment in the case of *Kozinets v. Ukraine*[3] must have been the first ECtHR tax case to contemplate inhuman treatment in a tax context. Kozinets was the beneficial owner of a company that was subject to a tax investigation and was apprehended trying to record a conversation he held at the Kharkiv State Tax Police Inspectorate. Kozinets alleged that when the Head of the Tax Police Inspectorate realised that Kozinets was taping him, he flew into a rage, broke the tape recorder and beat him up, causing him head and abdominal injuries. Kozinets' allegations were corroborated by a medical report. Kozinets filed a case at the ECtHR complaining that he had been subjected to inhuman and degrading treatment by the Ukrainian tax authorities and that the competent authorities had failed to investigate the gross abuse caused by the tax inspector.

In delivering judgment, the ECtHR reiterated that Article 3 ECHR enshrines one of the most fundamental values of a democratic society prohibiting torture or inhuman or degrading treatment or punishment, irrespective of the circumstances or the victim's behaviour in absolute terms. The ECtHR's observations of what constitutes treatment falling within the scope of Article 3 ECHR are interesting because it acknowledges that the concept of inhuman treatment includes premeditated mental suffering that could occur in a particularly heavy-handed tax investigation:

> 52. To fall under Article 3 of the Convention, ill-treatment must attain a minimum level of severity. The assessment of this minimum level of severity is relative; it depends on all the circumstances of the case, such as the duration of the treatment, its physical and mental effects and, in some cases, the gender, age and state of health of the victim (see Valašinas v. Lithuania, no. 44558/98, §§ 100-01, ECHR 2001-VIII). The Court has considered treatment to be 'inhuman' because, inter alia, it was premeditated, was applied for hours at a stretch and caused either actual bodily injury or intense physical and mental suffering. It has deemed treatment to be 'degrading' because it was such as to arouse in the victims feelings of fear, anguish and inferiority capable of humiliating and debasing them (see Kudła v. Poland [GC], no. 30210/96, § 92, ECHR 2000-XI).

The ECtHR held that the standard of proof applied to establish inhuman treatment is the standard of proof 'beyond reasonable doubt', a degree of proof that was not present in the case in front of it. The case file materials had not established that Kozinets entered the Tax Police premises in good health but left it injured. Therefore, for lack of evidence, the ECtHR did not find a violation of the substantive limb of Article 3 of the Convention. Nonetheless, it reached a different conclusion with respect to the complaint referring to the alleged inadequacy of the investigation:

3. Application no. 75520/01.

> 59. The Court reiterates that where an individual raises an arguable claim that he has been seriously ill-treated by the State authorities in breach of Article 3, that provision, read in conjunction with the State's general duty under Article 1 of the Convention, requires by implication that there should be an effective official investigation. ...
>
> 60. The investigation into arguable allegations of ill-treatment must also be thorough. This means that the authorities must always make a serious attempt to find out what happened and should not rely on hasty or ill-founded conclusions to close their investigation or as the basis of their decisions ... .

The ECtHR unanimously held that there had been a violation of the procedural limb of Article 3 because of lack of effective investigation. Mr Kozinets was awarded a compensation of EUR 2,000 in respect of non-pecuniary damage and EUR 23,788 for costs and expenses.

The second and third known tax cases incorporating an allegation of inhuman and degrading treatment belong to the Yukos saga.

The second case was the 2011 case of *Mikhail Borisovich Khodorkovskiy v. Russia* (Khodorkovskiy no. 1)[4] when the complainant alleged inhuman treatment in the course of his criminal trial for tax evasion. The complainant objected to the fact that during the trial he was made to sit on a wooden bench in a small cage in the courtroom and forced to instruct his lawyers through the bars. He was aggrieved by the fact that on court days, he received little food, no exercise, and no fresh air. The ECtHR accepted the complaint:

> 125. ... Thus, the applicant was accused of non-violent crimes, he had no criminal record, and there was no evidence that he was predisposed to violence ...
>
> 126. In sum, the security arrangements in the courtroom, given their cumulative effect, were, in the circumstances, excessive and could have been reasonably perceived by the applicant and the public as humiliating.
>
> There was, therefore, a violation of Article 3 of the Convention in that the treatment was degrading within the meaning of this provision.

The same ordeal was described in the case of *Khodorkovskiy and Lebedev v. Russia* (Khodorkovskiy no. 2).[5] The ECtHR did not find any reason to depart from its findings in the Khodorkovskiy no. 1 case in this regard. Both complainants were detained in the courtroom in identical conditions; their personal profiles, if not identical, were similar in essence. Therefore, it found a violation of Article 3.

2.4 CONCLUSIONS

The ECtHR's conclusions on the application of Articles 2 and 3 ECHR in a tax context did not involve intriguing interpretational issues. They are interesting because they represent early precedents in a jurisprudential line that contains heavy growth potential. Tax procedures are not immune from the basic standards of humanity.

4. Application no. 5829/04.
5. Applications nos. 11082/06 and 13772/05.

Probably, future tax complaints based on Article 3 will be based on less clumsy human rights infringements than those discussed, and the Articles 2 and 3 tax cases of the future will be based on more subtle forms of inhumanity. The facts in issue in the judgment in Article 2 are highly unusual, but the ECtHR's comments are a reminder that the actions of tax collectors and assessors must always remain subject to careful scrutiny.

CHAPTER 3

Prohibition of Slavery and Forced Labour

ARTICLE 4

1. No one shall be held in slavery or servitude.

2. No one shall be required to perform forced or compulsory labour.

3. For the purpose of this Article the term 'forced or compulsory labour' shall not include:

(a) any work required to be done in the ordinary course of detention imposed according to the provisions of Article 5 of this Convention or during conditional release from such detention;

(b) any service of a military character or, in case of conscientious objectors in countries where they are recognised, service exacted instead of compulsory military service;

(c) any service exacted in case of an emergency or calamity threatening the life or well-being of the community;

(d) any work or service which forms part of normal civic obligations.

3.1 UNPAID SERVANTS OF THE STATE

Tax laws of State Signatories contemplate situations when private citizens and companies owe their States burdensome compliance obligations that leave no visible benefit to them. Thus, laws in the vein of Council Directive 2006/112/EC of 28 November 2006 on the common system of VAT contemplate a system wherein suppliers of goods and services are bound to act as non-remunerated tax collectors and failures to abide by their compliance obligations expose them to administrative and criminal penalties. Similarly, many State Signatories bind employers with the obligations of a 'Pay-as-you-earn' (PAYE) mechanism contemplating mandatory obligations to calculate, withhold and collect tax on salaries paid. Employers covered by PAYE are not remunerated for their services to their State, but failures to meet mandatory obligations tend to be heavily punished. In many States, notaries and intermediaries appearing on certain transactions are bound to act as unremunerated tax collectors. Similarly, in the course of tax investigations, failure to provide information on third parties is punishable, but there are no rewards for those who comply.

Recent base erosion and profit shifting driven initiatives like Council Directives (EU) 2018/822 and 2011/16/EU (DAC) on mandatory automatic exchange of information in the field of taxation in relation to reportable cross-border arrangements imposing reporting obligations on tax planning intermediaries contemplate the mandatory, unremunerated rendering of services to the State. In 2020, as part of an (Organisation for Economic Co-operation and Development) OECD-inspired Tax Package adopted in July of the same year, the European Commission proposed to amend DAC to extend the remit of its transparency rules to digital platforms operating in certain sectors. In November 2020, the European Commission launched an initiative to amend DAC to cover crypto-assets and e-money.[1]

Tax authorities have been given powerful tools with the backing of the G7, OECD and EU, and such measures rely on the power to collect data from third parties. Recent legislative trends enhancing tax authorities' powers to exact unremunerated services from innocent third parties create concerns under Article 4, especially in view of the definition of forced labour contained in Article 2 of the Forced Labour Convention, 1930 (No. 29), a Convention that was used by the ECHR as an interpretational instrument:[2]

> 1. For the purposes of this Convention the term forced or compulsory labour shall mean all work or service which is exacted from any person under the menace of any penalty and for which the said person has not offered himself voluntarily.[3]

3.2 'FORCED OR COMPULSORY LABOUR'

Article 4 contemplates delimitations; forms of forced labour that are excluded from the ECHR definition of forced labour *ex lege*; Article 4 prescribes that 'forced or compulsory labour ... shall not include: any work or service which forms part of normal civic obligations'.

1. https://ec.europa.eu/commission/presscorner/detail/en/ip_20_2253.
2. Including especially the 1983 case of *Van Der Mussele v. Belgium*, Application no. 8919/80.
3. Even Article 29 International Labour Organization Forced Labour Convention comes with a delimitation clause which excludes from the definition '(e) minor communal services of a kind which, being performed by the members of the community in the direct interest of the said community, can therefore be considered as normal civic obligations incumbent upon the members of the community, provided that the members of the community or their direct representatives shall have the right to be consulted in regard to the need for such services'.

The issue of forced labour in a tax context arose early in the day. The Strasbourg organs delivered their first pronouncement on the matter as early as 1976, but jurisprudence has not evolved much since.

The decision in *four companies W., X., Y. et Z. c v. Austria*[4] dealt precisely with the application of Article 4, paragraph 3 (d) ECHR in a tax collection context. The complaint referred to the Austrian PAYE system.

The four companies complained that they were obliged, without any return to themselves, to calculate and withhold from the wages and salaries of their employees the tax on wages, the contributions to social security and other similar contributions and to pay them to the competent authorities, to withhold from wages and salaries any sums taken in execution of a court judgment, to pay to their employees family allowances and wages and salaries in case of sickness and to claim compensation from the competent public authorities. The complainants argued that the obligations contemplated in Austrian Law amounted to compulsory labour that went beyond normal civic obligations.

Interestingly, the European Commission on Human Rights observed that it could not assume:

> that the concept of forced labour is applicable at all in a case like the present one where the applicants are not natural persons but corporate bodies, and where the duty to do certain work is not a personal obligation but can be carried out with the assistance of employees, the Commission considers that the deduction of taxes, social security contributions etc. from salaries and wages cannot in itself be considered as forced or compulsory labour. The Commission therefore finds that the facts of the present case as they have been submitted by the applicant companies do not disclose any appearance of a violation of the Convention on the ground that the duties imposed on the applicant companies go beyond normal civic obligations within the meaning of Art. 4(3) (d) of the Convention. It follows that this complaint of the applicant companies is manifestly ill-founded.

Thus, the Commission dismissed the application on multiple counts.

3.3 '(D) ANY WORK OR SERVICE WHICH FORMS PART OF NORMAL CIVIC OBLIGATIONS'

The Commission analysed a similar matter in the 1995 case *Adriano Borghini v. Italy*,[5] involving the Italian tax mechanism known as 'sostituti d'imposta' binding employers of workers in the liberal arts with withholding tax obligations.

The fact that this case involved a physical person and not a legal person did not change the conclusions reached by the Commission. Borghini's case was dismissed, because the Italian mechanism did not exceed the parameters of normal civil obligations:

4. Application no. 7427/76.
5. Application no. 21568//93.

> Cependant, la Commission a déjà établi que l'obligation pour une entreprise de calculer et de retenir sur le salaire de ses employés les impôts perçus à la source, ainsi que diverses cotisations et contributions, n'excède pas les obligations civiques normales, au sens de l'article 4, par. 3 d) (art. 4-3-d) de la Convention, et ne saurait dès lors être considérée comme un travail forcé ou obligatoire interdit par le premier paragraphe de cette même disposition (cf., mutatis mutandis, No 7427/76, déc. 27.9.76, D.R. 7 p. 148). En l'espèce, la Commission ne dégage aucun élément justifiant un départ de cette jurisprudence.

3.4 CONCLUSIONS

The conclusions reached in the Four Companies case classifying PAYE tax obligations as not going beyond normal civic obligations do not come as a surprise, but in a tax world dominated by legal persons, the decision's premise is very worrying. Excluding legal persons from the remit of Article 4 implies that State Signatories have an unfettered discretion in exacting unremunerated services from taxpayers that are legal persons.

Nowadays, authorities take it for granted that the article discussed in this chapter 'applies to human beings but not to legal persons,'[6] but tax cases especially the *Yukos* cases discussed in this book invite a reconsideration of such a restrictive approach; after all, Article 34 ECHR does not make such distinctions:

> The Court may receive applications from any person, non-governmental organisation or group of individuals claiming to be the victim of a violation by one of the High Contracting Parties of the rights set forth in the Convention or the Protocols thereto. The High Contracting Parties undertake not to hinder in any way the effective exercise of this right.

Writing in 2000, Philip Baker pointed out that:

> There remains still the possibility that certain duties imposed in connection with taxation might be regarded as going beyond normal civic obligations. An example might be a revenue authority requiring a third party – and not the taxpayer concerned – to expend significant effort and incur significant expenditure in supplying information in connection with an investigation ... .

Since 2000, the powers of tax authorities have been enhanced exponentially, and the exclusion of legal persons from the protection of Article 4 renders Article 4 ineffective in many tax contexts because the largest data holders are legal persons who the ECtHR excludes from the purview of Article 4. Possible solutions to the debacle include a new approach to Article 4 by 'looking-through' it and extending the protection of Article 4 to the individuals bearing the physical responsibility of abiding by the requirement to provide the unremunerated labour, an approach that has been endorsed in an Article 8 ECHR context. In the 2013 tax judgment in the case of *Bernh*

6. David Harris, Michael O'Boyle, Ed Bates and Carla Buckley, *Harris, O'Boyle, and Warbrick: Law of the European Convention on Human Rights* (4th ed.), Oxford, OUP, 2018, p. 235.

Larsen Holding AS and Others v. Norway,[7] the ECtHR made a very relevant observation:

> 107 ... This said, the applicant companies had legitimate interests in ensuring the protection of the privacy of individuals working for them and such interests should be taken into account in the assessment of whether the conditions in Article 8 § 2 were fulfilled in the instant case.

7. Application no. 24117/08.

CHAPTER 4

Right to Liberty and Compensation for Wrongful Conviction

ARTICLE 5
Right to liberty and security

1. Everyone has the right to liberty and security of person. No one shall be deprived of his liberty save in the following cases and in accordance with a procedure prescribed by law:

(a) the lawful detention of a person after conviction by a competent court;

(b) the lawful arrest or detention of a person for noncompliance with the lawful order of a court or in order to secure the fulfilment of any obligation prescribed by law;

(c) the lawful arrest or detention of a person effected for the purpose of bringing him before the competent legal authority on reasonable suspicion of having committed an offence or when it is reasonably considered necessary to prevent his committing an offence or fleeing after having done so;

...

2. Everyone who is arrested shall be informed promptly, in a language which he understands, of the reasons for his arrest and of any charge against him.

3. Everyone arrested or detained in accordance with the provisions of paragraph 1 (c) of this Article shall be brought promptly before a judge or other officer authorised by law to exercise judicial power and shall be entitled to trial within a reasonable time or to release pending trial. Release may be conditioned by guarantees to appear for trial.

4. Everyone who is deprived of his liberty by arrest or detention shall be entitled to take proceedings by which the lawfulness of his detention shall be decided speedily by a court and his release ordered if the detention is not lawful.

5. Everyone who has been the victim of arrest or detention in contravention of the provisions of this Article shall have an enforceable right to compensation.

4.1 THE CRIMINAL TWIST

Tax cases involving Article 5 ECHR are uncommon, but the *Yukos* cases created awareness of the relevance of Article 5 ECHR in a tax context. In tax investigations, Article 5 ECHR becomes relevant whenever the investigation takes a criminal twist. Article 5 (1) ECHR allows an encroachment into the right to liberty after a conviction by a competent court. Article 5 (3) ECHR and Article 5 (4) ECHR provide for pre-trial detention providing for the necessary safeguards.

Article 5 on the right to liberty is read in conjunction with Article 3 of Protocol 7 providing for compensation for wrongful conviction prescribing that when a person has by a final decision been convicted of a criminal offence and when subsequently his conviction has been reversed, or he has been pardoned, on the ground that a new or newly discovered fact shows conclusively that there has been a miscarriage of justice, the person who has suffered punishment as a result of such conviction shall be compensated according to the law or the practice of the State concerned, unless it is proved that the nondisclosure of the unknown fact in time is wholly or partly attributable to him.

4.1.1 Conviction Cases

Article 5 (1) ECHR contemplates a 'lawfulness requirement', allowing conviction only when it follows 'a procedure prescribed by law'.

The 1996 case of *Benham v. the United Kingdom* is the first known conviction case dealing with taxation and Article 5 ECHR.[1] In 1990 Mr Benham became liable to pay Poll Tax, and since he did not pay it, the Poole Magistrates' Court ordered the issue of a liability order, entitling Poole Borough Council to commence enforcement proceedings against Benham.

Bailiffs visited Mr Benham's parents' house but were told that he had no goods of any value there or elsewhere which could be seized by them and sold in order to pay the tax debt. Domestic law provided that if a person was found to have insufficient goods on which to levy outstanding community charge, the charging authority could apply to a magistrates' court for an order committing him to prison. On such an application being made, the domestic court had to enquire in the presence of the debtor as to his present means and also whether his failure to pay which led to the liability order being made was due to wilful refusal or culpable neglect. The charging authority

1. Application no. 19380/92.

applied for such an order and, on the basis of evidence, the magistrates concluded that Benham's failure to pay the community charge was due to his culpable neglect. Accordingly, the domestic court decided that he ought to be sent to prison for thirty days unless he paid what was owing. Subsequently, the Magistrate's decision was revoked in judicial review proceedings because it transpired that Mr Benham had a valid legal reason not to pay the poll tax. Benham was released after serving ten days of his jail term. Benham took his case to the ECHR on the basis that his detention constituted a violation of Article 5 (1) ECHR, and his case went to the Grand Chamber.

The ECtHR explained that it is in the first place for the national courts to interpret domestic law, but since Article 5 (1) ECHR provides for a lawfulness requirement implying that failure to correctly apply domestic law entails a breach of the ECHR, it follows that the ECHR retains a supervisory function.

The ECtHR pointed out that a period of detention will, in principle, be lawful if it is carried out pursuant to a court order, but a subsequent finding that the court erred under domestic law in making the order will not necessarily retrospectively affect the validity of the intervening period of detention. Consequently, the ECtHR dismissed the part of the application that referred to Article 5:[2]

> 46. Against the above background, it cannot be said with any degree of certainty that the judgment of the Divisional Court was to the effect that the magistrates acted in excess of jurisdiction within the meaning of English law. It follows that the Court does not find it established that the order for detention was invalid, and thus that the detention which resulted from it was unlawful under national law (see the above-mentioned Bouamar judgment p. 21, para. 49). The mere fact that the order was set aside on appeal did not in itself affect the lawfulness of the detention (see paragraph 42 above).
>
> 47. Nor does the Court find that the detention was arbitrary. It has not been suggested that the magistrates who ordered Mr Benham's detention acted in bad faith, nor that they neglected to attempt to apply the relevant legislation correctly (see the above-mentioned Bozano judgment, pp. 25-26, para. 59). It considers the question of the lack of legal aid to be less relevant to the present head of complaint than to that under Article 6 (art. 6) (see paragraph 64 below). Accordingly, the Court finds no violation of Article 5 para. 1 of the Convention (art. 5-1).

The 1997 case *S. D. v. the United Kingdom*[3] shared similar merits with the *Benham* case but had a different outcome. In 1992, S.D. appeared at Wolverhampton Magistrates' Court, on application of Wolverhampton Metropolitan Borough Council, for an enquiry to be made into his means and the reasons for his failure to pay the Poll Tax. S.D. who was not represented gave evidence that he was then living on support and could not afford to pay the tax.

The magistrates rejected the applicant's proposals to pay the arrears under a repayment programme. They concluded that the applicant's failure to pay the poll tax was due to his culpable neglect and issued a warrant committing him to prison for fourteen days.

2. The application was upheld under Article 6 (3) ECHR.
3. Application no. 25286/94.

The applicant spent at least six days in custody before release on bail. S.D. complained to the ECHR that the courts which imprisoned him for not paying poll tax did not have power to commit him to prison, so that his detention was in violation of Article 5 (1) ECHR. The ECHR upheld the complaint, because it transpired that Court that had convicted the complainant had, contrary to requirements of domestic law, failed to enquire whether the failure to pay was due to the applicant's wilful refusal or culpable neglect.

The 1999 case *Ian Poole v. the United Kingdom*[4] was another Article 5 (1) Case contesting a Poll Tax Conviction. Given that the facts of the case were similar to those in S.D., the outcome was entirely predictable:

> 49. In these circumstances the Commission considers that it can be said, with the practically possible degree of certainty, that the magistrates when ordering the applicant's imprisonment acted in excess of jurisdiction and that, therefore, the applicant's detention was unlawful under domestic law.

A similar conclusion was reached in *Shaun Thomas Johnson v. the United Kingdom.*[5]

4.1.2 Pre-trial Detention Cases

The 1968 case of *Neumeister v. Austria*[6] involved a challenge to pre-trial detention under Article 5 (3) ECHR. The Austrian Tax Authorities had denounced Neumeister for being an accomplice in helping third parties improperly obtain turnover tax refunds. At the request of the Vienna Public Prosecution, a Judge decided to open a preliminary investigation concerning Neumeister's activities and ordered that Neumeister be taken into detention on remand. Neumeister filed proceedings contesting pre-trial detention but was detained for two years, two months and four days nonetheless. Neumeister took his case to Strasbourg alleging a violation of Article 5 (3) ECHR on several counts. The ECtHR upheld his complaint:

> Under Article 5 (3) (art. 5-3) 'everyone arrested or detained in accordance with the provisions of paragraph 1 (c)' of that Article (art. 5-1-c) 'shall be entitled', inter alia, 'to trial within a reasonable time or to release pending trial'; it is also provided that 'release may be conditioned by guarantees to appear for trial' ...
>
> 4. The Court is of the opinion that this provision cannot be understood as giving the judicial authorities a choice between either bringing the accused to trial within a reasonable time or granting him provisional release even subject to guarantees. The reasonableness of the time spent by an accused person in detention up to the beginning of the trial must be assessed in relation to the very fact of his detention ...
>
> 15. For these reasons, the Court finds that Neumeister's continued provisional detention until 16 September 1964 constituted a violation of Article 5 (3) (art. 5-3) of the Convention.

4. Application no. 28190/95.
5. Application no. 28455/95.
6. Application no. 1936/63.

The 2007 case of *Mooren v. Germany*[7] was another interesting case. Mooren was suspected of tax evasion (around EUR 200,000), and a District Court ordered his pre-trial detention.

The District Court noted that the applicant, who had availed himself of the right to remain silent, was strongly suspected of tax evasion on the basis of the business records that had been seized when his home was searched. The District Court held that Mooren had to be placed in pre-trial detention, because there was a risk that the applicant, if released, might destroy the missing documents or conceal further business transactions and accounts.

Mooren was released from detention after four months of complicated judicial proceedings. Mooren complained that, in the proceedings for review of his pre-trial detention, the Court of Appeal, by remitting his case back to the Court of First Instance instead of quashing the detention order which it had found not to comply with domestic law, had unlawfully deprived him of his liberty and had unduly delayed the judicial review proceedings. Furthermore, he claimed that his defence counsel had been refused access to the investigation files. The ECtHR held unanimously that there had been two violations of Article 5 § 4 on account of the lack of speedy review of the lawfulness of the applicant's detention and the refusal to grant access to the case files in those review proceedings. The applicant was awarded EUR 1,500 in respect of non-pecuniary damage and EUR 5,150 for costs and expenses.

A similar issue to the one debated in Mooren was discussed in the 2010 case of *Marian Sobczyński v. Poland*.[8] Marian who was suspected of tax fraud complained that the length of his detention on remand had been excessive.

The ECtHR pointed out that in cases such as Marian's, the risk that a detainee, if released, might bring pressure to bear on witnesses or other co-accused or might otherwise obstruct the proceedings often is, by the nature of things, high. The ECtHR accepted that the reasonable suspicion against the applicant of having committed serious offences could initially warrant his detention, and the likelihood of a severe sentence being imposed on Marian created a presumption that the applicant would obstruct the proceedings. Thus, the ECtHR concluded that the grounds given for Marian's pre-trial detention were 'relevant' and 'sufficient' to justify holding him in custody for the entire relevant period, that is one year, two months and ten days. In addition, the ECtHR observed that the investigation was of considerable complexity, regard being had to the number of witnesses, the extensive evidentiary proceedings and the implementation of special measures required in cases concerning organised crime. Therefore, the ECtHR concluded that during the relevant period, the domestic authorities handled the applicant's case with relative expedition and did not find a violation of Article 5 (3) ECHR.

The 204-page 2013 judgment in the case of *Khodorkovskiy and Lebedev v. Russia*[9] (Khodorkovskiy) included, among others, a complaint under Article 5 (3) ECHR and Article 5 (4) ECHR. Lebedev and Khodorkovskiy qua officers of the Yukos company

7. Application no. 11364/03.
8. Application no. 35494/08.
9. Applications nos. 11082/06 and 13772/05.

contested their criminal conviction for tax evasion and fraud, as well as the events related to the criminal proceedings against them. Both complainants had been subjected to pre-trial detention.

Lebedev argued that his detention was in breach of Article 5 (3) ECHR, because it lacked relevant and sufficient reasons. In addition, he submitted complaints under Article 5 (4) ECHR on account of the delayed examination of the detention orders and the fairness and speediness of the other detention proceedings. Lebedev also contested the domestic courts' failure to address his arguments in the detention proceedings.

The ECtHR pointed out that Lebedev had been kept in custody within the meaning of Article 5 (3) ECHR for one year, ten months, and eighteen days. Given the complexity of the case and the fact that there were no long periods of inactivity during the proceedings, the period did not per se appear unreasonable. However, the ECtHR added that the reasonable time requirement cannot be assessed in abstracto. It quoted the 1993 judgment in *W. v. Switzerland* which had established that continued detention can be justified only if there are specific indications of a genuine requirement of public interest which outweigh the rule of respect for individual liberty. The ECtHR proceeded to examine whether the domestic courts adduced relevant and sufficient reasons for extending the applicant's detention. Referring to its previous admissibility judgment involving the same applicant,[10] it observed that the context of the case did not render the complainant 'non-bailable', because the tax accusations adduced were non-violent. In addition, Lebedev did not have any criminal record and he lived permanently with his family in Moscow, where he had his main business interests.

The ECtHR concluded that Lebedev's continuous detention was not justified by compelling reasons outweighing the presumption of liberty. Furthermore, the existence of a risk of absconding was not convincingly demonstrated in the detention extension orders. References to Lebedev's 'international connections' were too vague and not supported by any evidence. The ECtHR noticed that judgments extending detention orders used a stereotyped wording, suggesting an absence of proper judicial review. Finding a violation of Article 5 (3) ECHR, the ECtHR concluded that the domestic courts failed to demonstrate that the applicant's detention during the period under consideration was justified by 'relevant and sufficient' reasons:

> '... In the present case the authorities did not consider the possibility of ensuring the second applicant's attendance by the use of a more lenient preventive measure, such as bail, house arrest, or other measures provided by the Russian law, and the context of the case was not such as to make the applicant obviously "non-bailable" (see Khodorkovskiy (no. 1), § 196, with further references).'

The ECtHR proceeded to examine the complaint under 5 (4) ECHR finding that whereas some of the detention extension orders were regular, one of the extension orders was not compliant with Article 5 (4) ECHR, because long public holidays had been used as an excuse for delaying the examination of the application for release. The

10. *Lebedev v. Russia*, Application no. 4493/04 partial decision on admissibility of 25 November 2004, decision on admissibility of 18 May 2006, and judgment of 25 October 2007 referred to by the ECtHR as Lebedev (no. 1).

ECtHR concluded that the appeal against one of the detention orders was not examined 'speedily', as required by Article 5 § 4 of the Convention. There was therefore a violation of that provision in this respect.

The ECtHR was critical of the quality of the judicial proceedings confirming the detention orders, reiterating that proceedings must be adversarial and must always ensure equality of arms between the parties. In detention proceedings, the detainee should have access to the documents in the investigation file which are essential for assessing the lawfulness of his detention and should also have an opportunity to comment on the arguments put forward by the prosecution. Mindful of the legal principle that Article 5 ECHR contains more flexible procedural requirements than Article 6 ECHR (Fair Hearing) while being much more stringent as regards speediness, the ECtHR concluded that although the prosecution had more time to develop their arguments, given the nature of the proceedings, this disparity between the parties did not disturb the principle of equality of arms to an extent incompatible with Article 5 (4) ECHR.

4.2 THE CONCEPT OF REASONABLE SUSPICION AND GOOD FAITH

In 2016, the ECtHR delivered another Article 5 ECHR judgment in the case of *Rasul Jafarov v. Azerbaijan*.[11] Rasul, a human rights lawyer, was investigated for large-scale tax evasion and tax avoidance and was both convicted and detained. Among others, Rasul alleged that his conviction and pre-trial detention had not been justified and had been carried out in bad faith. He submitted a case that referred both to Article 5 (1) (c) ECHR and Article 5 (4) ECHR.

The wording of Article 5 (1) (c) ECHR expressly states that for there to be an arrest, there must be a reasonable suspicion. The ECtHR had an opportunity to explain the application of the concept both in a non-tax and a tax environment without distinguishing between the two. No special ring-fenced concept of 'reasonable suspicion' was applied in this tax case.

Referring to non-tax cases, the ECtHR explained that in order for an arrest on reasonable suspicion to be justified under Article 5 (1) (c) ECHR, it is not necessary for the police to have obtained sufficient evidence to bring charges, either at the point of arrest or while the applicant is in custody;[12] nor is it necessary that the person detained should ultimately have been charged or taken before a court. The object of detention for questioning is to further a criminal investigation by confirming or discontinuing suspicions which provide the grounds for detention. Facts which raise a suspicion need not be of the same level as those necessary to justify a conviction or even the bringing of a charge, which comes at the next stage of the process of criminal investigation.[13]

11. Application no. 69981/14.
12. *Brogan and Others v. the United Kingdom*, Applications nos. 11209/84, 11234/84, 11266/84 and 11386/85.
13. *Murray v. the United Kingdom*, Application no. 22384/93.

The ECtHR added that the requirement that a suspicion must be based on reasonable grounds forms an essential part of the safeguard against arbitrary arrest and detention. The fact that a suspicion is held in good faith is insufficient. The words 'reasonable suspicion' mean the existence of facts or information which would satisfy an objective observer that the person concerned may have committed the offence. What may be regarded as 'reasonable' will depend upon all the circumstances,[14] adding that the length of the deprivation of liberty may also be material to the level of suspicion required.

In an Article 5 (1) ECHR case, the respondent Government carries the burden of proof that the arrested person was reasonably suspected of having committed the alleged offence.

Turning to the case before it, the ECtHR noted that Rasul complained of the lack of 'reasonable' suspicion against him throughout the entire period of his pre-trial detention, including both during the initial period following his arrest and the subsequent periods when his remand in custody was authorised and extended by court orders. The ECtHR reiterated that the persistence of reasonable suspicion that an arrested person has committed an offence is a prerequisite for the lawfulness of his continued detention. Accordingly, while reasonable suspicion must exist at the time of the arrest and initial detention, in cases of prolonged detention it must also be shown that the suspicion persisted and remained 'reasonable' throughout the detention.

In Rasul's case, the description of the three original charges brought against him lacked a certain level of coherence, order and clarity expected. The misconduct attributed to Rasul essentially stemmed from the fact that he had operated an Non-Governmental Organisation lacking State registration and had failed to report grants received. In the course of domestic proceedings, it transpired that a proper reporting procedure did not even exist. No other information or evidence supporting the suspicion was shown to exist, either at the time he was accused or throughout the entire period of pre-trial detention. The ECtHR held that:

> 132. In any event, the Court notes that, as with the original charges, the description of the new charges essentially remained the same and lacked a sufficient level of coherence. ... Taking into account the manifest unreasonableness of the original three charges against the applicant (see paragraph 130 above) and the heightened level of scrutiny required by the specific context of the present case (see paragraph 120 above), the Court considers that the respondent Government also failed to satisfy the Court that the applicant was reasonably suspected of having committed the alleged offences under Articles 179.3.2 and 313 of the Criminal Code.

Even the fact that Rasul was taken to trial was held to be insufficient:

> 133. The Court is mindful of the fact that the applicant's case has been taken to trial. That, however, does not affect the Court's findings in connection with the present complaint, where it is called upon to consider whether the deprivation of

14. *Fox, Campbell and Hartley v. the United Kingdom*, Applications nos. 12244/86, 12245/86 and 12383/86.

> the applicant's liberty during the pre-trial period was justified on the basis of the information or facts available at the relevant time. In this respect, having regard to the above analysis, the Court finds that the material put before it does not meet the minimum standard set by Article 5 § 1 (c) of the Convention for the reasonableness of a suspicion required for an individual's arrest and continued detention. Accordingly, during the period the Court is considering in the present case, the applicant was deprived of his liberty in the absence of a 'reasonable suspicion' of his having committed a criminal offence.
>
> 134. Accordingly, there has been a violation of Article 5 § 1 of the Convention.

In addition, Rasul complained that the domestic courts had not properly assessed the arguments the defence had put forward in favour of his release. Echoing the conclusions reached in the case of *Lebedev* cited above, the ECtHR found for Rasul on this point too:

> 143. As the Court has observed above, the domestic courts in the present case consistently failed to verify the reasonableness of the suspicion underpinning the applicant's arrest (see paragraph 129 above). In their decisions, the domestic courts limited themselves to copying the prosecution's written submissions and using short, vague and stereotyped formulae for rejecting the applicant's complaints as unsubstantiated. In essence, the domestic courts limited their role to one of automatic endorsement of the prosecution's applications, and they cannot be considered to have conducted a genuine review of the 'lawfulness' of the applicant's detention. That is contrary not only to the requirements of Article 5 § 4, but also to those of the domestic law as interpreted and clarified by the Plenum of the Supreme Court (see paragraphs 79-80 above).
>
> 144. The foregoing considerations are sufficient to enable the Court to conclude that the applicant was not afforded proper judicial review of the lawfulness of his detention. Accordingly, there has been a violation of Article 5 § 4 of the Convention.

4.3 CONCLUSIONS

The ECtHR's cases involving the Application of Article 5 ECHR in a tax context are remarkable. The egregious nature of the violations committed by Russia and Azerbaijan gave the ECHR every opportunity to take a firm stand, and the ECtHR did not decline the offer, setting standards.

The outcome of the Article 5 ECHR tax judgments of the ECtHR discussed above could not be taken for granted. Laudably, the ECtHR did not fall to the temptation of creating some dangerous precedent for the sake of the fiscal stability and cohesion of the State Signatories.

Tax evasion endangers the economic well-being of State Signatories, but a red line must be drawn in matters relating to the core right to liberty. The ECtHR's tax judgments on Article 5 ECHR are remarkable because they do not create some special ring-fenced tax rules creating some prohibitive margin of appreciation giving State Signatories wide powers in prosecuting their tax offenders.

Tax cases are treated as normal cases with the Yukos case pointing out that tax evasion remains a non-violent crime. With the best of intentions, over the past few years, the European Parliament[15] has been exerting significant pressures aimed at protecting State Revenues, and there was a concern that the ECtHR would be prepared to allow special interpretational tax exceptions for the sake of protecting State Revenues. The ECtHR's minimum standards are welcome because they help to achieve a fair balance.

15. *See* https://www.europarl.europa.eu/doceo/document/A-7-2013-0162_EN.html and https://www.europarl.europa.eu/doceo/document/B-9-2021-0530_EN.html.

CHAPTER 5

Right to a Fair Trial

ARTICLE 6
Right to a fair trial

1. In the determination of his civil rights and obligations or of any criminal charge against him, everyone is entitled to a fair and public hearing within a reasonable time by an independent and impartial tribunal established by law. Judgment shall be pronounced publicly but the press and public may be excluded from all or part of the trial in the interests of morals, public order or national security in a democratic society, where the interests of juveniles or the protection of the private life of the parties so require, or to the extent strictly necessary in the opinion of the court in special circumstances where publicity would prejudice the interests of justice.

2. Everyone charged with a criminal offence shall be presumed innocent until proved guilty according to law.

3. Everyone charged with a criminal offence has the following minimum rights:

(a) to be informed promptly, in a language which he understands and in detail, of the nature and cause of the accusation against him;

(b) to have adequate time and facilities for the preparation of his defence;

(c) to defend himself in person or through legal assistance of his own choosing or, if he has not sufficient means to pay for legal assistance, to be given it free when the interests of justice so require;

(d) to examine or have examined witnesses against him and to obtain the attendance and examination of witnesses on his behalf under the same conditions as witnesses against him;

(e) to have the free assistance of an interpreter if he cannot understand or speak the language used in court.

5.1 SCOPE OF ARTICLE 6 ECHR

A dispute falls within the scope of Article 6 ECHR and is governed by the right to a fair trial only if such dispute falls either to be classified as a 'determination of … civil rights and obligations' or if it concerns 'a criminal charge' with the meaning of the ECHR. Therefore, if a matter neither involves civils rights and obligations nor a criminal charge it falls into a vacuum and the application of the procedural guarantees contemplated in Article 6 ECHR is not mandatory.[1] The right to a fair trial cannot be taken for granted and the ECtHR's many tax cases prove this. In a tax context, knowledge of the way the ECtHR has interpreted the key terms 'civil right and obligations' and 'criminal charge' is crucial. This is the area where tax disputes have created the greatest interpretational challenges to the ECtHR, and this is the area where pronouncements have not always been entirely predictable. Judgments on the matter have reserved surprises to taxpayers and Revenue authorities alike.

Equally importantly, Article ECHR has two limbs. The first limb contemplated in Article 6 (1) ECHR, 'the civil limb', lists the rights applicable to normal civil proceedings; the second contemplated in Article 6 (2) ECHR and Article 6 (3) ECHR, the criminal limb, lists additional guarantees applicable whenever a person is charged with 'a criminal offence'. Questions relating to the application of the criminal limb of Article 6 ECHR to tax disputes have created an interesting line of judgments.

5.2 'IN THE DETERMINATION OF HIS CIVIL RIGHTS AND OBLIGATIONS'

The ECtHR's leading case on the meaning of 'In the determination of his civil rights and obligations' applied in a tax context is the 2001 Grand Chamber judgment in *Ferrazzini v. Italy*.[2]

The facts of the case must be carefully considered. Ferrazzini, a businessman in the agritourism sector, had transferred land, property and a sum of money to a limited liability company and applied to the tax authorities for a reduction in property transfers tax namely INVIM, *imposta sull'incremento di valore immobiliare*, stamp duty, mortgage-registry tax and capital-transfer tax (*imposta di registro, ipotecaria e voltura*).

In 1988, in the procedures determining whether the tax concession was due, the tax authorities concluded that the property had been incorrectly valued for tax purposes and instead of reducing the tax due, increased it. In 1988 Ferrazzini applied to have the decision of increasing the tax reversed. Subsequently, the tax authorities accepted the applicant's comments and requested the case to be struck out of the list.

In separate proceedings, the tax authorities issued two supplementary tax assessments on the grounds that Ferrazzini was ineligible for the reduced rate of tax to which it had referred. The revised assessments stated that the company would be liable to an administrative penalty of 20% of the amounts requested if payment was not made

1. On this point, *see* cases of *Schouten and Meldrum v. The Netherlands*, Applications nos. 19005/91 and 19006/91.
2. Application no. 44759/98.

within sixty days. In 1988 Ferrazzini contested this decision too, but in 1998 the District Tax Commission adjourned the cases *sine die* and gave the applicant thirty days in which to appoint a lawyer. Subsequently, a hearing was listed for 24 April 1999. In 1999, the District Tax Commission dismissed the request for a reduction of tax on the basis that the transferred property, which included, among other things, a swimming pool and a tennis court, could not be regarded as the normal assets of an agricultural company falling within the purview of the reduction. In 2000, Ferrazzini lodged an appeal with the Regional Tax Commission and in 2001 filed a complaint under Article 6 (1) ECHR on the grounds that the length of the proceedings had exceeded the 'reasonable time' requirement.

Italy argued that Article 6 ECHR was inapplicable to the proceedings in question, considering that they did not concern a 'civil right'. The existence of an individual's tax obligation vis-à-vis the State belonged, in their submission, exclusively to the realm of public law. That obligation was part of the civic duties imposed in a democratic society, and the purpose of the specific provisions of public law was to support national economic policy. Ferrazzini, on his part, stressed the pecuniary aspect of his claims and contended that the proceedings accordingly concerned 'civil rights and obligations'.

The ECtHR reiterated that, according to its case law, the concept of 'civil rights and obligations' cannot be interpreted solely by reference to the domestic law of the respondent State; the concept is 'autonomous', within the meaning of Article 6 (1) ECHR.[3] The ECtHR proceeded to analyse the particular nature of the tax dispute in front of it:

> 25. Pecuniary interests are clearly at stake in tax proceedings, but merely showing that a dispute is 'pecuniary' in nature is not in itself sufficient to attract the applicability of Article 6 § 1 under its 'civil' head (see Pierre-Bloch v. France, judgment of 21 October 1997 ...). In particular, according to the traditional case-law of the Convention institutions,
>
> 'There may exist "pecuniary" obligations vis-à-vis the State or its subordinate authorities which, for the purpose of Article 6 § 1, are to be considered as belonging exclusively to the realm of public law and are accordingly not covered by the notion of "civil rights and obligations". Apart from fines imposed by way of "criminal sanction", this will be the case, in particular, where an obligation which is pecuniary in nature derives from tax legislation or is otherwise part of normal civic duties in a democratic society ... .'

It observed that:

> 27. Relations between the individual and the State have clearly evolved in many spheres during the fifty years which have elapsed since the Convention was adopted, with State regulation increasingly intervening in private-law relations. This has led the Court to find that procedures classified under national law as being part of 'public law' could come within the purview of Article 6 under its 'civil' head if the outcome was decisive for private rights and obligations, in regard to such matters as, to give some examples, the sale of land, the running of a private clinic, property interests, the granting of administrative authorisations relating to the conditions of professional practice or of a licence to serve alcoholic beverages ... .

3. *König v. Germany*, Application no. 6232/73, and *Baraona v. Portugal*, Application no. 10092/82.

Concluding that:

> 29. In the tax field, developments which might have occurred in democratic societies do not, however, affect the fundamental nature of the obligation on individuals or companies to pay tax. In comparison with the position when the Convention was adopted, those developments have not entailed a further intervention by the State into the 'civil' sphere of the individual's life. The Court considers that tax matters still form part of the hard core of public-authority prerogatives, with the public nature of the relationship between the taxpayer and the community remaining predominant. Bearing in mind that the Convention and its Protocols must be interpreted as a whole, the Court also observes that Article 1 of Protocol No. 1, which concerns the protection of property, reserves the right of States to enact such laws as they deem necessary for the purpose of securing the payment of taxes (see, mutatis mutandis, Gasus Dosier- und Fördertechnik GmbH v. the Netherlands, judgment of 23 February 1995, Series A no. 306-B, pp. 48-49, § 60). Although the Court does not attach decisive importance to that factor, it does take it into account. It considers that tax disputes fall outside the scope of civil rights and obligations, despite the pecuniary effects which they necessarily produce for the taxpayer ...
>
> 31. Accordingly, Article 6 § 1 of the Convention does not apply in the instant case ... .

Thus, the long and the short of it was that tax disputes similar to those arising in the *Ferrazzini* case were out of scope of Article 6 ECHR implying that the right to a fair trial did not apply.

Sadly, the conclusion reached in *Ferrazzini* which could be called the *Ferrazzini* dictum was not reversed in subsequent judgments to the extent that it was re-affirmed in 2020. In the controversial judgment case of *Alojzy Formela v. Poland*[4] when, referring to the *Ferrazzini* dictum, the ECtHR dismissed Formela's allegation of a violation of his right to a fair hearing on the basis that according to its settled case law, tax disputes fall outside the scope of civil rights and obligations, despite the pecuniary effects which they necessarily entail for the taxpayer.

Nonetheless, the fact that the dangerous precedent set in the *Ferrazzini* dictum was so heavily criticised by dissenting judges[5] and academics alike[6] implied that the draconian conclusion would find limited application. In fact, Bonello's dissenting

4. Application no. 31651/08.
5. Namely the dissenting opinion of Judge Bonello:

> The travaux préparatoires relating to Article 6 of the Convention – closely linked to those of Article 14 of the Covenant – demonstrate in my opinion the following: (1) it was the intention of the drafters to exclude disputes between individuals and governments on a more general basis mainly owing to difficulties at that time in making a precise division of powers between, on the one hand, administrative bodies exercising discretionary powers and, on the other hand, judicial bodies; (2) no specific reference was made to taxation matters, which are normally not based on a discretion but on the application of more or less precise legal rules; (3) the exclusion of the applicability of Article 6 should be followed by a more detailed study of the problems relating to 'the exercise of justice in the relations between individuals and governments'; accordingly, (4) it seems not to have been the intention of the drafters that disputes in the field of administration should be excluded forever from the scope of applicability of Article 6 § 1.

opinion predicted that the ECtHR's wide definition of the concept of 'criminal charge' would cause major restrictions to the application of the Ferrazzini dictum.

5.3 'OR OF ANY CRIMINAL CHARGE'

Whereas, in the 2001 judgment in *Ferrazzini*, the ECtHR adopted a restrictive interpretation of the term 'civil rights and obligations', in its earlier judgment in *Bendenoun v. France*,[7] the same Court had adopted a very liberal interpretation of the concept of criminal charge. Frequently, 'administrative penalties' imposed by tax authorities are treated as criminal charges within the meaning of Article 6 ECHR attracting the protection of the criminal limb of Article 6 ECHR.

In fact, the Bonello dissenting opinion pointed out that:

> Since Bendenoun v. France (judgment of 24 February 1994, Series A no. 284), the Court has consistently considered proceedings relating to tax disputes to be 'criminal' if tax fines, surcharges, etc., with a deterrent and punitive purpose are imposed or even if there is a risk that they may be imposed (see, most recently, J.B. v. Switzerland, no. 31827/96, ECHR 2001-III). The result is no different if the proceedings also concern the tax assessment as such (see the admissibility decision of 16 May 2000 in Georgiou v. the United Kingdom, no. 40042/98, unreported). This implies that the level of protection under Article 6 § 1 of the Convention varies depending on how the legal framework for tax proceedings is organised in the different legal systems; and even within one legal system it may be purely a matter of coincidence whether penalty proceedings and tax assessment proceedings are joined or not. An interpretation of the Convention that leads to such random results is far from satisfactory.

In 2000, Philip Baker had anticipated that, after *Bendenoun*, determinations over tax penalties would not only not be subject to the *Ferrazzini* dictum but that the day would come when determinations of tax penalties would attract the protection of Article 6 ECHR under its criminal head:

> One practical consequence of this decision is likely to be a further extension of the criminal aspects of Article 6 to tax proceedings. The European Court has already established that the determination of a liability to substantial penalties for incorrectly completed tax returns involves the determination of a criminal charge, and all the criminal guarantees in Article 6 will then apply. The issue of which tax penalties involve a criminal charge is gradually being clarified. There may also be a tendency in some countries for taxpayers to ask for the determination of their tax liability and the determination of any penalties to be considered at the same court hearing: in those circumstances, the Court has held that it is not possible to separate out the different parts of the proceedings and that Article 6 applies to the entire proceedings. One of the bizarre consequences of the decision in Ferrazzini is that Article 6 will apply in those countries where penalties and liability to tax are determined at the same time, but not in those countries were the determinations are separate.

6. Philip Baker, 'The Decision in Ferrazzini: Time to Reconsider the Application of the European Convention on Human Rights to Tax Matters', Intertax, Volume 29, Issue 11 (2001) pp. 360-361.
7. Application no. 12547/86.

Concluding that:

> It now seems clearly established, therefore, that a tax-geared penalty can entail a criminal charge, and that the issue of liability to penalties of 25% or higher has been regarded as involving the determination of a criminal charge.[8]

According to the ECtHR, the classification of a tax penalty is not determined by reference to formal designation, but a substance over form is applied. In the non-tax case of *Engel v. Netherlands*, the ECtHR concluded that the criteria to be used in determining whether an administrative penalty is to be treated as a 'criminal charge' within the meaning of the ECHR are the following:

(a) The legal classification of the offence under national law.
(b) The very nature of the offence.
(c) The degree of severity of the penalty that the person concerned risks incurring.

The ECtHR has held that the second and third criteria are alternative and not necessarily cumulative. This, however, does not exclude a cumulative approach where separate analysis of each criterion does not make it possible to reach a clear conclusion as to the existence of a criminal charge.

In a tax context, the application of the *Engel* criteria has resulted in the re-categorisation of most tax penalties as criminal charges within the meaning of the criminal limb Article 6 ECHR.

The case of *Bendenoun v. France*[9] cited in Bonello's dissenting opinion was a case involving administrative penalties (denominated as tax surcharges) imposed for non-compliance with the Tax Code. The ECtHR observed that the tax surcharges were not intended as pecuniary compensation for damage but essentially as a punishment to deter reoffending. In addition, the tax penalties were both deterrent and punitive. The tax surcharges were very substantial, and failure to pay the tax penalties exposed the taxpayer an effective prison term to be determined by the criminal courts.

The ECtHR weighed on the 'predominance' of the criminal connotation of the tax surcharges concluding that although the French legal system classified the tax penalties in dispute as administrative penalties, the ECtHR was to treat such tax surchages as 'criminal charges' within the meaning of Article 6 ECHR. Cases involving the re-characterisation of tax surcharges as criminal penalties abound with some later cases taking an even more liberal approach towards the reclassification of tax surcharges than Bendenoun.

The watershed moment came in the 2006 Grand Chamber judgment *Jussila v. Finland*,[10] a case involving a tax surcharge of only 10% of the reassessed tax liability

8. Baker, *supra* note 6, p. 30.
9. Application no. 12547/86.
10. Application no. 73053/01.

(the additional tax surcharges amounted to EUR 308.80). The ECtHR concluded that even this tiny surcharge was a 'criminal charge' within the meaning of the ECHR. The ECtHR examined whether a special concept of 'criminal charge' was to be considered in fiscal or tax cases. The ECtHR noted that in Bendenoun, the Court did not refer expressly to *Engel and Others v. the Netherlands*, leaving room for doubt.

The ECtHR referred to the case in *Janosevic v. Sweden*,[11] when the ECtHR had placed a great deal of emphasis on the severity of the actual and potential penalty (a surcharge of EUR 17,284) as a criterion to classify the charge pointing out that in the subsequent case of *Morel v. France*[12] a 10% tax surcharge of EUR 678, which was 'not particularly high' and was deemed to be a 'a long way from the "very substantial" level' needed for it to be classified as criminal.

The Grand Chamber highlighted the importance of the second criterion, the nature of the offence as being the most important criterion. The fact that the tax surcharges were not intended as pecuniary compensation for damage but as a punishment to deter reoffending was the determining factor. The deterrent and punitive element was held to be decisive. A distinction was drawn between *malum in se/malum quia prohibitum*, applying it to tax surcharges, and Jussila states that Article 6 rights and guarantees are not always applicable to *malum quia prohibitum* cases; for example, the right to be present may not be applicable to *malum quia prohibitum* cases. In *Jussila*, the Court confirmed the approach taken in *Janosevic* emphasising that no established or authoritative basis has therefore emerged in the case law for holding that the minor nature of the penalty, in taxation proceedings or otherwise, may be decisive in removing an offence, otherwise criminal by nature, from the scope of Article 6 ECHR. Moreover, in a clear signal of its intention not to deprive taxpayers of their fundamental safeguards in dealings with the State, the ECtHR added that:

> ... while there is no doubt as to the importance of tax to the effective functioning of the State,
>
> the Court is not convinced that removing procedural safeguards in the imposition of punitive penalties in that sphere is necessary to maintain the efficacy of the fiscal system or indeed can be regarded as consonant with the spirit and purpose of the Convention.

In so doing, the Court 'to a certain extent' abandoned the rationale of *Ferrazzini*, since it admitted that matters of pure tax assessment did not fall outside the ECHR's material scope. *Ratione materiae* issues relating to tax penalties may involve the Court in an evaluation of the States' sovereign power of tax assessment. The neutralisation of the public power prerogative in Jussila led the Court to an apparent reframing of the specificity of tax obligations in the context of European human rights law.

Even where the tax surcharges were not classified in national law as criminal, that fact alone was not decisive for the Court. The fact that tax surcharges were imposed by legal provisions applicable to taxpayers generally, with a deterrent purpose, was considered far more relevant. As a matter of principle, tax surcharges

11. Application no. 34619/97.
12. Application no. 54559/00.

were not intended solely as pecuniary compensation for certain damage caused to the State, but as a form of punishment of offenders and a means of deterring recidivism and potential new offenders. In the eyes of the Court, tax surcharges were thus imposed by a rule, the purpose of which was simultaneously deterrent and punitive, even where a 10% tax surcharge had been imposed, with an overall maximum possible surcharge of 20%. For the Court, the punitive nature of tax surcharges trumped the de minimis consideration of *Bendenoun*. Consequently, proceedings involving tax surcharges were also found to be 'criminal proceedings' for the purpose of Article 6 ECHR.

The ECtHR's 2007 case of *Paykar Yev Haghtanak Ltd v. Armenia*[13] is a perfect illustration of how, in practice, the *Bendenoun* rule frequently excludes the application of the *Ferrazzini* dictum. Paykar Yev Haghtanak Ltd was involved in a dispute with the Tax Inspectorate over a tax assessment which included a surcharge. The point at the issue was, in light of the judgment in *Ferrazzini*, whether Article 6 applied to the case in point. The issue revolved around a matter of classification. Article 6 does not apply (in terms of *Ferrazzini*) to pure tax disputes, but still applies to disputes over a criminal charge. The crux of the issue was whether the Armenian tax surcharge amounted to 'a criminal charge' for the purposes of Article 6. The ECtHR held that the surcharges attached to the assessment in dispute were deterrent and punitive. Furthermore, penalties were substantial and went up to 43%. The ECtHR concluded that the case in point was not a pure tax dispute subject to the *Ferrazzini* dictum, but it was a case over a criminal charge to which all the guarantees of Article 6 applied. The ECtHR found that applicant had been denied access to Court in violation of Article 6:

> 35. As regards the second criterion, the Court notes that the relevant provisions of the Law on Taxes and the Law on Value Added Tax are applicable to all persons – both physical and legal – liable to pay tax and are not directed at a specific group. Furthermore, the surcharges and the fines are not intended as pecuniary compensation for any costs that may have been incurred as a result of the taxpayer's conduct. The purpose pursued by these measures is to exert pressure on taxpayers to comply with their legal obligations and to punish breaches of those obligations. The penalties are thus both deterrent and punitive.
>
> 36. The Court considers that the above is sufficient to establish the criminal nature of the offence (ibid., § 38). It would, nevertheless, also point out that in the present case the applicant company had quite substantial penalties imposed on it: the fines ranging from 10 to 50 per cent and the surcharges for the period of delay cumulatively amounting from about 5 to 43 per cent of the tax due.
>
> 37. In the light of the above, the Court concludes that the proceedings to which the applicant company was a party can be classified as 'criminal' for the purposes of the Convention. It follows that Article 6 applies.

In the 2008 cases *Hannu Lehtinen v. Finland*[14] and *Kallio v. Finland*,[15] the ECtHR proceeded to classify tax surcharges as criminal charges without delving into the Engel criteria in any detail:

13. Application no. 21638/03.
14. Application no. 32993/02.
15. Application no. 40199/02.

> Article 6 is applicable under its criminal head to tax surcharge proceedings (see Jussila v. Finland, § 38). Regarding the parties' differing views on the role or impact of the taxation procedure as regards criminal proceedings, the Court notes that under Finnish practice the imposition of a tax surcharge does not prevent criminal charges being brought for the same conduct. That is, however, done in separate proceedings before a criminal court ...
>
> In view of the Administrative Court's firm conclusion that an oral hearing could be dispensed with, the Court considers that it is not necessary to examine separately whether the rights of the defence were violated by reason of the court's refusal to hear oral evidence.

In two articles analysing many years in the tax jurisprudence of the ECtHR, Philip Baker reached the following conclusions, both of which are endorsed by the authors:

> Following Jussila, it is likely that virtually all penalties computed as a percentage of the tax under-charged will be regarded as involving the determination of a criminal charge for the purposes of Art 6 of the ECHR. It is likely that only small, fixed penalties (for example, for delay in submitting a tax return) would not be regarded as involving the determination of a criminal charge. The consequence is, therefore, that virtually every tax case in which an administrative penalty is assessed will engage the criminal guarantees in Art 6 of the ECHR.[16]

And that:

> The case law here evolved in a run of cases that begins with Bendenoun v. France (12547/86)18 and ends with Jussila v. Finland (73053/01).19 That line of cases gradually determined that fixed penalties based on a percentage of the tax avoided or evaded constituted 'criminal charges' for the purposes of article 6. In Bendenoun the penalty was a potential 100% of the tax avoided for manoeuvres frauduleuses, but the run of cases gradually brought the borderline of a criminal charge down to a 10% tax surcharge (EUR 308 in that particular case) in Jussila.[17]

As a matter of fact, in the past seven years, the ECtHR has been quite 'liberal' in its interpretation of the term 'criminal charge', classifying most (if not all) tax penalties as criminal charges.

In 2015 in the case of *Rinas v. Finland*,[18] Finnish tax surcharges amounting to EUR 6,727 levied on a taxpayer for having received disguised dividends from foreign companies were held to constitute criminal charges, because tax surcharges were imposed by general legal provisions applying to taxpayers generally. The ECtHR's classification of the tax surcharges as criminal penalties was influenced by the fact that the 'surcharges were not intended as pecuniary compensation for damage but as a punishment to deter re offending. The surcharges were thus imposed by a rule, the purpose of which was deterrent and punitive'. The ECtHR reiterated that 'the minor nature of the penalty did not remove the matter from the scope of Article 6. Hence,

16. Philip Baker, 'The "Determination of a Criminal Charge" and Tax Matters', European Taxation, Volume 47, Issue 12 (2007).
17. Philip Baker, '60 Years of the European Convention on Human Rights and Taxation', European Taxation, Volume 61, Issue 12 (2021).
18. Application no. 17039/13.

Article 6 applied under its criminal head notwithstanding the minor nature of the tax surcharge'.[19]

In 2016, in the case of *Žaja v. Croatia,*[20] a case involving a customs-related administrative fine that was not routed in the Criminal Code, not entered in a person's criminal record, and not calculated by reference to income, the ECtHR held that the fine was to be classified as a criminal penalty because the offence emanated from legislation that applied to the whole population and not just to a particular group and the fine imposed on the applicant was punitive in nature as it was not intended to serve as pecuniary compensation for unpaid customs duties but as a penalty to deter reoffending.

In 2017, in the case of *Chap ltd v. Armenia,*[21] an Armenian late payment administrative penalty equivalent to 60% of the amount of tax due was held to be a criminal charge. The ECtHR referred to its earlier case law reiterating that proceedings concerning the imposition of fines and surcharges for unpaid or underpaid profit tax and VAT fall under the criminal head of Article 6.[22]

In 2018, in the case of *Matthildur Ingvarsdottir v. Iceland,*[23] an Icelandic 25% tax surcharge on undeclared income was treated as a criminal charge without much debate.

In 2019, in the two separate Icelandic cases, *Bjarni Ármannsson v. Iceland*[24] and *Ragnar Thorisson v. Iceland,*[25] there was not even a dispute as to whether a 25% surcharge for an underpayment of tax amounted to a criminal charge, with the ECtHR treating the issue as being obvious.

The 2022 Grand Chamber judgment in the case of *Vegotex International S.A. v. Belgium*[26] sums up the ECtHR's current approach to the *Ferrazzini* and *Bendenoun* dicta.

After excluding the application of Article 6 ECHR based on the *Ferrazzini* line of judgments:

> 66. ... Tax matters form part of the hard core of public-authority prerogatives, with the public nature of the relationship between the taxpayer and the community remaining predominant, despite the pecuniary effects which tax disputes necessarily produce for the taxpayer (see Ferrazzini, cited above, § 29). It follows that Article 6 § 1 of the Convention is not applicable under its civil limb.

It proceeded to apply the criminal limb of Article 6 ECHR based on *Bendenoun*:

> 69. It is true that the tax surcharge imposed did not fall within the scope of Belgian criminal law but was covered by fiscal legislation. Nevertheless, as in the case of Jussila (cited above), the surcharge was based on a general provision applicable to

19. Similar conclusions were reached by the ECtHR in the case of *Kiiveri v. Finland,* Application no. 53753/12 and the case of *Österlund v. Finland,* Application no. 53197/13.
20. Application no. 37462/09.
21. Application no. 15485/09.
22. *Namely Paykar Yev Haghtanak Ltd v. Armenia,* Application no. 21638/03.
23. Application no. 22779/14.
24. Application no. 72098/14.
25. Application no. 52623/14.
26. Application no. 49812/09.

> taxpayers generally (Article 444 of the 1992 Income Tax Code – see paragraph 35 above) and served a purpose that was both deterrent and punitive. Furthermore, the penalty which the applicant company was liable to incur was substantial: in view of the administrative decision, the applicant company risked incurring a surcharge of up to 50% of the tax it had been found to owe, a figure that could not be increased by the domestic courts.
>
> 70. It follows that the criminal limb of Article 6 of the Convention is 'applicable'.

In 2021, in the case of *Milošević v. Croatia*,[27] an excise fuel surcharge of over 100% was to be treated as a criminal charge because it was intended as a punishment to deter reoffending, a recognised characteristic feature of criminal penalties. In addition, the fact that purpose of the surcharge was not merely compensatory but also deterrent and punitive was sufficient to establish the criminal nature of the proceedings.

In 2021, in the case of *Bragi Guðmundur Kristjánsson v. Iceland*,[28] an 25% surcharge on the unreported tax base was treated as a criminal charge without any discussion.

In conclusion, the current judicial trend seems to treat most, if not all, tax penalties as criminal charges giving rise to major implications that go beyond Article 6 ECHR. The re-characterisation of tax administrative penalties as criminal charges has given rise to important developments in the interpretation of Article 7 ECHR and Article 4 of Protocol 7 ECHR.[29]

5.4 FERRAZZINI CASES, BENDENOUN CASES, PURE CRIMINAL PROSECUTIONS, CIVIL DETERMINATIONS AND THE TAX CASES IN-BETWEEN

It must be emphasised that the cases falling under the *Ferrazzini* dictum are only the 'pure' tax cases, cases involving the issuance of a tax assessment by the tax authority and the contestation of same. The *Ferrazzini* cases not covered by the ECHR right to a fair hearing are only cases involving the determination of pure tax.

Conversely, should tax assessments consist in administrative penalties satisfying certain criteria, then proceedings to determine the matter will be fully covered by the right to a fair trial under Article 6 ECHR. What is more, *Bendenoun* cases attract the protection of Article 6 under its criminal head. Nonetheless, the November 2022 Grand Chamber Judgment in *Vegotex International S.A. v. Belgium*[30] highlighted the special nature of tax disputes even in the context of the application of the criminal limb of Article 6 emphasising that:

> 76. Furthermore, in accordance with the case-law of the Court, as tax surcharges differ from the hard core of criminal law, the guarantees of Article 6 do not necessarily apply with their full stringency (see Jussila, cited above, § 43; see also,

27. Application no. 12022/16.
28. Application no. 12951/18.
29. Discussed *infra*.
30. Application no. 49812/09.

to similar effect, Segame SA v. France, no. 4837/06, §§ 56-60, ECHR 2012 (extracts); Chap Ltd v. Armenia, no. 15485/09, §§ 41 and 44, 4 May 2017; and, from the standpoint of Article 4 of Protocol No. 7, A and B v. Norway, cited above, § 133).

Needless to say, 'pure' criminal proceedings for tax offences would always be governed by Article 6 ECHR under its criminal limb. Thus, in the 2007 judgment *Juha Nuutinen v. Finland*,[31] the application of Article 6 ECHR was almost taken for granted. Mr Nuutinen was qua shadow director of a company prosecuted criminally on two counts of aggravated tax fraud and two counts of tax fraud (producing false invoices and entering false data in the books and records of the company). He was eventually, at the Appellate stage, found guilty of aiding and abetting the offences he had been charged with as principal offender and guilty of an offence which he had not been charged in the indictment. Nuutinen argued that his right to a fair hearing had been infringed because he had not been granted an opportunity to defend himself-he was convicted of offences different from those with which he had been originally charged. The ECtHR treated the case as a 'pure criminal case' and did not delve into Ferrazzini issues.

The 2007 case of *Lilja v. Sweden*[32] involved a two-pronged approach with the competent authorities pursuing Lilja both administratively and criminally. The ECtHR did not hesitate to apply Article 6 ECHR, finding a violation of the same. The same approach was adopted in the 2021 case of *Gančo v. Lithuania* involving a complaint relating to the reasonable requirement test in the context of a criminal tax case.[33]

There is a genre of cases that does not fall within the parameters described in the previous paragraphs, and these are the cases that fall between *Ferrazzini* and *Bendenoun*; cases that neither involve a 'pure' tax assessment nor a criminal charge, the cases that Baker classifies as 'Civil Cases'.[34] The ECtHR has acknowledged that there are cases that, because of their predominant private law character, would still fall within the parameters of the definition of 'civil rights and obligations'.

Baker cites the 1989 case of *Tre Traktörer Aktiebolag v. Sweden*[35] as an example. Given that the *Traktörer* case involved the revocation of trade licence as a punitive measure for a tax infringement, the ECtHR conceded that Article 6 ECHR applied because:

> features of public law mentioned by the Government do not suffice to exclude from the category of 'civil rights' within the meaning of Article 6 para. 1 (art. 6-1).

More recently, the ECtHR adopted a similar approach in the Article 1 Protocol 1 case of *Bimer S.A. v. Moldova*,[36] a case involving the revocation of a licence to operate a duty-free business.

31. Application no. 45830/99.
32. Application no. 36689/02.
33. Application no. 42168/19.
34. Philip Baker, 'Taxation and the European Convention on Human Rights', British Tax Review, Volume 40, Issue 4 (2000) pp. 211–377.
35. Application no. 10873/84.
36. Application no. 15084/03.

The Strasbourg organs applied Article 6 ECHR in cases involving actions in damages filed against the State for failure to grant tax concessions.[37] In the 1992 case of *Editions Periscope v. France*,[38] it was explained that:

> 40. The Court notes that the subject-matter of the applicant company's action was 'pecuniary' in nature and that the action was founded on an alleged infringement of rights which were likewise pecuniary rights. The right in question was therefore a 'civil right', notwithstanding the origin of the dispute and the fact that the administrative courts had jurisdiction (see, inter alia, the Ringeisen v. Austria judgment of 16 July 1971, Series A no. 13, p. 39, para. 94, and the König v. Germany judgment of 28 June 1978, Series A no. 27, p. 30, para. 90) ... .
>
> 41. Accordingly Article 6 para. 1 (art. 6-1) applies in this case.

The ECtHR's case law on disputes involving tax refunds and tax credits has not always been entirely consistent.

In the 1992 case *D. C. v. Italy*[39] involving a suit for a tax refund that was certain liquidated and due ('les procédures litigieuses visaient le recouvrement de crédits d'impôts liquides, certains et exigibles') Article 6 ECHR was applied and a violation on account of unreasonable delays in settling the refund was found.

A year later, the case of the *National & Provincial Building Society, the Leeds Permanent Building Society and the Yorkshire Building Society v. the United Kingdom*[40] did not find a violation but was prepared to entertain the case under Article 6 ECHR. The *Building Society* case involved claims to restitution of monies paid under invalidated tax provisions that had been extinguished under the effects of retrospective legislation. Article ECHR applied because:

> ... both sets of restitution proceedings (see paragraphs 30, 31 and 41 above) were private-law actions and were decisive for the determination of private-law rights to quantifiable sums of money. This conclusion is not affected by the fact that the rights asserted in those proceedings had their background in tax legislation and the obligation of the applicant societies to account for tax under that legislation.

A slightly different approach was taken in the case *Riccardo D'Andrea v. Italy*[41] a case involving a claim for a tax refund ('remboursement d'une somme qu'il avait versée à titre d'impôt sur le revenu') when, paradoxically, Article 6 ECHR was found to be inapplicable, because the case was dismissed as a case involving the interpretation of tax law:

> La demande du requérant devant les autorités nationales portait dès lors sur l'interprétation des lois fiscales quant à la détermination de revenus imposables. Par conséquent le point en litige n'était pas seulement le calcul du montant de

37. Application no. 11760/85.
38. *Ibid.*
39. Application no. 13120/87.
40. Applications nos. 21319/93, 21449/93 and 21675/93.
41. Application no. 30601/96.

> l'impôt dû et le remboursement de ce qui avait été payé en surplus, mais une interprêtation relative à la détermination de l'assiette fiscale.

Notwithstanding the outcome of the Italian case cited above, in the 1993 case *S. v. Austria*,[42] a case involving decisions of the Austrian tax authorities to seize jewellery pledged to them, Article 6 ECHR was still found to be applicable. It was pointed out that although tax proceedings are normally outside the scope of Article 6 ECHR,[43] the case before the Commission involved decisions taken by the Customs Office to seize and claim tax liability. The administrative decisions in question conflicted with the applicant's civil right of pledge. The customs authorities exercised a discretionary power in claiming tax liability in rem, and, in this context, were required to consider civil rights of third parties who for this purpose were recognised as parties to the proceedings. Against this background, the customs proceedings in question involved a determination of the question whether and to what extent the applicant could actually make use of its civil right of pledge. Accordingly, the civil limb of Article 6 ECHR was found to be applicable.

Similar challenges of classification are posed by 'mixed' cases involving tax assessments that, besides incorporating an assessment to raw tax, incorporate punitive measures. Arguably, such cases are 'indivisible' with the criminal nature of the case re-characterising the whole dispute.[44]

5.5 'FAIR AND PUBLIC HEARING'

The general rule is that the right to a fair hearing is intended to comprise the right of access to court, a right that must not be merely theoretical or illusory but a right that must be both practical and effective. Second, the right to fair hearing implies equality of arms in adversarial proceedings. In this respect, there is an overlap between Article 6 (1) ECHR and Article 6 (3) ECHR discussed below.

42. Application no. 18778/91.
43. *X. v. Austria*, Application no. 8903/80, *X. v. France*, Application no. 9908/82.
44. On this point *see* Philip Baker, 'Taxation and the European Convention on Human Rights' (Amended to 10 September 2000):

> One point which has not perhaps been highlighted in the cases on fiscal penalties and criminal charges is the distinction between the proceedings to determine the tax liability and the proceedings to determine the penalty. In most of the cases the proceedings under examination involved both issues. Strictly speaking, the question of applicability of Article 6 turns on whether the proceedings can be regarded as involving the determination of a criminal charge. Where the tax liability and the penalties are contained in the same assessment, or the penalty is automatic, it would seem impossible – as a practical matter, if nothing else – to apply Article 6 to part only of the proceedings ... Where substantial penalties are involved, it seems logical to say that Article 6 applies to the entire proceedings. This issue has not been conclusively resolved by the Strasbourg organs.

5.5.1 Access to Court

The ECtHR's leading cases on the matter are the non-taxes *Golder v. the United Kingdom*[45] and *Artico v. Italy*[46] when the ECtHR established that access to justice must be reasonably achievable. Access to a Tribunal must not be cluttered by unnecessary barriers, but certain restrictions are allowed. Allowable restrictions include reasonable peremptory deadlines and reasonable court fees that do not prejudice 'the very essence of the right'.[47]

The tax judgments of the ECtHR follow the principles laid down in *Golder* and *Artico* quite closely. Thus, in the case of *Scordino v. Italy* (no. 1), the ECtHR pointed out:

> 201 ... It might appear paradoxical that, by imposing various taxes – payable prior to the lodging of an application or after the decision – the State takes away with one hand what it has awarded with the other to repair a breach of the Convention. Nor should the costs be excessive and constitute an unreasonable restriction on the right to lodge such an application and thus an infringement of the right of access to a tribunal ... .

In the case of the insolvent company *Paykar Yev Haghtanak Ltd v. Armenia*,[48] cited previously, the fact that access to a tax court was denied because the company was unable to pay a court fee of EUR 370 was found to be a violation of Article 6 ECHR:

> 48. The Court observes that the requirement to pay court fees cannot be regarded as a restriction on the right of access to a court which is incompatible per se with Article 6 § 1 of the Convention. However, the amount of such fees assessed in the light of the particular circumstances of a given case, including the applicant's ability to pay them, and the stage of proceedings at which such a restriction is imposed, are factors which are material in determining whether or not a person enjoyed his right of access ...
>
> 50. In view of the above, the Court concludes that the applicant company was denied access to court in violation of Article 6 § 1 of the Convention.

5.5.2 Equality of Arms

Interestingly, but predictably, Article 6 (1) ECHR has been applied to both criminal tax cases and administrative proceedings. Thus, in the 1998 case of *J.J. v. the Netherlands*, the applicant's claim that he had been a victim of a violation of Article 6 (1) ECHR because he had not been able to reply to the advisory opinion submitted to the Supreme Court by the advocate general was upheld:

> 43 ... the outcome of the proceedings before the Supreme Court determined a 'criminal charge' against the applicant (see paragraphs 39–40 above). Regard being had, therefore, to what was at stake for the applicant in the proceedings and

45. Application no. 4451/70.
46. Application no. 6694/74.
47. *Ashingdane v. the United Kingdom*, Application no. 8225/78.
48. Application no. 21638/03.

> to the nature of the advisory opinion of the advocate-general, the fact that it was impossible for the applicant to reply to it before the Supreme Court took its decision infringed his right to adversarial proceedings. That right means in principle the opportunity for the parties to a criminal or civil trial to have knowledge of and comment on all evidence adduced or observations filed, even by an independent member of the national legal service, with a view to influencing the court's decision (see the above-mentioned Vermeulen judgment, p. 234, § 33, and the Van Orshoven judgment, p. 1051, § 41). There has accordingly been a violation of Article 6 § 1 of the Convention.

The 1996 case of *Miailhe v. France* (no. 2)[49] acknowledged the application of the equality of arms principle in a tax context but the case was dismissed on the merits.

The ECtHR's leading case on the application of the equality of arms principle in tax trials is the 2011 case *Oao Neftyanaya Kompaniya Yukos v. Russia*[50] involving, among others, complaints under Article 6 (1) ECHR and Article 6 (3) (b) ECHR. Yukos alleged that in the tax trial that led to its collapse it had not been afforded a fair hearing because:

(1) The Moscow City Court had allowed the tax authorities to seize Yukos' assets as a security for the claim before their claim had become final and conclusive.
(2) In the course of the tax proceedings, Yukos has not been allowed to adequately prepare for trial, the time within which it had to submit its case had been manifestly short and the time limit within which Yukos could file an appeal had been unjustifiably abridged.
(3) The Russian tax courts had pronounced judgment without studying all evidence.

According to the ECtHR, the seizure of Yukos' assets pending the outcome of the tax claim was neither arbitrary nor unfair. The ECtHR added that the immediate enforcement of the appeal did not prevent Yukos from filing its cassation appeal. The ECtHR observed that the right of access to court did not guarantee the right to an automatic stay of enforcement of an unfavourable court decision. Thus, on this count, it decided in favour of Russia.

The ECtHR observed that, at first instance, Yukos had not been granted access to all documents in the court file. The time which Yukos' lawyer was allowed to examine the court dossier had been extremely short. The ECtHR held that Yukos had only been given four days to prepare its case, concluding that it had not been granted facilities for the preparation of its defence. The ECtHR found that it was incumbent on the Russian court to ensure that Yukos was granted a sufficiently long period of time to study a voluminous case file. The ECtHR found a violation of Yukos' right to a fair hearing.

The ECtHR found some of Yukos' allegations as being 'vague', 'unspecific' and 'unsubstantiated', but it held that Yukos' complaints about the early beginning of the appeal hearings were justified. The ECtHR concluded that the effective shortening of

49. Application no. 18978/91.
50. Application no. 14902/04.

the time limit within which Yukos was to submit its case amounted to another violation of Yukos' right to a fair hearing.

The ECtHR concluded that there had been a violation of Yukos' right to a fair hearing:

> 551. Having regard to the above, the Court finds that the applicant company's trial did not comply with the procedural requirements of Article 6 of the Convention for the following reasons: the applicant company did not have sufficient time to study the case file at first instance, and the early beginning of the hearings by the appeal court unjustifiably restricted the company's ability to present its case on appeal. The Court finds that the overall effect of these difficulties, taken as a whole, so restricted the rights of the defence that the principle of a fair trial, as set out in Article 6, was contravened. There has therefore been a violation of Article 6 § 1 of the Convention, taken in conjunction with Article 6 § 3 (b).

The 2020 Chamber judgment in the case of *Vegotex International S.A. v. Belgium*[51] (as broadly confirmed by the Grand Chamber in 2022) is another important tax judgment on the right to a fair trial. One of the complaints was based on the nature of the adversarial proceedings. This specific complaint was dismissed on the merits, but the ECtHR made some important observations. The ECtHR pointed out that the concept of a fair hearing also includes the right to adversarial proceedings, according to which the parties must have the opportunity to make known any evidence needed for their claims to succeed, but also to have knowledge of, and comment on, all evidence adduced or observations filed, with a view to influencing the court's decision. The principle of adversarial proceedings requires that courts should not base their decisions on elements of fact or law which have not been discussed during the proceedings and which give the dispute an outcome which neither party would have been able to anticipate.

The fact that a tax debt that was time-barred by retrospective effect of case law was subsequently reinstated by retrospective but foreseeable legislation was not held to breach Article 6 ECHR either. The ECtHR did not find a violation, because it was not impervious to the Government's argument that the legislature's intervention was necessary in order to restore legal certainty after the latter had been undermined by the domestic Courts. In its November 2022 judgment, the Grand Chamber pointed out that:

> 123. Having regard to the specific circumstances of the present case, the Court finds that in seeking to combat large-scale tax fraud, avoid arbitrary discrimination between taxpayers and offset the effects of the Court of Cassation judgment of 10 October 2002 in order to restore legal certainty by re-establishing the settled administrative practice, reflected furthermore in the predominant case-law of the lower courts in the matter, the foreseeable intervention by the legislature was justified on compelling grounds of the general interest.
>
> 124. Accordingly, there has been no violation of Article 6 § 1 of the Convention on this account.

51. Application no. 49812/09.

The concept of fair hearing implies the equal access to the contents of the court file. One of the reasons why the ECtHR found violations of Article 6 ECHR in the 2012 case of *Chambaz v. Switzerland*[52] was because Chambaz was not allowed access to his tax investigation file. The ECtHR found that the Swiss authorities' denial to grant Chambaz access to the investigation file did not pursue a legitimate aim because the authorities' denial to provide access to the investigation file was ascribed exclusively to Chambaz's uncooperative 'attitude' in the course of the proceedings. The ECtHR observed:

> 67. Au vu de ce qui précède, la Cour en déduit que le refus de communiquer au requérant l'intégralité du dossier détenu par l'administration n'était pas justifié par des motifs en adéquation avec les principes se dégageant de la jurisprudence de la Cour en matière d'égalité des armes. Le processus décisionnel n'a en outre pas été assorti de garanties aptes à protéger les intérêts de l'accusé. Celui-ci a donc été placé dans une situation de net désavantage (Bendenoun c. France, précité, § 52).
>
> 68. Ces éléments suffisent à la Cour pour conclure que le droit à l'égalité des armes, tel que garanti par l'article 6 § 1 de la Convention a été violé en l'espèce.

Fair trial contemplates properly motivated judicial decisions. The issue was raised and acknowledged in the 2012 case *Segame SA v. France*,[53] a case that was dismissed on the merits. Conversely, a complaint on lack of sufficient reasoning was upheld in the 2021 case of *Melgarejo Martinez de Abellanosa v. Spain*.[54] The ECtHR found that the Spanish Audiencia Nacional had failed to explain why despite the fact that the surcharge and interest were considered ancillary under section 25 of the General Tax Act, the enforcement proceedings concerning the surcharge and interest could be pursued even in the absence of a valid enforcement title for the main debt. Similarly, when the applicant lodged the application for annulment, the Audiencia Nacional did not expressly respond to certain submissions. Consequently, the ECtHR found a violation of Article 6 (1) ECHR:

> It therefore required a specific and express reply, which the domestic courts did not provide. In such circumstances, it is impossible to ascertain whether the Audiencia Nacional failed to examine the applicant's submission at all, or whether it assessed and dismissed it and, if so, what were the reasons for so deciding (see, mutatis mutandis, Farzaliyev v. Azerbaijan, no. 29620/07, § 39, 28 May 2020).
>
> 43. The foregoing considerations are sufficient to enable the Court to conclude that the applicant's right to a reasoned judgment has been breached.

5.5.3 *Nemo Tenetur se Ipse Accusare*

The judgment in *Chambaz* is important from the perspective of nemo tenetur se ipso accusare too, because fair hearing implies freedom from self-incrimination. The ECtHR confirmed that the implied protection from self-incrimination contained in Article 6 (1)

52. Application no. 11663/04.
53. Application no. 4837/06.
54. Application no. 11200/19.

ECHR applies in a tax context too. The ECtHR found a violation of Article 6 (1) ECHR, because the Swiss Courts had forced Chambaz to incriminate himself. The ECtHR noted that by putting Chambaz under pressure to provide, in the course of an investigation for tax evasion, documentation which was potentially incriminating the Swiss authorities had violated Chambaz's right to silence:

> 54. La Cour observe, par ailleurs, que le requérant ne pouvait exclure que toute information relative à des revenus supplémentaires de sources non imposées l'exposait à être accusé d'avoir commis l'infraction de soustraction d'impôt (J.B. c. Suisse, précité, § 65) et était de nature à compromettre sa position dans l'enquête pour soustraction d'impôts. ...
>
> 58. Ces éléments suffisent à la Cour pour conclure que le droit de ne pas être contraint de s'incriminer soi-même, tel que garanti par l'article 6 § 1 de la Convention, a été violé en l'espèce.

The Commission has delivered a number of decisions on freedom from self-incrimination with the most frequently quoted decision being the 1995 case *Maximilian Abas v. the Netherlands*,[55] a case involving a false claim relating to a change in tax residence. Abas complained that he had been unjustly forced to disclose self-incriminating information which is contrary to the principle of nemo tenetur inherent in the notion of a fair hearing. The case was dismissed on the merits, but it was acknowledged that:

> The Commission recalls that, although not specifically mentioned in Article 6 (Art. 6) of the Convention, the right to silence and the right not to incriminate oneself, are generally recognised international standards which lie at the heart of the notion of a fair procedure under Article 6 (Art. 6). Their rationale lies, inter alia, in the protection of the accused against improper compulsion by the authorities thereby contributing to the avoidance of miscarriages of justice and to the fulfilment of the aims of Article 6 (Art. 6) of the Convention. The right not to incriminate oneself, in particular, presupposes that the prosecution in a criminal case seeks to prove its case against the accused without resort to evidence obtained through methods of coercion or oppression in defiance of the will of the accused (Eur. Court H.R., Saunders v. United Kingdom judgment of 17 December 1996, to be published in Reports 1996, para. 68).

In the 2001 case of *J.B. v. Switzerland*,[56] it was pointed out that by providing the accused with protection against improper compulsion by the authorities, their right to silence contributes to avoiding miscarriages of justice and securing the aims of Article 6 ECHR.[57] In J.B's case, it transpired that after the Swiss competent authorities had instituted tax evasion proceedings against the applicant, he was requested to submit all documents concerning the companies in which he had invested money. When the applicant failed to do so, he was requested on three further occasions to declare the source of the income invested. A fine was imposed for non-compliance. Clearly, the authorities were attempting to compel the applicant to submit documents which would

55. Application no. 27943/95.
56. Application no. 31827/96.
57. *See* Funke, cited above; *John Murray v. the United Kingdom*, Application no. 18731/91; *Saunders v. the United Kingdom*, Application no. 19187/91.

have provided information as to his income with a view to the assessment of his taxes. Consequently, the ECtHR concluded that there had been a violation of the right not to incriminate oneself.

The decision in *Maurice Marcellin Marie Van Weerelt v. the Netherlands*[58] is particularly interesting. It led Baker to conclude that information provided in violation of the *nemo tenetur si ipsum accusare* principle should never result in exposure to criminal charges:

> ... To respect the freedom from self-incrimination, they will need to guarantee that any information supplied will not be used for the purpose of imposing fines or criminal prosecution. Those advising a taxpayer would equally need to advise him not to supply information unless such as a guarantee was offered.[59]

The ECtHR delivered a thorough decision on the matter in the October 2022 case of *De Legé v. the Netherlands*[60] when the applicant complained, under Article 6 (1) ECHR, that documents concerning a foreign bank account had been obtained from him under coercion for use in tax proceedings in which tax fines were imposed on him, in violation of the privilege against self-incrimination. The ECtHR explained that protection from self-incrimination does not extend to the use in criminal proceedings of materials obtained from an accused through methods of coercion when these materials have an existence independent of his will. The use of documentary evidence obtained under threat of penalties in the context of financial law matters use does not fall within the scope of protection of the privilege against self-incrimination where the authorities are able to show that the compulsion is aimed at obtaining specific pre-existing documents (i.e., documents that have not been created as a result of the very compulsion for the purpose of the criminal proceedings, which documents are relevant for the investigation in question and of whose existence those authorities are aware). The ECtHR distinguished the merits of the facts before it from those in *J.B. v. Switzerland* where the authorities had attempted to compel the complainant to provide the evidence of offences through pure 'fishing expeditions'.[61] Consequently, the ECtHR did not find a violation of Article 6 (1) ECHR.

5.5.4 'Public Hearing'

In the 1991 case *K. v. Sweden*,[62] cited previously, the Commission explained that the public character of court hearings is a fundamental principle enshrined in Article 6 ECHR which may be waived expressly or tacitly. Such a waiver must be unequivocal and not contrary to any important public interest.

58. Application no. 784/14.
59. Philip Baker, 'Some Recent Decisions of the European Court of Human Rights on Tax Matters (And Related Decisions of the European Court of Justice)', European Taxation, Volume 56, Issue 8 (2016) pp. 342–351.
60. Application no. 58342/15.
61. Namely an attempt to compel an individual to provide evidence that was only suspected to exist.
62. Application no. 13800/88.

The same approach was adopted in 1994 in the Commission's detailed decision in *H. B. v. Switzerland*[63] when it was explained that the public hearing requirement exists to protect litigants against the administration of justice in secret with no public scrutiny. It is also one of the means whereby confidence in the courts, superior and inferior, can be maintained. By rendering the administration of justice visible, publicity contributes to the aim of Article ECHR, namely a fair trial, the guarantee of which is one of the fundamental principles of any democratic society within the meaning of the Convention. According to the case law, the fact that a public hearing is held in first instance implies that the absence of a hearing before a second or third instance may be justified by the special features of the case. Moreover, in both criminal and civil cases, it is possible to waive a right guaranteed by the Convention. However, insofar as the waiver is permissible, it must be established in an unequivocal manner. In the case of procedural rights, furthermore, a waiver, in order to be effective for Convention purposes, requires minimum guarantees commensurate to its importance. Neither the letter nor the spirit of Article 6 prevents a person from waiving of his own free will and in an unequivocal manner, the entitlement to have his case heard in public. The Commission concluded that:

> 48. It may reasonably be considered, therefore, that the applicant unequivocally waived his right to a public hearing before the Cantonal Tax Appeals Commission.
>
> 49. The Commission concludes, by 9 votes to 4, that in the present case there has been no violation of Article 6 para. 1 (Art. 6-1) of the Convention.

5.5.5 'Within a Reasonable Time'

The application of Article 6 ECHR entails that proceedings must be concluded within a reasonable time. The 1992 case of *Editions Periscope v. France*[64] is one of the ECtHR's earliest tax cases on this point. The ECtHR drew from its 'general' non-tax jurisprudence:

> 44. The reasonableness of the length of proceedings is to be determined with reference to the criteria laid down in the Court's case-law and in the light of the circumstances of the case, which in this instance call for an overall assessment.
>
> Examination of the two decisions of the administrative courts shows that the case was not a particularly complex one. In addition, the applicant company did nothing to delay the conclusion of the proceedings; on the contrary, it made repeated attempts to compel the ministries concerned to submit their memorials more rapidly (see paragraphs 18 and 20 above). It follows that the Court cannot regard as reasonable in this instance a lapse of time of more than eight years.
>
> There has accordingly been a violation of Article 6 para. 1 (art. 6-1).

In this respect judgments of the ECtHR are unequivocal. In 2006, in the case of *Dukmedjian v. France*,[65] a case involving tax surcharge proceedings, while the ECtHR

63. Application no. 17951/91.
64. Application no. 11760/85.
65. Application no. 60495/00.

did not find the tax surcharges calculated as a percentage of tax payable incompatible with Article 1 of Protocol 1 ECHR, it did not hesitate to conclude that proceedings that took over fifteen years to conclude violated the reasonable time requirement.

The detailed 2006 judgment in the case of *Scordino v. Italy* (no. 1) explained how the core value of justice within a reasonable time is to apply in a tax context. In complaints involving the reasonable time requirement, the ECtHR considers complainant's proactivity, stakes involved in the dispute, complexity of the cases and, of course, the interval of time between the institution of proceedings and their conclusion:

> 214. In the instant case the Court notes that the Court of Appeal did not find that the conduct of the applicants had had a significant effect on the length of the proceedings. Nor did it find that the case was particularly complex. The Court of Appeal's decision appears to take account only of the excessive length, assessed at three years and six months, and the stakes involved in the dispute. The Court reiterates that the stakes involved in the dispute cannot be assessed with regard only to the final outcome, otherwise proceedings that are still pending would have no value. Regard has to be had to the overall stakes involved in the dispute for the applicants.

The reasonable time requirement was examined in the 2005 case of *Marpa Zeeland B.V. and Metal Welding B.V. v. the Netherlands*,[66] a case when the ECtHR was prepared to accept that, unlike other cases, tax cases tend to be complex warranting proceedings that take long to conclude:

> 61 ... Moreover, the Court is prepared to accept that an investigation into offences of the kind at issue – forgery and company tax fraud – is by definition relatively complex. Nevertheless, it notes that the pre-trial phase also encompasses two periods of apparent inactivity, which together amount to more than a year, which cannot be attributed either to the complexity of the case or to the conduct of the applicant companies.

Nonetheless, due to the unjustifiable period of inactivity, the length of the proceedings was deemed to be excessive and failed to meet the 'reasonable-time' requirement. Consequently, the ECtHR found a breach of Article 6 (1) ECHR.

The ECtHR returned to the reasonable time requirement in the 2007 case of *Lilja v. Sweden*[67] mentioned above. Lilja was a director and shareholder of around twenty companies and was charged on suspicion of aggravated tax fraud and keeping false books. Criminal proceedings were taken against him, and tax proceedings were instituted separately. Criminal proceedings lasted for eight years. Tax proceedings were instituted separately and lasted five years (proceedings included proceedings over a tax surcharge). Lilja was acquitted of criminal charges, but he lost his tax dispute and was ordered to pay substantial tax surcharges. The ECtHR concluded that the length of the proceedings had been incompatible with the 'reasonable time' requirement in Article 6 ECHR. The ECtHR held that the five-year term of the tax proceedings and the seven-year term of the criminal proceedings were both unreasonable.

66. Application no. 46300/99.
67. Application no. 36689/02.

The ECtHR's important 2021 judgment in the case of *Vegotex International S.A. v. Belgium*[68] confirmed by the Grand Chamber in November 2022 included an analysis of a complaint relating to the reasonable time requirement too. In all, the proceedings had lasted for thirteen years and six months, at one administrative level and three levels of court jurisdiction. The financial interests at stake were considerable and the case was complex, but the ECtHR considers that these factors were insufficient per se to explain the duration of the proceedings which, taken overall, were unreasonably long. Accordingly, the Grand Chamber confirmed a violation of Article 6 (1) ECHR on account of the failure to comply with the reasonable time requirement:

> 157. The Court accepts that the complexity of the present tax-related case may justify lengthier periods than in other types of cases, especially those which call for particular expedition owing to their subject matter. This is particularly so given that the State has a greater interest than the individual in prompt recovery of the tax. Nevertheless, even assuming that the reasonable-time guarantee should not apply with its full stringency (see paragraph 76 above), the Court considers that, taken overall and in the circumstances of the case, the proceedings brought by the applicant company exceeded a reasonable time.

In 2021, the ECtHR heard another case over the reasonable time requirement, the case of *Gančo v. Lithuania*.[69] The complaint was that the length of the criminal proceedings – almost six years and five months – had been excessive, and that it had not been justified by the alleged complexity of the case. There had been multiple periods of inactivity, and furthermore, the time taken by the State Tax Inspectorate to prepare its conclusion had been unreasonable. The complainant argued that he had not done anything to prolong the proceedings, and consequently their length was attributable solely to the authorities. Although the ECtHR was prepared to accept that the criminal case was complex concerning allegations of financial crimes and multiple suspects, the complexity of the case did not justify long periods of inactivity on the part of the tax authorities. The ECtHR found a violation:

> 35. Lastly, having examined the material in its possession, the Court is unable to find that the applicant abused his procedural rights or unreasonably prolonged the proceedings in any other way. Therefore, their overall length must be attributed to the authorities.
>
> 36. There has accordingly been a violation of Article 6 § 1 of the Convention.

5.5.6 'Independent and Impartial Tribunal Established by Law'

5.5.6.1 Independence and Impartiality

The non-tax case law of the ECtHR has established that a tribunal is considered to be independent if it is free from external pressures via transparent rules relating to appointment, duration, and security of tenure of the members of the tribunal:

68. Application no. 49812/09.
69. Application no. 42168/19.

> Only an institution that has full jurisdiction and satisfies a number of requirements, such as independence of the executive and also of the parties, merits the designation 'tribunal' within the meaning of Article 6 para. 1 (art. 6-1).

The existence of a suspicion of collusion is not held to be sufficient to establish a lack of 'independence'.[70]

According to the ECHR Handbook on European law relating to access to justice,[71] the concept of impartiality comprises two elements, namely:

- a subjective element relating to an individual judge's personal prejudices or bias;
- an objective element relating to issues such as the appearance of bias.

In the non-tax case of *Morice v. France*,[72] the ECtHR observed that impartiality denotes absence of prejudice or bias. The existence of impartiality must be determined according to a subjective test relating to the personal conviction and behaviour of a particular judge and also according to an objective test, by ascertaining whether the tribunal in its composition offered sufficient guarantees of impartiality.

The principles established in the non-tax cases of the ECtHR were applied in its tax jurisprudence without special considerations. Thus, in the 1994 tax evasion case of *H. W. K. v. Switzerland*,[73] it was observed:

> 2. It is true that the applicant complains under Article 6 (Art. 6) of the Convention that his fine for tax evasion was not decided by an 'independent ... tribunal' within the meaning of this provision. He submits in particular that the Appeals Commission for Federal Taxes appears as part of the cantonal administration.
>
> In determining whether this body can be considered to be 'independent', notably of the executive and of the parties to the case, the Commission has had regard to the manner of appointment of its members and the duration of their term of office, the existence of guarantees against outside pressures and the question whether the body presents an appearance of independence (cf. Eur. Court H.R., Campbell and Fell judgment of 28 June 1984, Series A no. 80, p. 39 et seq., para. 78) ...
>
> Moreover, the duration of office of the members of the Appeals Commission, lasting four years, is not so short as to raise an issue as to their independence. The absence in the applicable legislation of a formal recognition of the irremovability from office again cannot in itself imply lack of independence (loc. cit. p. 40, para. 80) ...
>
> As a result, the Commission is satisfied that the Appeals Commission was an 'independent tribunal' within the meaning of Article 6 para. 1 (Art. 6-1) of the Convention.

The impartiality of a Russian Tax Court was questioned in the 2013 case of *Khodorkovskiy and Lebedev v. Russia*[74] when applicants alleged that one of the judges

70. *Campbell and Fell v. The United Kingdom*, Applications nos. 7819/77 and 7878/77.
71. *Ibid.*, p. 38.
72. Application no. 29369/10.
73. Application no. 23399/94.
74. Applications nos. 11082/06 and 13772/05.

had not been impartial because, before hearing their case, the judge had convicted an individual who was connected to their case. The ECtHR did not find a violation because the judge was not bound by her earlier findings. The judge's earlier judgment did not contain any finding directly incriminating the applicants: they were not referred to as 'perpetrators', 'offenders', 'co-authors', etc. The judgment did not analyse their involvement in the crime imputed to the personal tax evasion imputed to the complainant's associate and did not establish the constituent elements of the applicants' criminal liability:

> 556. The Court concludes that the judgment in Mr Shakhnovskiy's case did not contain findings that prejudged the question of the applicants' guilt in subsequent proceedings, and that Judge XX was not bound by her previous findings, either legally or otherwise.

The same parties submitted complaints of partiality in their 2020 case of *Khodorkovskiy and Lebedev v. Russia* (no. 2).[75] This time, complainants argued that one's of the judge's bias emerged in information published in the media after the trial and in procedural decisions during the trial. The ECtHR held that to overcome the presumption of impartiality, which is a starting point under the subjective test, the ECtHR must have strong evidence. The ECtHR held that certain allegations were unsubstantiated. While the applicants alleged that a particular judge had been unduly influenced by the Inferior Court, allegations did not go beyond the conduct of a particular judge and did not involve allegations of a lack of judicial impartiality that is functional in nature, such as hierarchical links with another person involved in the proceedings. Having regard to the material before it, the ECtHR did not find any appearance of a lack of independence and impartiality under the objective test either.

5.5.6.2 'Tribunal'

In the case of *Julius Kloiber Schlachthof Gmbh and Others v. Austria,*[76] a case involving surcharges, the ECtHR explained that the concept of '"tribunal" is characterised in the substantive sense of the term by its judicial function, determining matters within its competence applying the law and after proceedings conducted in a prescribed manner. A degree of permanence is needed. It must also satisfy a series of further requirements: independence of the executive; impartiality; the duration of its members' terms of office; and the guarantees afforded by its procedure'. Referring to *Umlauft v. Austria*, the ECtHR added that decisions taken by administrative authorities which do not themselves satisfy the substantive requirements of a fair hearing must, in their own turn, be subject to higher review by a 'judicial body that has full jurisdiction'. The ECHR handbook, cited previously, quotes the following characteristics as being inherent in a tribunal:

- be established by law;

75. Applications nos. 51111/07 and 42757/07.
76. Applications nos. 21565/07, 21572/07, 21575/07 and 21580/07.

- be permanent;
- be independent and impartial;
- include an inter-partes procedure;
- have compulsory jurisdiction;
- apply rules of law.[77]

The ECtHR's tax judgments follow the ECtHR's traditional judgment in this respect. Thus, in the case of *Ravon and Others v. France*,[78] the ECtHR pointed out:

> La Cour rappelle à cet égard que seul mérite l'appellation de 'tribunal' un organe répondant à une série de critères – telle l'indépendance à l'égard de l'exécutif et des parties – et jouissant de la plénitude de juridiction, et que, pour qu'un tel 'tribunal' puisse décider d'une contestation sur des droits et obligations de caractère civil en conformité avec cette disposition, il faut qu'il ait compétence pour se pencher sur toutes les questions de fait ou de droit pertinentes pour le litige dont il se trouve saisi (voir, par exemple, l'arrêt Chevrol précité, §§ 76-77). Par ailleurs, à l'instar des autres droits garantis par la Convention, le droit d'accès aux tribunaux doit être concret et effectif (voir, par exemple, mutatis mutandis, les arrêts Airey c. Irlande, du 9 octobre 1979, série A no 32, § 24, et Steel et Morris c. Royaume-Uni du 15 février 2005, no 68416/01, CEDH 2005-II, § 59).

In *Ravon*, the ECtHR found a violation because the grievance procedure made available to him lacked the necessary procedural guarantees to be considered a 'tribunal' within the meaning of the ECtHR:

> 33. Il reste la possibilité évoquée par le Gouvernement d'engager une action à l'encontre de l'agent judicaire du Trésor pour rupture du principe d'égalité devant les charges publiques ou de saisir le juge judiciaire sur le fondement de l'article 9 du code civil. ...
>
> 34. Il résulte de ce qui précède que les requérants n'ont pas eu accès à un 'tribunal' pour obtenir, à l'issue d'une procédure répondant aux exigences de l'article 6 § 1 de la Convention, une décision sur leur 'contestation'.
>
> 35. En conséquence, la Cour conclut au rejet de l'exception du Gouvernement tirée du non-épuisement des voies de recours internes et à la violation de l'article 6 § 1 de la Convention.

The issues raised in *Ravon* were discussed in more detail in *André and Other v. France*[79] which will be analysed in the chapter examining Article 8 ECHR.

5.6 THE CRIMINAL LIMB

The criminal limb of Article 6 ECHR consisting in the special rules in Article 6 (2) and 6 (3) ECHR creates additional guarantees to those contemplated in Article 6 (1) ECHR. When the criminal guarantees apply, they apply over and above the guarantees in 6 (1)

77. *Ibid.*, p. 32.
78. Application no. 18497/03.
79. Application no. 18603/03.

ECHR, but there is undoubtedly an element of overlap between the civil limb and the criminal limb, especially between Article 6 (1) ECHR and Article 6 (3) (b) ECHR.

5.6.1 'Criminal offence'

Article 6 (2) ECHR listing the additional safeguards of the criminal limb ties the application of the criminal limb to 'a charge with a criminal offence'. Curiously, Article 6 (2) ECHR does not faithfully replicate the Article 6 (1) ECHR jargon 'determination ... of a criminal charge' but judgments of the ECtHR, including its tax judgments, suggest that 'a charge with a criminal offence' and a 'determination ... of a criminal charge' are the same thing.

5.6.2 'Presumed innocent until proved guilty according to law'

Issues relating to the presumption of innocence in a tax context were raised early in the day in the history of the ECHR. The first known case is the landmark judgment in *Funke v. France*,[80] a complex case involving complaints under a number of articles. In one of the complaints, Funke alleged that his conviction for refusing to disclose the documents asked for by the customs had violated the right not to give evidence against oneself. The complaint was upheld:

> 44. The Court notes that the customs secured Mr Funke's conviction in order to obtain certain documents which they believed must exist, although they were not certain of the fact. Being unable or unwilling to procure them by some other means, they attempted to compel the applicant himself to provide the evidence of offences he had allegedly committed. The special features of customs law (see paragraphs 30-31 above) cannot justify such an infringement of the right of anyone 'charged with a criminal offence', within the autonomous meaning of this expression in Article 6 (art. 6), to remain silent and not to contribute to incriminating himself.
>
> There has accordingly been a breach of Article 6 para. 1 (art. 6-1).

In the 1994 case of *H. B. v. Switzerland*,[81] the applicant complained that the Swiss Tax Court's incomplete establishment of the facts violated his right to the presumption of innocence. It was noted that the presumption of innocence will be violated if, without the accused's having previously been proved guilty according to law, a judicial decision concerning him reflects an opinion that he is guilty. The mere criticism of the assessment of evidence made by the Courts was not sufficient to constitute infringement of presumption of innocence. The casefile did not contain evidence that during the proceedings the courts anticipated the finding that the applicant had committed the acts with which he was charged. Consequently, the case was dismissed as manifestly ill-founded.

80. Application no. 10828/84.
81. Application no. 17951/91.

The 1994 case *K.S. and K.S. AG*[82] *v. Switzerland* was another early case when the issue of presumption of innocence was raised in a tax context. The applicant complained of a breach of the presumption of innocence in that he had to prove that he had not used certain moneys for private purposes. It was held that the ECHR does not prohibit presumptions of fact or of law in principle. Rather, it requires States to confine presumptions within reasonable limits which take into account the importance of what is at stake and maintain the rights of the defence. The complaint was dismissed:

> Thus, the Federal Court in fact found that it fell to the tax authorities to establish the applicants' guilt. However, the Federal Court also considered that it was up to the applicant, who wished to claim a reduction of taxes, to demonstrate that he had not used certain moneys for personal purposes. In the Commission's opinion, the Federal Court thus duly took into account the presumption of innocence in criminal proceedings, while fully maintaining the applicants' rights of defence.

The judgment in the case *E.L., R.L. and J.O. –L. v. Switzerland* is singled out as one of the ECtHR's most important judgments because of its ingenious combination of its rules on the classification of tax penalties and the presumption of innocence. The classification of tax administrative penalties as criminal penalties was taken to imply that such penalties were not inheritable. The ECtHR's conclusion on the non-inheritability of tax penalties was considered to be a corollary of the rule on presumption of innocence:

> 52. In this case the Court does not find it necessary to decide whether the guilt of the deceased was lawfully established. Pursuant to Article 130 § 1 of the Ordinance on Direct Federal Tax, the proceedings were brought against the applicants themselves and the fine was imposed on them (see paragraphs 11 and 21 above). It must therefore be accepted that, whether or not the late Mr L. was actually guilty, the applicants were subjected to a penal sanction for tax evasion allegedly committed by him.
>
> 53. It is a fundamental rule of criminal law that criminal liability does not survive the person who has committed the criminal act … .
>
> In the Court's opinion, such a rule is also required by the presumption of innocence enshrined in Article 6 § 2 of the Convention. Inheritance of the guilt of the dead is not compatible with the standards of criminal justice in a society governed by the rule of law. There has accordingly been a violation of Article 6 § 2.

The ECtHR reached a different conclusion in the 2007 case of the *Estate of Nitschke v. Sweden*,[83] but the merits of the case were different. While reiterating that it is a fundamental rule of criminal law that criminal liability does not survive the person who committed the criminal act and that imposing criminal sanctions on the living in respect of acts apparently committed by a deceased person calls for careful scrutiny, the ECtHR observed that there were some fundamental differences between the cited Swiss cases and its case. According to Swiss law, the deceased's assets and liabilities fall directly to the heirs, whereas, under Swedish law, the estate of a deceased person

82. Application no. 19117/91.
83. Application no. 6301/05.

is a separate legal person responsible for settling the deceased's financial, and other, matters. Hence, the heirs have no personal responsibility for the deceased's debts or other liabilities (unless in some very particular circumstances which were not present in the instant case). Furthermore, in the two Swiss cases, proceedings had been brought against the applicants and fines imposed on them personally, after the death of their father, for tax evasion allegedly committed by him. In contrast, Mr Nitschke was never accused of having committed a crime, such as tax evasion, but the tax surcharges were imposed on him on objective grounds and after it had been established that no reasons for remission existed. Neither Mr Nitschke's heirs nor his estate was ever held personally liable for the tax surcharges since they had already been imposed on Mr Nitschke while he was alive and paid by him. The ECtHR concluded that:

> 55. In these circumstances, and in particular as the Court has found that the presumption of innocence was respected in relation to Mr Nitschke and that neither his estate nor his heirs have in any way been held personally liable for the tax surcharges, the Court considers that the presumption of innocence in Article 6 § 2 of the Convention has been complied with.

The 2014 case of *Melo Tadeu c. Portugal*[84] contemplated issues of vicarious liability. A shadow manager was held to be personally liable for a tax debt due by the company in which she was deemed to serve in despite acquittal in the Criminal Courts. Melo Tadeu's personal assets were seized by the tax authorities in tax enforcement procedures that seemed to assume that Melo Tadeu was responsible for the underlying tax offence. The ECtHR did not hesitate to find a violation of the presumption of innocence:

> 66. Tant l'administration fiscale que les juridictions administratives saisies ont méjugé l'acquittement de la requérante par le tribunal criminel d'Almada du chef d'abus de confiance fiscal pour des faits commis par la société V. au motif que la requérante n'en était pas gestionnaire de fait. Elles ont ainsi considéré comme établi un élément qui avait été jugé non-prouvé par les juridictions pénales. La Cour considère que cette manière d'agir a jeté un doute sur le bien-fondé de l'acquittement de la requérante, ce qui apparaît incompatible avec le respect de la présomption d'innocence. Dans ces conditions, la Cour conclut qu'il y a eu violation de l'article 6 § 2 de la Convention.

Issues relating to vicarious responsibility of directors and presumption of innocence returned to the ECtHR in the 2021 case of *Busuttil v. Malta*.[85] Busuttil complained that a presumption of guilt was applied against him on the basis that he was the director of the company. The ECtHR did not find any indication that the domestic courts had applied the domestic rules on the burden of proof in a manner incompatible with the presumption of innocence. The complainant had not explained in what way the burden of proof imposed on him was unattainable to the extent that his defence could have no prospect of success. There was nothing indicating that the criminal courts in fulfilling their functions started from the assumption that the applicant was

84. Application no. 27785/10.
85. Application no. 48431/18.

guilty. The ECtHR explained that State Signatories may, in principle and under certain conditions, penalise a simple or objective fact as such, irrespective of whether it results from criminal intent or from negligence. The ECtHR felt that it had to single out the particular nature of tax law:

> ... In the Court's view, it is therefore judicious for the law to provide that the latter, in taking up his or her responsibilities as director, takes up the obligation to pay the relevant tax dues, in order to allow for a functional system in the interests of all those concerned, as long as some means of defence remains available to an accused.
>
> Bearing in mind the above, the Court considers that the presumption under Maltese law, that a director is responsible for any act which by law must be performed by the company, was not unreasonable in the circumstances of the present case.
>
> There has accordingly been no violation of Article 6 § 2 of the Convention.

Issues relating to presumption of innocence were raised in the case of *Agapov v. Russia*,[86] when the applicant argued that, in the civil proceedings, his right to be presumed innocent had been breached, because the outcome of a tax case was heavily influenced by observations made in a criminal tax evasion case. It transpired that the civil courts based their decision to grant the claims against the applicant exclusively on the findings as to his criminal liability set out in an investigator's file without evaluating any further evidence or making any independent assessment. Criminal liability had been presumed. The ECtHR concluded that the applicant was treated in a manner inconsistent with his right to be presumed innocent, finding a violation of Article 6 (2) ECHR.

Complaints relating to presumption of innocence were submitted in another Yukos case, the 2020 case of *Khodorkovskiy and Lebedev v. Russia* (no. 2).[87] Applicants complained about various statements made by the Russian Prime Minister. Applicants complained that the Russian Prime Minister had compared them to Al Capone, the famous American mobster convicted of tax evasion and other criminals. Repeating that Article 6 (2) will be violated if a statement of a public official concerning a person charged with a criminal offence reflects an opinion that he is guilty before he has been proved so according to law, the ECtHR did not find a violation of Article 6 (2) ECHR.

5.6.3 '(a) to be informed promptly, in a language which he understands and in detail, of the nature and cause of the accusation against him;'

The ECtHR found a violation of 6 (3) ECHR in the *Juha Nuutinen v. Finland*,[88] cited previously. The ECtHR held that in criminal matters, the accused must be provided with full, detailed information concerning the charges and the legal characterisation of

86. Application no. 52464/15.
87. Applications nos. 51111/07 and 42757/07.
88. Application no. 45830/99.

a charge is a prerequisite. The factual situation set out in the indictment changed in the proceedings and accused's right to defend himself was impaired. The ECtHR concluded that Nuutinen rights to be informed in detail of the nature and cause of the accusations against him and his right to have adequate time and facilities for his defence were infringed.

5.6.4 '(b) to have adequate time and facilities for the preparation of his defence; (c) to defend himself in person or through legal assistance of his own choosing or, if he has not sufficient means to pay for legal assistance, to be given it free when the interests of justice so require; (d) to examine or have examined witnesses against him and to obtain the attendance and examination of witnesses on his behalf under the same conditions as witnesses against him; (e) to have the free assistance of an interpreter if he cannot understand or speak the language used in court.'

Matters pertinent to this limb of the right to a fair hearing were raised in the 1994 case *K.S. and K.S. AG*[89] *v. Switzerland* when applicants complained that in the proceedings before the Tax Court they did not have an oral hearing. In addition, applicants complained that they had not been not given the opportunity to question key witnesses. They also complained that they were not able to put forward certain evidence and were not properly informed of the charges brought against them. The case was dismissed on the basis of failure to exhaust ordinary remedies.

The 2019 case of *Düriye Karalar v. Turkey*[90] involved a complaint under Article 6 (3) (b) and (c) ECHR. Karalar, a qualified accountant, complained that she had not had a fair trial, because she had not been given the time and facilities necessary to prepare her defence against the tax penalty imposed on her. Furthermore, the deadline to institute the tax contestation proceedings fell when Karalar was serving a prison term. Although the ECtHR was mindful of the inherent difficulties Karalar might have faced in her attempts to challenge the tax penalty within the time limit provided for by law, it was not prepared to accept that the mere fact of being in prison is per se sufficient to constitute a 'special circumstance' absolving her from the requirement to use the above-mentioned effective domestic remedy:

> 66. More importantly, no material before the Court suggests that the applicant had the report in full when lodging an objection against the payment order with the Antalya Tax Court, which is another indication that she was not prevented from, at the very least, complying with the time-limit laid down in section 7 of Law no. 2577. In the Court's view, this is another element which in fact militates against her contention that she was prevented from effectively challenging the tax penalty on time because she did not receive the tax report in full.

89. Application no. 19117/91.
90. Application no. 1964/07.

> 67. In view of the above, the Court cannot accede to the view that the above-mentioned circumstances were such as to render impossible the effective exercise by the applicant of the remedy provided for in section 7 of Law no. 2577, which was in principle an effective remedy in respect of her complaints.

Matters pertinent to most aspects of Article 6 (3) ECHR were discussed in the lengthy judgment in the 2013 case of *Khodorkovskiy and Lebedev v. Russia*[91] when, understandably, the ECtHR examined complaints under Article 6 (3) with complaints under 6 (1) ECHR.

The ECtHR explained that it is a fundamental aspect of the right to a fair trial that criminal proceedings, including the elements of such proceedings which relate to procedure, should be adversarial and that there should be equality of arms between the prosecution and the defence, which means that both the prosecution and defence must be given the opportunity to have knowledge of and comment on the observations filed and the evidence adduced by the other party. The accused must have the opportunity to organise his defence in an appropriate way and without restriction as to the possibility to put all relevant defence arguments before the trial court and thus to influence the outcome of the proceedings. The facilities which should be enjoyed by everyone charged with a criminal offence include the opportunity to acquaint himself, for the purposes of preparing his defence, with the results of investigations carried out throughout the proceedings.

The ECtHR took umbrage with the conditions in which the applicants had to work with their case files finding the conditions uncomfortable at best. Nonetheless, the fact that the complainants were experienced businessmen coupled with the fact that their lawyers worked in high-performing teams led the ECtHR to dismiss this part of the complaint:

> 586. The above five elements lead the Court to the conclusion that although the defence had to work in difficult conditions at the pre-trial stage, the time allocated to the defence for studying the case file (compare with the judgment in the Yukos case, cited above, § 536) was not such as to affect the essence of the right guaranteed by Article 6 §§ 1 and 3 (b). It follows that there was no violation of those Convention provisions on this account.

In addition, Khodorkovskiy and Lebedev complained of a separate violation of Article 6 (3) ECHR on the basis that they had not been given sufficient time to study the trial materials. The ECtHR found that the difficulties experienced by the defence during the appeal proceedings did not affect the overall fairness of the trial and that there was no violation of Article 6 (1) ECHR and Article 6 (3) (b) ECHR on this account.

The ECtHR proceeded to examine the complaint that the two applicants had not been allowed lawyer-client confidentiality, a right that stems from the right to a defence. The ECtHR conceded that not every measure hindering communication between a defendant and his lawyer must necessarily lead to a violation to Article 6 (3) (c) ECHR, but in the case in front of it, the complainants did not have 'an opportunity for private communication' with their lawyers, due to the permanent presence of escort

91. Applications nos. 11082/06 and 13772/05.

officers near the metal cage they were held in and the minimal distance the lawyers had to respect. Even though the complainants benefited from legal assistance from several lawyers, the secrecy of their exchanges, both oral and written, was seriously impaired during the hearings. The ECtHR found a breach:

> In conclusion the Court finds that throughout the investigation and the trial the applicants suffered from unnecessary restrictions of their right to confidential communication with their lawyers, and that the secrecy of their communications was interfered with in a manner incompatible with Article 6 § 3 (c) of the Convention. There was therefore a breach of Article 6 §§ 1 and 3 (c) of the Convention on that account.

The ECtHR also found that one of the Russian tax courts created a disbalance between the defence and the prosecution in the area of collecting and adducing 'expert evidence', thus breaching the equality of arms between the parties in violation of Articles 6 (1) and 3 (d) ECHR on that account.

Complaints under the same articles were submitted in another Yukos case, the 2020 case of *Khodorkovskiy and Lebedev v. Russia* (no. 2)[92] when applicants' lengthy complaints concerning the taking and examination of evidence and breach of the principles of equality of arms and presumption of innocence in the proceedings were divided into six groups namely:

(i) Inability to cross-examine most of the expert witnesses for the prosecution.
(ii) Partial treatment of expert evidence.
(iii) Failure to summon witnesses for the defence, to secure forced attendance of a number of witnesses and to obtain their questioning by video-conference or through letters rogatory.
(iv) Refusal to consider exculpatory material to the case file or to order disclosure of exculpatory material or 'source materials' in general.
(v) The trial court's reliance on judgments in other criminal cases.
(vi) Refusal to exclude inadmissible evidence for the prosecution, including evidence obtained in breach of lawyer-client confidentiality.

The ECtHR agreed that the omission of the Khamovnicheskiy District Court to hear in person the expert witnesses whose reports were later used against the applicants was capable of substantially affecting their fair trial rights, in particular the guarantees for 'adversarial proceedings' and 'equality of arms'. The ECtHR found a breach of Articles 6 (1) and 3 (d) ECHR.

The ECtHR found an imbalance between the defence and the prosecution in the area of collecting and adducing 'expert evidence', thus breaching the principle of equality of arms between the parties finding another breach of Articles 6 (1) and 3 (d) ECHR on that account as well.

The trial court's failure to examine the defence witness in question was found to have adversely affected the overall fairness of the proceedings in violation of Articles 6 (1) and 3 (d) ECHR. The manner in which the trial court relied on judgments in other

92. Applications nos. 51111/07 and 42757/07.

proceedings was found not to be compatible with the guarantees of a fair trial, in breach of Article 6 (1) ECHR.

Lastly, the 1996 case of *Benham v. the United Kingdom*[93] was unusual because it involved the right to free legal assistance under Article 6 (3) (c) ECHR. In view of the severity of the penalty risked by Mr Benham and the complexity of the applicable law, the interests of justice demanded that, in order to receive a fair hearing, Mr Benham ought to have benefited from free legal representation during the proceedings before the magistrates. The ECtHR reached a different conclusion in *Afram Barsom and Levent VARLI v. Sweden*,[94] a case involving tax surcharge proceedings. The fact that the complainant had been denied legal aid was not held to be a breach:

> In view of all of the above, the Court finds that there is no indication that legal aid was indispensable to give the applicants effective access to court or that the refusal of legal aid adversely affected their ability to present their case properly and satisfactorily (see, Airey v. Ireland, 9 October 1979, §§ 24 and 26, Series A no. 32, and Gnahoré v. France, no. 40031/98, §§ 39-41, ECHR 2000-IX). Consequently, in the present case, the interests of justice did not require the applicants to be granted free legal assistance and the fact that legal aid was refused by the domestic courts was therefore not a violation of their rights under Article 6 § 3(c) of the Convention.

5.7 CONCLUSIONS

The ECtHR's Article 6 ECHR tax judgments are complex, and the permutations of the judgments are infinite. The judgment in *Ferrazzini* shocked the tax world and the conclusion that tax proceedings are not covered by the right to a fair trial is odious giving rise to undesirable results. *Bendenoun* balances *Ferrazzini* and comes as a balm to tax litigators, but it creates another extreme position. Most, if not all, tax penalties are criminal charges within the meaning of Article 6 ECHR implying that, despite qualifications and hesitations typical of the ECtHR,[95] even the criminal limb of Article 6 ECHR will apply to tax surcharge proceedings. The reclassification of tax penalties as

93. Application no. 19380/92.
94. Applications nos. 40766/06 and 40831/06.
95. On this point *see Segame SA v. France*, Application no. 4837/06:

> 59. La Cour observe tout d'abord que la loi elle-même proportionne dans une certaine mesure l'amende à la gravité du comportement du contribuable, puisque celle-ci est fixée en pourcentage des droits éludés, dont en l'espèce la requérante a pu amplement discuter l'assiette (cf. mutatis mutandis Valico S.r.l. c. Italie (déc.), no. 70074/01, CEDH 2006-III). La Cour admet par ailleurs, comme le souligne le Gouvernement, le caractère particulier du contentieux fiscal impliquant une exigence d'efficacité nécessaire pour préserver les intérêts de l'Etat et observe, en outre, que ce contentieux ne fait pas partie du noyau dur du droit pénal au sens de la Convention (cf. mutatis mutandis Jussila c. Finlande [GC], no. 73053/01, § 43, CEDH 2006-XIII). Elle considère enfin que le taux de l'amende, fixé à 25 % par l'ordonnance du 7 décembre 2005, n'apparaît pas disproportionné (Malige précité, § 49; a contrario et mutatis mutandis Mamidakis c. Grèce, no. 35533/04, § 48, 11 janvier 2007 et Grifhorst c. France, no. 28336/02, § 105, 26 février 2009).

criminal charges within the meaning of the ECHR has given rise to major repercussions under Article 7 ECHR, Article 4 of Protocol 7 ECHR and other articles.

It is difficult to anticipate what the future lies in store. The Grand Chamber's judgment in *Regner v. the Czech Republic*[96] aliments hopes that eventually the ECtHR will revoke the *Ferrazzini* dictum. Hopefully, the day will come when the application of the right to a fair trial in all tax cases will be taken for granted in the same way it is taken for granted by the Court of Justice of the European Union (CJEU). Thus, in *Jiří Sabou v. Finanční ředitelství pro hlavní město Prahu*,[97] a case involving the tax directive known as the Mutual Assistance Directive,[98] the Grand Chamber of the CJEU observed:

> ... In accordance with that principle, the addressees of decisions which significantly affect their interests must therefore be placed in a position in which they can effectively make known their views as regards the information on which the authorities intend to base their decision (see, inter alia, C-32/95 P Commission v Lisrestal and Others [1996] ECR I-5373, paragraph 21, and Sopropé, paragraph 37).[99]

The ECtHR sides more frequently with the State than with the taxpayer, in evidentiary issues pertaining to the guilt of the defendant. Aggressive tax planning and tax optimisation techniques are severely reproached, sometimes assuming that the defendant is guilty until proven innocent which is not compatible with the benefit of the presumption of innocence and the prohibition of *Nemo tenetur* stated in foundational cases.[100]

The same *in dubio contra reum* approach is to be seen in criminal procedure against tax payers when applying detention on remand.[101] Sometimes the presumption of dangerousness is entirely unrelated to the concrete person and personal circumstances of the tax payer.

96. Application no. 35289/11. The observation in §102 is especially noteworthy because it tends to overrule the *Ferrazzini* dictum, 'There can be no doubt about the fact that there is a right within the meaning of Article 6 § 1 where a substantive right recognised in domestic law is accompanied by a procedural right to have that right enforced through the courts. The mere fact that the wording of a legal provision affords an element of discretion does not in itself rule out the existence of a right ... .'
97. CJEU, Case C-276/12.
98. Directive 77/799 (repealed by Council Directive 2011/16/EU of 15 February 2011 on administrative cooperation in the field of taxation).
99. Nonetheless it concluded that 'that respect for the rights of the defence of the taxpayer does not require that the taxpayer should take part in the request for information sent by the requesting Member State to the requested Member State. Nor does it require that the taxpayer should be heard at the point when inquiries, which may include the examination of witnesses, are carried out in the requested Member State or before that Member State sends the information to the requesting Member State'.
100. Augusto Silva Dias and Paula Dourado, 'Information Duties, Aggressive Tax Planning and Nemo Tenetur se Ipsum Accusare in the Light of Article 6 ECHR', in Georg Kofler, Miguel Poiares Maduro and Pasquale Pistone (org.) (eds), *Human Rights and Taxation in Europe and the World*, Amsterdam, IBFD, 2011, pp. 131–152.
101. *Marian Maciejewski v. Poland*, Application no. 34447/05.

CHAPTER 6

No Punishment Without Law

ARTICLE 7
No punishment without law

1. No one shall be held guilty of any criminal offence on account of any act or omission which did not constitute a criminal offence under national or international law at the time when it was committed. Nor shall a heavier penalty be imposed than the one that was applicable at the time the criminal offence was committed.

2. This Article shall not prejudice the trial and punishment of any person for any act or omission which, at the time when it was committed, was criminal according to the general principles of law recognised by civilised nations.

6.1 'NO ONE'

The ECtHR's tax judgments suggest that the protection contemplated in Article 7 ECHR applies both to physical persons and legal persons. Thus, the 2009 admissibility decision in *OAO Neftyanaya Kompaniya Yukos v. Russia*[1] tackled several complex procedural issues, but the company's right to file a complaint under Article 7 ECHR was not questioned.

6.2 'CRIMINAL OFFENCE UNDER NATIONAL OR INTERNATIONAL LAW'

While, the referenced Yukos admissibility decree did not express any reservations on the company's *locus standi*, the issue as to whether proceedings were criminal was debated at length because a matter falls within the scope of Article 7 ECHR only if such

1. Application no. 14902/04.

matter involves a 'criminal offence'. The Russian Government argued that the proceedings had not been criminal within the meaning of the Russian law and that there had not been criminal proceedings within the meaning of Article 7 ECHR. According to the Russian Government, the dispute was the adjudication of a tax debt of an administrative-law nature, a purely public policy issue falling outside of the Court's jurisdiction.

Yukos argued that the proceedings had been 'criminal' within the meaning of Article 7 ECHR, and the ECtHR agreed:

> 498. As regards the Government's argument that Article 7 of the Convention was inapplicable, the Court observes that it has earlier established the criminal nature of the tax offence ... .

Interestingly, the tools that, earlier on, the ECtHR had used to determine the existence of the 'criminal offence' for the purposes of Article 7 ECHR were the tools it had used to determine the existence of a 'criminal charge' for the purposes of Article 6 ECHR:

> 453. On the facts, the company was found guilty of tax evasion and ordered to pay the default interest surcharges and a 40 percent fine. The latter fine, representing a very substantial sum of over half a billion euros, was imposed in proportion to the amount of the tax avoided, had no upper limit and was clearly intended as a punishment to deter re-offending (compare with 20 to 40 percent surcharge rates in the case of Janosevic v. Sweden, no. 34619/97, § 69, ECHR 2002-VII and a 20 percent surcharge rate in the mentioned Jussila case). The Court considers that this establishes the criminal nature of the offence for the purposes of Article 6 of the Convention. Hence, Article 6 applies under its criminal head to the 2000 Tax Assessment proceedings.

In fact, in the 2002 tax case of *Göktan v. France*,[2] the ECtHR concluded that imprisonment in default of payment of the customs fine was not a means of enforcing the fine, but a penalty, within the meaning both of Article 7 ECHR and of Article 4 of Protocol No. 7 ECHR. The notion of what constitutes a 'penalty' cannot vary from one Convention provision to another. The implication is that if a penalty meets the Engel criteria for the purposes of Article 6 ECHR it is to be treated as a 'criminal charge' and a 'criminal offence' for the purposes of all the articles of the ECHR.

The above does not mean that all adverse tax consequences are to be treated as attracting the protection of Article 7 ECHR. Thus, in *Société Oxygène plus v. France*[3] compensatory interest on late payment of tax was not held to be a criminal punitive measure for the purposes of Article 7 ECHR and the case was dismissed:

> 50. S'agissant, enfin, du troisième critère, la Cour note l'importance significative des montants réclamés à la requérante. Elle constate cependant qu'ils se limitent au rappel d'impôt, assorti d'un intérêt de retard. Elle ne relève pour le surplus aucune pénalité mise à la charge de la requérante, dont la bonne foi n'apparaît pas contestée par l'administration fiscale. Le terme de 'pénalités' employé par la

2. Application no. 33402/96.
3. Application no. 76959/11.

> requérante et par les juridictions internes se borne en effet à désigner les intérêts de retard. À cet égard, la Cour rappelle que de simples intérêts de retard, qui impliquent que la bonne foi du contribuable est admise, ne constituent pas une accusation en matière pénale au sens de l'article 6 § 1 (voir, notamment, Mieg de Boofzheim, précité, et Poniatowski, précité).

6.3 THE LAWFULNESS REQUIREMENT

Like Article 1 of Protocol 1 ECHR, Article 7 ECHR contemplates a lawfulness test implying that the law must be clear, foreseeable and predictable. For the purposes of the lawfulness test under Article 7 ECHR, the ECHR adopts the same definition it applies in the interpretation of Article 1 of Protocol 1 ECHR. Thus, in the earliest known ECtHR tax case dealing with Article 7 ECHR, the 1997 tax fraud case of *L.-G. R. v. Sweden*,[4] the term 'law' was taken to include both written and unwritten law and judicial precedent:

> However, as noted above, the concept of 'law' under Article 7 (Art. 7) of the Convention comprises not only written but also unwritten law, most importantly the case-law of the national courts.
>
> Consequently, if the applicant, on account of the existing case-law, was able to foresee, with a reasonable degree of certainty, that the aiding and abetting in question would make him criminally liable, his conviction was not incompatible with Article 7 (Art. 7) ... This case-law had been published and was therefore accessible. Accordingly, as admitted by the applicant himself, it was foreseeable that his conduct would make him criminally liable.

Two of the cases in the Yukos saga gave the ECtHR an excellent opportunity to create important tax precedents on the practical application of Article 7 ECHR, and the ECtHR obliged.

The 2013 case of *Khodorkovskiy and Lebedev v. Russia*[5] was a complex case that involved, among others, a complaint under Article 7 ECHR on the basis that the interpretation of the tax law which had led to the complainants' conviction for tax evasion had been unforeseeable, and that, as a result, they had been convicted for acts which had not been regarded as 'criminal' when they had been committed. The complaint referred to the fact that tax evasion charges related to the tax cuts obtained by the trading companies and by them personally, as well as to the payment of taxes with promissory notes, where unpredictable. In the opinion of the applicants, the tax-minimisation techniques they had used (selling oil through the trading companies registered in the Lesnoy town and receiving consulting fees in the capacity of individual entrepreneurs) had been perfectly legal at the time.

The ECtHR singled out the special nature of tax law. It reflected on the complainant's use of various tax-minimisation techniques in respect of both company taxes and personal income taxes. Noting that Russian law interpreted 'tax evasion' in very general terms it held that, by itself such a broad definition, did not raise any issue

4. Application no. 27032/95.
5. Applications nos. 11082/06 and 13772/05.

under Article 7 ECHR. The ECtHR held that forms of economic activity are in constant development, and so are the methods of tax evasion. In order to define whether a particular behaviour amounts to 'tax evasion' in the criminal-law sense, the domestic courts may invoke legal concepts from other areas of law, in particular the tax law. The law in this area may be sufficiently flexible to adapt to new situations, without, however, becoming unpredictable.

The ECtHR examined the special nature of anti-tax avoidance laws and the 'substance-over-form' approach existing in the field of tax law, finding that such an approach is neither unreasonable nor unusual. Such an approach was held to be legitimate even in the context of transfer pricing arrangements. Russian practices to transfer pricing were held to be compliant. In conclusion, despite flaws in the domestic proceedings, the proceedings could not be characterised as a 'flagrant denial of justice'. The substantive findings of the Russian courts were not 'arbitrary or manifestly unreasonable', the Court found.

While acknowledging that the applicants' case had no precedents, the ECtHR remarked that Article 7 ECHR is not incompatible with judicial law-making and does not outlaw the gradual clarification of the rules of criminal liability through judicial interpretation from case to case, provided that the resultant development is consistent with the essence of the offence and could reasonably be foreseen. The applicants may have fallen victim to a novel interpretation of the concept of 'tax evasion', but it was based on a reasonable interpretation of Russian Law and 'consistent with the essence of the offence'. Therefore, the ECtHR concluded that there was no violation of Article 7 ECHR.

The 2020 case of *Khodorkovskiy and Lebedev v. Russia* (no. 2)[6] had a different outcome, and the Article 7 ECHR complaint was dismissed because, despite the tax element, the charges in this case involved the hard-core of criminal law, misappropriation, embezzlement and money laundering. Unlike tax offences which are perceived as novel and extremely complex, rules on more traditional crimes should give rise to less interpretational issues, and the ECtHR is less tolerant of moving goal posts.

The ECtHR highlighted the fact that the Article 7 ECHR complaint in the case before it was substantially different from that it had to examine in the previous case brought by the applicants which concerned the charge of tax evasion in the first set of criminal proceedings against them. In that case, the Court observed that while 'tax evasion' was defined in the domestic criminal law in very general terms, this did not in itself raise any issues under Article 7 ECHR. Conversely, none of the considerations of the previous case applied to the case at hand. The special nature of tax law was emphasised:

> 585. In the light of the foregoing the Court concludes that in the determination of the criminal charges against the applicants the offence set out in Article 160 § 4 of the Criminal Code, as in force at the time of their conviction, was extensively and unforeseeably construed, to their detriment. It considers that such an interpretation could not be said to have constituted a development consistent with the essence of the offence ... In view of the above, it was not possible to foresee that

6. Applications nos. 51111/07 and 42757/07.

> the applicants' conduct in entering into the transactions on the sale of oil from the Yukos production entities to the Yukos trading companies would constitute misappropriation or embezzlement.
>
> 586. In the light of its findings above, the Court considers that it was equally unforeseeable that the profits from the sale of the oil from the Yukos production entities to the Yukos trading companies would be found to constitute the proceeds of a crime, the use of which could amount to laundering of money or of other assets under Article 174.1 of the Criminal Code (see Navalnyye, cited above, § 68, 17 October 2017).
>
> 587. It follows that there has been a violation of Article 7 of the Convention.

The implication seems to be that a lower threshold of foreseeability and predictability is contemplated for tax offences characterised by an element of novelty. A similar approach was adopted in 2019 *Heinrich Josef Bley v. Germany*,[7] where the highly specialised nature of tax law was emphasised once more. Although the ECtHR acknowledged that criminal liability was indeed based on a complex chain of provisions referring to one another, the ECtHR accepted the domestic courts' conclusion that the applicant must have been aware of the illegality of his acts. He had invented a sophisticated leasing system, which required knowledge of the basic mechanisms of the system in place. As acknowledgeable operator in his industry, Bley should have been expected to be aware of the rules governing his operations. With regard to Bley's submissions that he had sought advice from his tax accountant, the ECtHR observed that the Regional Court, having heard the accountant as a witness, considered that he had only advised the applicant on general taxation law, but not on the specific regulations governing the distribution of quotas. Under these circumstances, the ECtHR accepted the domestic courts' assessment that the applicant would have been informed of the criminal implications of his actions had he sought appropriate advice of a specialist.

Thus, the ECtHR considered that the criminal implications of the applicant's actions were, as required by Article 7 ECHR, sufficiently foreseeable for him as a person working in a highly regulated market.

Of course, this does not mean that the tax threshold for Article 7 ECHR complaints is a prohibitive one. In fact, the ECtHR upheld Article 7 ECHR complaints both before and after the *Khodorkovskiy* judgments.

In 2018, the ECtHR struck down a fiscal measure in the case *Prigală c. République de Moldova*[8] on the basis of Article 7 ECHR because the disputed penalty regime was found to be unpredictable.

In 2019 the ECtHR returned to the point in the case of *Lopac and Others v. Croatia*,[9] a case involving, *inter alia*, criminal proceedings for customs offences. When it transpired that the legislative instrument underlying the prosecution was based on a misinterpretation of the Istanbul Convention which Croatia had inconsistently applied, the violation of Article 7 ECHR became glaring. Important rules relating to tax

7. Application no. 68475/10.
8. Application no. 36763/06.
9. Applications nos. 7834/12 and 3 others.

exemptions were extensively and unforeseeably construed to complainant's detriment. The ECtHR found infringements of Article 1 of Protocol 1 ECHR and Article 7 ECHR. Principles established in Lopac could be easily exported to the 'tax mainland' and could become useful in managing situations involving the transposition of EU tax directives, Tax Treaty instruments and transfer pricing.

6.4 CONCLUSIONS

Nullem Crimen Sine Lege is a core value of criminal law and a core value of the ECtHR. Seeing the principle being applied in a mutilated fashion in tax law gives rise to legitimate concerns. General principles of law should apply to all areas of law indiscriminately without any qualifications based on the peculiarities of particular laws. The fact that the judgments that developed the qualified approach to taxation happened to be cases involving complex tax arrangements was very unfortunate. Predictably, the ECtHR does not have time for artificial arrangements intended to shift profits to low-tax jurisdictions and erode legitimate tax bases. The ECHR was not intended to offer artful tax dodgers any shelter. The ECtHR gives State Signatories leeway in designing general anti-avoidance provisions leaving them plenty of room to manoeuvre their weapons in combatting tax avoidance, tax evasion and tax fraud. 'Substance-over-form' approaches imply that basing a tax mitigation scheme solely on the basis of literal interpretations has become a dangerous thing.

CHAPTER 7

Right to Respect for Private and Family Life

ARTICLE 8
Right to respect for private and family life

1. Everyone has the right to respect for his private and family life, his home and his correspondence.

2. There shall be no interference by a public authority with the exercise of this right except such as is in accordance with the law and is necessary in a democratic society in the interests of national security, public safety or the economic well-being of the country, for the prevention of disorder or crime, for the protection of health or morals, or for the protection of the rights and freedoms of others.

7.1 'EVERYONE'

Both legal persons and physical persons seem to benefit from the protection of Article 8 ECHR, because in the 2017 case *Lindstrand Partners Advokatbyrå AB v. Sweden*[1] the fact that the complainant was a law firm which was a legal person and not a physical person did not stop it from successfully arguing its case under Article 8 ECHR.

The ECtHR has adopted a wide interpretation of the term including within the scope of the protection of Article 8 ECHR parties other than the data subject himself. Interestingly, the ECtHR's paper on Legal professional privilege[2] incorporates many references to tax cases, evidencing the fact that it is in tax investigations that the State Signatories push Article 8 ECHR to its natural limits. In the 2015 case *Brito Ferrinho*

1. Application no. 18700/09.
2. https://www.echr.coe.int/Documents/FS_Legal_professional_privilege_ENG.pdf viewed in December 2019.

Bexiga Villa-Nova v. Portugal,[3] the data owner was a lawyer. In *M.N. and Others v. San Marino*,[4] interested parties included banks.

7.2 'INTERFERENCE'

The question whether tax authority intrusions into private matters amounted to an 'interference' within the meaning of Article 8 ECHR has rarely created much scope for academic debate. Telephone tappings, perquisitions, searches of premises, surveillance techniques, raids carried out by the anti-terrorist police in the context of economic crimes investigation,[5] forceful entry into homes and seizures of documents[6] were all treated as interferences within the meaning of Article 8 ECHR. The case of *Huvig v. France*[7] promptly concluded that the telephone tapping complained of amounted without any doubt to an 'interference by a public authority' paving the way for future cases.

The fact that requests for information, requests for explanations relating to private expenditure[8] and access to databases constituted an 'interference' appears to have been taken almost for granted too.[9] Predictably, even the dissemination of data collected by tax authorities was held to be an interference.[10]

The case of *Lindstrand Partners Advokatbyrå AB v. Sweden*[11] was a rare case when there was a contestation relating as to whether there had been an 'interference' within the meaning of the law. The parties disagreed on whether the seizure and copying, respectively, of the external hard disk drive and the USB memory stick constituted an interference with the applicant's rights under Article 8. The ECtHR observed that the data was not seized on the premises of the applicant law firm, but at the flat belonging to a third party. The ECtHR treated the matter as a point of fact which had been finally decided by the domestic courts. In conclusion, the ECtHR held that the search of the offices of the applicant law firm interfered with its right to respect for its home and correspondence but that the search and seizures occurring at the flat belonging to the third party did not constitute an interference with the applicant's rights under that provision.

3. Application no. 69436/10.
4. Application no. 28005/12.
5. Application no. 28926/10.
6. Application no. 10828/84. The aspects of this and the two related judgments of *Crémieux and Miailhe* relevant to Article 8 are discussed in Part 7. Article 6 was only considered in the *Funke* judgment.
7. Application no. 11105/84.
8. Application no. 9804/82.
9. Application no. 24117/08.
10. Application no. 75292/10.
11. Application no. 18700/09.

7.3 'PRIVATE AND FAMILY LIFE, HIS HOME AND HIS CORRESPONDENCE.'

The ECtHR attributed a wide meaning to the terms above. The 2013 tax judgment in the case of *Bernh Larsen Holding AS and Others v. Norway*[12] interpreted the word 'home' as including business premises and corporate registered addresses:

> 104. The Court first reiterates that, as interpreted in its case-law, the word 'home', appearing in the English text of Article 8, – the word 'domicile' in the French text has a broader connotation – covers residential premises and may extend also to certain professional or business premises (see Niemietz, cited above, § 30). It includes not only the registered office of a company owned and run by a private individual (see Buck, cited above, § 32) but also that of a legal person and its branches and other business premises (see Sallinen and Others v. Finland, no. 50882/99, § 70, 27 September 2005). Such an interpretation would not unduly hamper the Contracting States, for they would retain their entitlement to 'interfere' to the extent permitted by paragraph 2 of Article 8; that entitlement might well be more far-reaching where professional or business activities or premises were involved than would otherwise be the case (see Niemietz, cited above, § 31).

A similar approach was adopted in the more recent Scandinavian case of *Lindstrand Partners Advokatbyrå AB v. Sweden,*[13] cited previously, when the ECtHR conceded that even a search of a lawyer's office may be regarded as an interference with 'private life', 'home' and 'correspondence' under Article 8 (1) ECHR. The term 'home' is to be construed as including also the registered office of a company run by a private individual, as well as a legal person's registered office, branches and other business premises.

In the 2015 judgment *M.N. and Others v. San Marino*[14] the terms 'private life' and 'correspondence' were deemed to include documents relating to banking and trust relationships which all fell within the remit of Article 8. The ECtHR held that information retrieved from banking documents 'undoubtedly' amounted to personal data concerning an individual, regardless of whether it incorporated sensitive personal data or not. The ECtHR held that even information relating to professional dealings was within the scope of Article 8 ECHR. The ECtHR held that Article 8 ECHR protects the confidentiality of all the exchanges in which individuals may engage for the purposes of communication.

The ECtHR returned to this point in 2021 in the case of *L.B. v. Hungary*[15] (referred to the Grand Chamber pending decision). The L.B. case involved an unorthodox 'naming and shaming' regime which provided for the publication of an online list of tax defaulters. The disputed publication concerned the applicant's name, home address, tax identification number and the amount of unpaid tax which he owed. While such data were not considered intimate details linked to the applicant's identity, they still provided extensive information about him. Although, the applicant's home address

12. Application no. 24117/08.
13. Application no. 18700/09.
14. Application no. 28005/12.
15. Application no. 36345/16.

was already publicly available, interest in the protection of the right to respect for his private life was still engaged by the disclosure of his home address along with the other information. The ECtHR acknowledged that the publication of personal data, including a home address, can have significant effects or even serious repercussions on a person's private life but information relating to a taxpayer's non-compliance did not concern a purely private matter and was not considered to fall within the remit of Article 8 ECHR.

7.4 'FAMILY LIFE'

The two *Khodorkovskiy and Lebedev v. Russia* cases (nos. 1 & 2)[16] attacked another aspect of the right to family life with the complaints referring to the fact that they had been sent to serve their prison terms in a remote penal colony in Siberia situated thousands of kilometres from their homes. Internship in remote penal colonies had seriously hindered their contacts with the outside world, and, in particular, with their families. The ECtHR conceded in this respect that any detention which is lawful for the purposes of Article 5 ECHR entails by its nature various limitations on private and family life and, as a starting point, the ECtHR accepted that the authorities had a wide discretion in matters related to execution of sentences, but the ECHR cannot stop at the prison gate, and there is no question that a prisoner forfeits all of his Article 8 ECHR rights merely because of his status as a person detained following conviction. Placing a convict in a particular prison may potentially raise an issue under Article 8 ECHR if its effects on his private and family life go beyond 'normal' hardships and restrictions inherent to the very concept of imprisonment. Although the ECtHR was prepared to accept that given the size of the population in Moscow and the corresponding number of convicts from that city, there were no free places for the applicants, it was hardly conceivable that there were no free places in any of the many colonies situated closer to Moscow. The ECtHR found a violation of Article 8 ECHR because margin of appreciation had been exceeded:

> There are other arguments speaking in favour of giving the authorities a large margin of appreciation in this sphere. However, that margin of appreciation is not unlimited. The distribution of the prison population must not remain entirely at the discretion of the administrative bodies, such as FSIN. The interests of the convicts in maintaining at least some family and social ties must somehow be taken into account ... In absence of a clear and foreseeable method of distribution of convicts amongst penal colonies, the system failed to 'provide a measure of legal protection against arbitrary interference by public authorities' (see Telegraaf Nederland Landelijke Media B.V. and Others v. the Netherlands, no. 39315/06, § 90, 22 November 2012). In the applicants' cases, that led to results incompatible with the respect for the applicants' private and family lives.
>
> 851. There was therefore a violation of Article 8 of the Convention on that account.

16. Applications nos. 11082/06, 13772/05, 51111/07 and 42757/07.

7.5 '... EXCEPT SUCH AS IS IN ACCORDANCE WITH THE LAW AND IS NECESSARY IN A DEMOCRATIC SOCIETY IN THE INTERESTS OF ... THE ECONOMIC WELL-BEING OF THE COUNTRY ...'

The ECtHR delivered a number of judgments relating to the tax authorities' right to interfere with data pertaining to taxpayers. Landmark judgments *Funke v. France*[17] (1984), *Volokhy v. Ukraine*[18] (2002) and *André and others v. France*[19] (2008) established that for an interference by a tax authority to be 'in accordance with the law and is necessary in a democratic society in the interests of ... the economic well-being of the country ...', it must follow these minimum standards:

(a) The interference must be in accordance with the law (i.e., based on a foreseeable and predictable legal instrument).
(b) The interference must pursue a legitimate aim (in the knowledge that combatting tax abuse would be considered to be a legitimate aim).
(c) The interference must be necessary in a democratic society (meeting requirements relating to proportionality).
(d) The interference must be accompanied by relevant effective and genuine procedural safeguards providing for effective control enabling data subjects to challenge measures they would have been subjected to.

7.5.1 'Necessary in a Democratic Society ... in Accordance with the Law'

Early tax cases took a very balanced approached to the meaning of the terms 'necessary in a democratic society' applying an implied proportionality test. Thus, in the 1993 case of *Miailhe v. France* (no. 1),[20] a tax residence investigation, the ECtHR acknowledged that Contracting States have a certain margin of appreciation in assessing the need for an interference, but it goes hand in hand with European supervision. Exceptions provided for in paragraph Article 8 (2) are to be interpreted narrowly, the ECtHR adding that the need for them in a given case must be convincingly established. The particular nature of tax law was singled out, but the ECtHR emphasised the need for safeguards which in this case were lacking:

> 37. Undoubtedly, in the field under consideration – the prevention of capital outflows and tax evasion – States encounter serious difficulties owing to the scale and complexity of banking systems and financial channels and to the immense scope for international investment, made all the easier by the relative porousness of national borders. The Court therefore recognises that they may consider it necessary to have recourse to measures such as house searches and seizures in order to obtain physical evidence of exchange-control offences and, where appropriate, to prosecute those responsible. Nevertheless, the relevant legislation and

17. Application no. 10828/84.
18. Application no. 23543/02.
19. Application no. 18603/03.
20. Application no. 12661/87.

> practice must afford adequate and effective safeguards against abuse (see, among other authorities and mutatis mutandis, the Klass and Others judgment previously cited, Series A no. 28, p. 23, para. 50).
>
> 38. This was not so in the instant case ... The seizures made on the applicants' premises were wholesale and, above all, indiscriminate, to such an extent that the customs considered several thousand documents to be of no relevance to their inquiries and returned them to the applicants (see paragraph 7 above).
>
> 40. In sum, there has been a breach of Article 8 (art. 8).

The ECtHR reached a similar conclusion in the case of *Cremieux v. France*,[21] decided in the same year. In the *Cremieux* case, the complaint referred to the unlimited scope of the investigations. The tax authorities had conducted eighty-three investigative perquisitions spread over three years, and the case was neither serious nor complex. To make matters worse, some of the documents seized did not have any relevance to the investigation. Reproducing the same wording in *Miailhe*, the ECtHR confirmed that tax cases gave rise to special considerations, but it found a violation because procedural safeguards relating to the issue of search warrants were found to be inadequate.

In the case of *Huvig v. France*,[22] the ECtHR explained the application of the lawfulness requirement in a tax context. Predictably, the ECtHR followed the Cantoni interpretational principles associated with Article 7 ECHR:

> 26. The expression 'in accordance with the law', within the meaning of Article 8 § 2 (art. 8-2), requires firstly that the impugned measure should have some basis in domestic law; it also refers to the quality of the law in question, requiring that it should be accessible to the person concerned, who must moreover be able to foresee its consequences for him, and compatible with the rule of law ...
>
> Settled case-law of this kind cannot be disregarded ... In sum, the interference complained of had a legal basis in French law.

The ECtHR did not find anything objectionable with the accessibility of the law requirement, but contested its 'foreseeability' adding that investigative techniques that were particularly intrusive had to be backed by a solid legal infrastructure:

> 32. Tapping and other forms of interception of telephone conversations represent a serious interference with private life and correspondence and must accordingly be based on a 'law' that is particularly precise. It is essential to have clear, detailed rules on the subject, especially as the technology available for use is continually becoming more sophisticated.

Adequate safeguards against possible abuses were lacking because the categories of people liable to have their telephones tapped by judicial order and the nature of the offences which may give rise to such an order were nowhere defined. No judicial limits to the duration of telephone tapping were set. Protocols relating to the processing of intercepted conversations were entirely lacking. French law, written and unwritten, did not indicate with reasonable clarity the scope and manner of exercise of the

21. Application no. 11471/85.
22. Application no. 11105/84.

relevant discretion conferred on the public authorities. Accordingly, the ECtHR found a violation.

Effective oversight is fundamental. In *Brazzi v. Italy*,[23] involving the perquisition of a family home, lack of effective judicial control *ex ante* and a posteriori led to the finding of a breach. Conversely, in *Claude Keslassy v. France*[24] the presence of strong judicial safeguards implied that the case was unfounded and was dismissed:

> Accordingly, having regard to the strict rules governing the issue of warrants for searches of residential premises and the fact that the search of the applicant's home was conducted in accordance with those rules, the Court finds that the interference with the applicant's right to respect for his private life and his home was proportionate to the legitimate aims pursued and therefore 'necessary in a democratic society', within the meaning of Article 8 § 2 of the Convention (see, mutatis mutandis, F.P. and Others v. France, Application nos. 33009/96 to 33013/96, Commission decisions of 10 September 1997; see also Banco de finanzas e inversiones S.A. v. Spain, (dec.), no. 36876/97, 27 April 1999).

In *Funke v. France*,[25] the ECtHR held that France violated the right to privacy when its fiscal police searched the premises and seized documents in such a way that did not contemplate sufficient safeguards. In *Volokhy v. Ukraine*,[26] the ECtHR held that in the course of criminal investigations, secret surveillance is allowed only when such surveillance is strictly necessary, in accordance with the law, and in pursuit of a legitimate aim. The ECtHR held that rules on surveillance must be foreseeable and proportional. In *Volokhy*, the ECtHR found a breach of the right to privacy because the rules relating to surveillance were unclear and did not incorporate adequate safeguards against abuse. In *André and others v. France*,[27] the ECtHR developed the principle a step further adding that searches and seizures which are 'in accordance with the law' and 'which have a legitimate aim' might still be irregular. An investigation is compatible with the ECHR only if it is not disproportionate to the aim pursued.

In the 2013 case of *Bernh Larsen Holding AS (B.L.H.) and Others v. Norway*,[28] the ECtHR consolidated its earlier case law. Applicant companies used a common server which contained the applicant's own data and private information pertaining to third parties (some of whom were individuals). In the course of a tax investigation, the tax authorities demanded that B.L.H. allow its inspectors to make a copy of all the data on the server. Although B.L.H. complied with the request to grant access to the server, it refused to provide the tax authorities with a mirror copy of the entire server.

The applicant companies complained to the ECtHR that their right to respect for privacy, home and correspondence under Article 8 of the Convention had been infringed as a result of the order to provide the tax authorities with a copy of the server. The applicant companies disputed that the interference with their right to property was 'in accordance with the law'. They argued that the order to provide a mirror copy of the

23. Application no. 57278/11.
24. Application no. 51578/99.
25. Application no. 10828/84.
26. Application no. 23543/02.
27. Application no. 18603/03.
28. Application no. 24117/08.

server had exceeded the wording of the relevant statutory provisions and that the law in question failed to fulfil the quality requirements in the Court's case law. According to B.L.H, there had not been effective safeguards against abuse. The ECtHR found that there had not been a violation because the nature of the interference complained of was not of the same seriousness and degree as is ordinarily the case of search and seizure carried out under criminal law. Moreover, the disputed measure had in part been made necessary by the applicant companies' own choice to opt for 'mixed archives' on a shared server, making the task of separation of user areas and identification of documents more difficult for the tax authorities. The ECtHR concluded that access to information had been supported by relevant and sufficient reasons because:

> 174. Having regard to the circumstances of the case as a whole, the Court finds that the impugned section 4-10 (1) measure in the instant case was supported by relevant and sufficient reasons. It also sees no reason to doubt that the tax authorities of the respondent State, acting within their margin of appreciation, struck a fair balance between the applicant companies' right to respect for 'home' and 'correspondence' and their interest in protecting the privacy of persons working for them, on the one hand, and the public interest in ensuring efficiency in the inspection of information provided by the applicant companies for tax assessment purposes, on the other hand.
>
> 175. Accordingly, there has been no violation of Article 8 of the Convention in the present case.

In the same year, a similar approach was adopted in the case of *Rousk v. Sweden*[29] involving tax enforcement procedures that included forceful access to a home. The ECtHR acknowledged that it accepts that it will sometimes be necessary for the State to attach and sell property, including an individual's home, in order to secure the payment of taxes due to the State through enforceable debts, but these measures must be enforced in a manner which ensures that the individual's right to his or her home is properly considered and protected. Having regard to the lack of effective procedural safeguards for the applicant to protect his interests, the ECtHR found violations of Article 8 ECHR and Article 1 of the First Protocol ECHR.

The 2015 case of *Othymia Investments BV v. the Netherlands*[30] is interesting, because it involved dissemination of tax data from a tax authority to another tax authority. Othymia Investments BV was being investigated and in the course of the investigation, tax data concerning it was shared by two tax authorities of different Member States. Othymia Investments B.V. claimed that a transfer of data by the Dutch Tax Authorities to the Spanish authorities pursuant to an exchange of information framework contemplated by EU law was incompatible with its right to privacy.[31,32]

The ECtHR agreed that there had been interference with the applicant company's rights under Article 8, adding that interference per se does not make a violation of Article 8. According to the ECtHR's settled case law, an interference amounts to a

29. Application no. 27183/04.
30. Application no. 75292/10.
31. Council Directive 77/799/EEC.
32. *Ibid.*

violation only if it is not 'in accordance with the law', does not pursue one or more of the 'legitimate aims' and is not 'necessary in a democratic society'.

The ECtHR pointed out that the interference in Othymia's right to privacy was based on a solid statutory basis and was clearly 'in accordance with the law'. There was no doubt that the aim pursued, which was the collection of taxes, was a legitimate one because the measure involved the protection of Spain's fiscal jurisdiction and the economies of the EU Member States form a unified whole.

The ECtHR concluded that a request for information under the Mutual Assistance Directive was part of an investigation and did not require either the requesting State or the requested State to inform the taxpayer. The ECtHR accepted that, in the context of 'the interests of national security' and 'public safety' and 'the prevention of crime', covert investigative techniques were allowed; even against persons who are not themselves objects of investigation or surveillance. The ECtHR held that the applicant company had no 'arguable claim' under Article 8, because it cannot be a requirement of Article 8 ECHR that prior notice of lawful tax investigations or exchanges of tax-related information be given to all persons potentially implicated.

In the 2015 judgment *M.N. and Others v. San Marino*[33] the ECtHR held that although the interference in question had been prescribed by law, the wide extent of the Italian tax authorities' powers was disproportionate, because it adversely effected the rights of third-party data holders too. When the ECtHR proceeded to assess whether an 'effective control' was available to the applicant to challenge the measure to which he had been subjected, the ECtHR noted that the applicant only became officially aware of the authorities' decision and its implementation following a notification served over a year after the measure was ordered. Proceedings challenging the decision could not extend to an examination on the merits, because according to the domestic courts the applicant did not have *locus standi* to impugn the measure. Therefore, the ECtHR concluded that the applicant did not have available to him the 'effective control' restricting the interference in question to what was 'necessary in a democratic society'. In view of the above, the ECtHR concluded that there had been a violation of Article 8 ECHR.

The ECtHR attributes a lot of importance to the element of judicial control. In *Brito Ferrinho Bexiga Villa-Nova v. Portugal*[34] the fact that the information accessed consisting in personal bank accounts of a lawyer was not held to be conclusive. What determined the outcome of the case was the lack of procedural guarantees linked to the processing of the data. In the 2016 case of *GSB v. Switzerland*,[35] a case involving bank data shared by Switzerland with the US interfering with the right to data privacy, the presence of 'several effective and genuine' necessary procedural safeguards implied that there had not been a violation of Article 8 ECHR. The 2017 case *Lindstrand Partners Advokatbyrå AB v. Sweden*[36] concerned a zealous tax investigation that involved a search in a lawyer's office, a search in his apartment and the seizure of

33. Application no. 28005/12.
34. Application no. 69436/10.
35. Application no. 28601/11.
36. Application no. 18700/09.

computer hardware. The ECtHR held that the search at the legal offices interfered with the right to home and correspondence under Article 8 ECHR, but that the search at a flat which was used as business premises did not constitute an interference. The ECtHR held that the decision to search applicant's offices was thoroughly reasoned and the enforcement proceedings had been properly documented, implying that the investigation had been conducted in accordance with law. Having regard to the fact that private information subject to professional secrecy had, by court intervention, not been made available for examination by the Tax Agency, the ECtHR held that investigative measures had not been disproportionate and that the seizure of the computer hardware and the damage to applicant's professional reputation arising from the investigation did not amount to a violation of the right to property. Similarly, coercive measures used in the course of the investigation did not breach the right to a fair hearing because they did not involve the determination of a criminal charge. The ECtHR held that the fact that the applicant had been denied the right to a judicial remedy challenging coercive measures used in the course of the proceedings amounted to a violation of his right to an effective remedy. The ECtHR awarded damages of EUR 5,000 to the applicant.

Philip Baker's take from the judgment was that:

> ... It is possible for a revenue authority to obtain information from a third party without notifying the taxpayer if it is justifiable to do so having regard to the margin of appreciation and the balance between the interests of the individual and of the community in general. Where the person about whom information is sought (from a bank, for example) is given notification, that person must have an adequate procedural guarantee to allow them to challenge the gathering of the information. That guarantee must also allow the individual adequate opportunity to present his legal position.[37]

In fact, in the 2019 case of *Erduran and EM Export DIS TIC. A.Ş. v. Turkey*,[38] the ECtHR did not find a violation only because the interference met the criteria of sufficient judicial control. Having regard to the circumstances of the case as a whole, the Court held that the search measure complained of was carried out in accordance with the relevant law and that the domestic authorities, acting within their margin of appreciation, struck a fair balance between the applicant company's right to respect for its 'home' and the legitimate aim pursued by means of the search and seizure of its documents for tax assessment purposes. The allegation that there had been a violation of the right to property was dismissed too, because the ECtHR observed that the taxation procedure against the applicant company, which led to the imposition of substantial amounts of taxes and penalties on it had followed proceedings which complied with Article ECHR. The applicant company had an opportunity to challenge before the courts both the procedure leading up to the imposition of those taxes and penalties, and their calculation. The domestic courts eventually delivered decisions partially in applicant's favour by reducing the amount of the penalties. The ECtHR

37. Philip Baker, 'Some Recent Decisions of the European Court of Human Rights on Tax Matters (And Related Decisions of the European Court of Justice)', European Taxation, Volume 56 (2016) pp. 342–351.
38. Applications nos. 25707/05 and 28614/06.

observed that the applicant company did not substantiate the complaints it raised in the second application regarding the calculation of the penalties.

The ECtHR places a lot of importance on the existence of procedural safeguards. In the 2020 case of *Vinks and Ribicka v. Latvia*,[39] a case involving an early morning raid by anti-terrorist police unit at the applicants' home in the context of an evasion for tax fraud was held to create a violation because of a lack of adequate and sufficient procedural safeguards against abuse:

> 118. To sum up, the Court reiterates that the States, when taking measures to prevent crime and to protect the rights of others, may well consider it necessary, for the purposes of special and general prevention, to resort to measures such as searches and seizures in order to obtain evidence of certain offences in a sphere in which it is otherwise impossible to identify a person guilty of an offence. In addition, the involvement of special police units may be considered necessary in certain circumstances. However, having regard to the severity of the interference with the right to respect for private life of persons affected by such measures, adequate and effective safeguards against abuse must be put in place. Given the particular circumstances of this case (see paragraphs 114-17 above), the Court finds that the available safeguards, as applied in the present case, failed to ensure effective protection of the applicants' right to have respect for their private life. Therefore, the interference with the applicants' right to have respect for their private life cannot be regarded as proportionate to the aim pursued.
>
> 119. Accordingly, there has been a violation of Article 8 of the Convention in the present case in respect of both applicants.

7.5.2 'For the Protection of the Rights ... of Others'

In the 1988 case *K. v. Sweden*,[40] the phrase 'for the protection of the rights ... of others' was taken to mean the interest of Revenue Authorities qua creditors.

7.5.3 'The Economic Well-Being of the Country'

Predictably, the fact that combatting tax evasion is perceived as a legitimate aim for the economic well-being of the country for the purposes of Article 8 ECHR has been considered to be obvious. Thus, in the 1987 case *Riemeke Visser v. the Netherlands*[41] the Commission pointed out:

> Secondly, as regards the objective concerned, the purpose of the provision mentioned above is precision in the collection of taxes and the prevention of fraud and tax evasion. The interference may, therefore, be considered to pursue a legitimate aim, namely, the economic well-being of the country.

39. Application no. 28926/10.
40. Application no. 13800/88.
41. Application no. 12662/87.

7.5.4 The Recent Phenomenon of Naming and Shaming

The ECtHR's judgment in the 2021 case of *L.B. v. Hungary*[42] (referred to the Grand Chamber pending decision) involved a different type of interference. The complaint referred to Hungary's decision to publish a list of tax defaulters, naming and shaming them online. The issue was whether such a controversial approach was 'in accordance with law' and 'necessary' for 'the economic well-being of the country'. The ECtHR had to determine whether Hungary had struck a fair balance between the applicant's interest in protecting his right to privacy, and the interest of the community as a whole and interested third parties. The specific context in which the information at issue was made public was considered to form part of the general framework of the State's tax policy. The ECtHR highlighted the instrumental role of taxes not only in financing State apparatus but also in implementing the economic and social policy of the State in a broader sense. Besides serving the interest of the state coffers, the publication of the list of tax defaulters was seen as being in the interest of third parties, creditors and prospective business associates especially. The inference is that third parties have a right to know whether their prospective supplier or client is a tax defaulter. Access to the list was held to impact on fair trading and the functioning of the economy. The ECtHR conceded that it was ready to accept that the disclosure of the list of persons who owed a large amount of tax had an information value for the public on a matter of general interest which did not concern a purely private matter or an issue merely satisfying public curiosity.

References to the 'margin of appreciation' even in such an extreme context anticipated the ECtHR's conclusions. The use of words like 'manifestly' is worrying because they tend to suggest that the ECtHR would condemn an interference only if it is manifestly without foundation:

> 54. Based on the above, and bearing in mind the margin of appreciation allowed to States as regards general measures of economic and social strategy, the Court finds that the legislature's choice to make public the identity of persons who fail to respect their tax obligations, in order to improve payment discipline and protect the business interests of third parties, and thereby contribute to the general economy, is not manifestly without reasonable foundation (see the case-law quoted in paragraph 49 above).

For the purposes of the fair balance test, the ECtHR placed a lot of importance on the fact that the data selected for publication was that which concerned major tax defaulters and major tax evaders. The fact that the publication rules drew a distinction between taxpayers limiting negative publicity to those whose conduct was the most detrimental to revenue was favourably considered. Even the feature which provided for an erasure from the list of defaulters as soon as the tax debt was settled was held to be a beneficial balancing characteristic. Drawing from Data Privacy law principles, the ECtHR concluded that the identification of data subjects on the Tax Authority's website was possible for no longer than was necessary for the purposes of publication.

---

42. Application no. 36345/16.

Although the publication of personal data on a portal such as the internet remained a concern which the ECtHR acknowledged, the publication of such data was 'necessary' in the circumstances:

> 60 … . The legislature cannot be criticised for the fact that in order to provide accurate information on tax evaders, it chose a person's home address as additional identifying information …
>
> 71. Given the specific context in which the information at issue was published, the fact that the publication was designed to secure the availability and accessibility of information in the public interest, and the limited effect of the publication on the applicant's daily life, the Court considers that the publication fell within the respondent State's margin of appreciation.
>
> 72. It follows that there has been no violation of Article 8 of the Convention.

Predictably, the judgment in *L.B.* caused the kind of furore which had been caused by the *Ferrazzini* judgment. The dissenting opinion was very strongly worded. The authors endorse the opinion of Judges Ravarani and Schukking which criticised the application of the proportionality test. The dissenting judges considered publication of personal data on the internet as unnecessary with the 'shaming' effect going overboard, publishing an individual's home address on the internet unnecessarily exposed the data subject to burglary. The dissenting judges did not mince their words:

> 16. Conclusion. To conclude, it is the lack of necessity in the means used to attain the partially doubtful purpose, and the very serious – and potentially dangerous – intrusion into the applicant's private life, that lead us to conclude that the domestic authorities, and ultimately the majority, conducted an unsatisfactory balancing exercise between the respective interests at stake. We have reached the conclusion that the proportionality assessment should have led to a finding of a violation of Article 8 of the Convention.

The judgment in *L.B* was heavily criticised in the academic world too. Liesa Keunen[43] was very critical in describing the judgment as being tolerant of a 'Modern Pillory'. Keunen rightly observed that the Hungarian publication regime comes at loggerheads with the State Signatory's obligation to take positive action to protect data privacy:

> In line with the dissenting opinion of judges RAVARANI and SCHUKKING, one must concede that the absence of a violation of Article 8 ECHR in this specific case is hard to accept. The arguments for this are twofold. The publication of the home address was, first of all, unnecessary to fulfil the objective of the law. Second, it was not necessary to have published the lists on the internet. Moreover, one could argue that excluding the impact of possible republication of the personal data by third parties conflicts with the positive obligation of States to protect the right to private life.

43. 'The Right to Privacy used as a Modern Pillory in L.B. v. Hungary', viewed in 1 March 2021 at https://strasbourgobservers.com/2021/03/01/the-right-to-privacy-used-as-a-modern-pillory-in-l-b-v-hungary/.

Furthermore, Keunan was mindful of the way data posted on the internet could be republished robotically and the damage such a republication could cause:

> Looking at the bigger picture, it becomes clear that this personal tax data can be integrated in big data sets and consequently be used for algorithmic decision making by, for example, insurance companies and banks. The personal tax data could be useful for these institutes in determining who does and who does not receive a mortgage or a certain discount on an insurance fee. The impact on one's private life can thus be considered enormous, although it might not be immediately visible.

The fact that the case has been referred to the Grand Chamber is very telling, creating hope for a more calibrated approach. Nonetheless, it must be borne in mind that naming and shaming is becoming a popular punitive measure which has been adopted even in the legal instruments of the EU. Article 59 of Directive (EU) 2015/849 binds Member States to ensure that in cases involving money laundering, the administrative sanctions and measures include 'at least' a public statement which identifies the natural or legal person and the nature of the breach.

Matters analogous to those discussed in the *L.B.* case were determined a few months later in the 2021 judgment in the case of *Tiriac v. Romania.*[44] Interestingly, the case involved State's positive obligation to protect Article 8 ECHR rights. The complainant, a celebrity soccer player was irked by comments made by a journalist suggesting that he had tax debts with the State. Citing the State's positive obligations, he complained about a breach of his right to honour and reputation, alleging that the domestic courts had failed to protect his rights under Article 8 ECHR. The ECtHR dismissed his case on the basis of margin of appreciation:

> 99. In the light of the above the Court considers that the national courts conducted a thorough balancing exercise between the competing rights at stake in conformity with the criteria laid down in the Court's case-law. Having regard to the margin of appreciation available to the national authorities when weighing up divergent interests, the Court sees no strong reasons to substitute its view for that of the domestic courts (see paragraph 77 above). It could not be said therefore that by dismissing the applicant's claim, the courts have failed to comply with the positive obligations incumbent on the national authorities of protecting the applicant's right to private life under Article 8 of the Convention (see, mutatis mutandis, Von Hannover (no. 2), cited above, § 126, and Petrie v. Italy, no. 25322/12, §§ 46-54, 18 May 2017). There has accordingly been no violation of that provision. For these reasons, the court, unanimously, 1. Declares the application admissible; 2. Holds that there has been no violation of Article 8 of the Convention.

The 2021 case of *Samoylova v. Russia*[45] was a case involving the publication of tax data pertaining to the wife of a senior civil servant who was at the heart of an investigation relating to unexplained wealth. The taxpayer complained under Article 8 ECHR that a television report amounted to an unlawful and unjustified invasion of her privacy in that, being assisted by the investigating authorities, the television company

---

44. Application no. 51107/16.
45. Application no. 49108/11.

had collected and disseminated her tax data. The publication under review had published the complainant's residential address and tax identification number. The ECtHR concluded that there had not been a violation of Article 8 ECHR in relation to the alleged defamation and the showing of the data presented as the applicant's declared income, but there had been a violation of Article 8 ECHR in relation to the showing of the applicant's address, her taxpayer identification number and the images of the interior of her house:

> 97. In the present case the Court has been given no reason to doubt the journalists' choice of investigative and reporting techniques, in particular, by enquiring into the sources of allegedly unlawful income received by the subjects of the narrative (public officials) through a wider regard to the income of that person's spouse ... Similarly, the Court takes note of the technique focusing on the disparity between declared income of the household and expenditure ...
>
> 100. When showing the tax authority's letter of 19 November 2008, the journalists disclosed to the public the applicant's exact registration address in Moscow (see paragraph 7 above) ... the disclosure of the address had resulted in her being harassed by others, including journalists, at home ...
>
> 102. Similarly, a person's taxpayer identification number may, depending on the national law and practices, disclose and/or facilitate further access to relatively sensitive data closely linked to his or her identity. In the present case it suffices to note that the civil courts did not attempt to delve into the necessity of disclosing it in the television report, in addition to the declared income data.

7.6 CONCLUSIONS

If taxation forms part of the hard-core of public prerogatives, investigative rights form part of the inner core of the hard-core of public prerogatives. Consequently, Article 8 ECHR cannot be used to disarm the tax authorities from their legitimate weapons to apprehend and combat tax evasion. Perquisitions, access to information, sharing of information between investigative authorities and seizure of data in the course of tax investigations are necessary in a democratic society in the interests of the economic well-being of the country. The ECtHR has developed state-of-the-art tools to balance private legitimate interests with public prerogatives. Judgments on the safeguard of effective oversight have evolved in the right direction. Proper judicial controls ensure that fairness is achieved without unduly hampering the legitimate powers of investigative authorities.

Public prerogative must evolve in the current ecosystem. Public prerogatives are not what they were sixty years ago. EU Tax Directives, International Conventions, Bilateral Arrangements and new technologies have enhanced investigative powers in a manner that was previously unconceivable. The traditional concept of professional secrecy has been eroded, and journalists have joined the fight against tax evasion. The current environment invites a revised approach to Article 8 ECHR. The judgment in *L.B. v. Hungary* is worrying because the system that has been allowed by the ECtHR went too far. The publication of a list of tax defaulters may be understandable, in a VAT context especially because the chapter discussing Article 35 will explain that the right to credit for input VAT has been interpreted as being partly dependent on supplier's compliance. The publication of a list of defaulters is in the interest of both the State and third parties too because they need to know who they contract with. Nonetheless, naming and shaming must be used as a constructive tool and not as a means itself. Criteria for publication and listing must be transparent and fair and subject to regular judicial scrutiny. Furthermore, the data published must not go beyond what is strictly necessary. The personal safety of the tax defaulter and his family members must be duly considered.

CHAPTER 8

Freedom of Thought, Conscience and Religion, Freedom of Assembly and Association

ARTICLE 9

Freedom of thought, conscience and religion

1. Everyone has the right to freedom of thought, conscience and religion; this right includes freedom to change his religion or belief and freedom, either alone or in community with others and in public or private, to manifest his religion or belief, in worship, teaching, practice and observance.

2. Freedom to manifest one's religion or beliefs shall be subject only to such limitations as are prescribed by law and are necessary in a democratic society in the interests of public safety, for the protection of public order, health or morals, or for the protection of the rights and freedoms of others.

ARTICLE 11

Freedom of assembly and association

1. Everyone has the right to freedom of peaceful assembly and to freedom of association with others, including the right to form and to join trade unions for the protection of his interests.

2. No restrictions shall be placed on the exercise of these rights other than such as are prescribed by law and are necessary in a democratic society in the interests of national security or public safety, for the prevention of disorder or crime, for the protection of health or morals or for the protection of the rights and freedoms of others. This Article shall not prevent the imposition of lawful restrictions on the exercise of these rights by members of the armed forces, of the police or of the administration of the State

8.1 'EVERYONE'

Both Article 9 ECHR and Article 11 ECHR are meant to apply to 'everyone'. The most important successful tax complaints under Article 9 ECHR read in conjunction with Article 1 of Protocol 1 ECHR, Article 11 ECHR and Article 14 ECHR were filed by associations of bodies of persons such as branches of the Jehovah witnesses.

The ECtHR has admitted tax complaints submitted by non-individuals. Complaints filed by associations of religious persons have been held to be admissible and, in certain instances, have been upheld, but the *locus standi* of all types of legal persons, limited liability companies especially, cannot always be taken for granted. In the 1996 decision *Kustannus OY Vapaa Ajattelija AB, Vapaa-Ajattelijain Liitto Fritänkarnas Förbund R.Y. and Kimmo Sundström v. Finland,*[1] the Commission noted:

> The Commission would therefore not exclude that the applicant association is in principle capable of possessing and exercising rights under Article 9 para. 1 (Art. 9-1). However, the complaint now before the Commission merely concerns the obligation of the applicant company to pay taxes reserved for Church activities. The company form may have been a deliberate choice on the part of the applicant association and its branches for the pursuance of part of the freethinkers' activities ...
>
> The Commission therefore concludes that in the circumstances of the present case the applicant company cannot rely on the rights referred to in Article 9 para. 1 (Art. 9-1). It follows that, insofar as the complaint has been lodged by the applicant company and insofar as it pertains to the taxes imposed on the company for 1990 and 1993-94 which were either directly or indirectly reserved for Church activities, it must be rejected as being manifestly ill-founded.

Predictably, tax policies causing religious discrimination create concern under a number of articles of the ECHR, and previous chapters have analysed some important religious discrimination cases already.

8.2 FREEDOM OF THOUGHT, CONSCIENCE AND RELIGION

Understandably, freedom to worship belongs to the so-called forum internum implying that although a person has freedom to worship, he is still bound to get taxed. Similarly, the fact that a religious association has a right to exist does not imply that it should be immune from taxation. In *Iglesia Bautista 'El Salvador' and José Aquilino Ortega Moratilla v. Spain,*[2] the Commission pointed out that:

> It follows that Article 9 does not confer on them any right to refuse, on that account, to submit to the tax legislation in force.

Comparisons between the tax treatment of minority religious associations and mainstream religious associations were made in a number of Article 9 ECHR cases, especially when it was invoked in conjunction with Article 14 ECHR. In the 1996 case

1. Application no. 20471/92.
2. Application no. 17522/90.

Sivananda De yoga Vedanta v. France,[3] a yoga association argued that, unlike the Catholic Church, it did not benefit from the blanket tax exemption available to non-profit making organisation, but its case failed on the merits. Similarly, in the *Iglesia Bautista 'El Salvador' and José Aquilino Ortega Moratilla v. Spain*[4] cited above, the fact that, unlike complainant, the Catholic Church benefitted from the privilege of a tax exemption was justified. The Commission recalled that Article 9 ECHR does not prohibit all differences in treatment in the exercise of the rights and freedoms recognised, equality of treatment being violated only where the difference in treatment has no objective and reasonable justification. The tax exemptions enjoyed by the Catholic Church in Spain were provided for by a special agreement with the Holy See contemplating reciprocal obligations. In a way, the tax exemption was a consideration for the Catholic Church's undertaking to place its historical, artistic and documentary heritage at the service of the Spanish people.

Many 'first generation' Article 9 ECHR complaints contested obligatory church taxes, but complaints were rejected whenever the obligation to pay the Church tax could be lifted upon leaving the congregation. Thus, in the 1984 case *E. and G.R. v. Austria,*[5] the Commission held:

> ... The obligation can be avoided if they choose to leave the church, a possibility for which the State legislation has expressly provided. By making available this possibility, the State has introduced sufficient safeguards to ensure the individual's freedom of religion. The individual cannot reasonably claim, having regard to the terms of Art. 9 of the Convention, to remain a member of a particular church and nevertheless be free from the legal obligations, including financial obligations, resulting from this membership according to the autonomous regulations of the church in question. The same considerations would also apply if the matter were to be considered under Art. I of the Convention (freedom of association).

Some other first-generation cases involved conscientious objectors who contested taxation because they alleged that the money from their taxes would contribute to the purchase of military equipment and that warfare was against their religious beliefs. Their cases were dismissed, because religious beliefs pertained to the *forum internum* and could not form the basis of their behaviour in the public sphere.[6]

Whereas all the known early cases were rejected, later cases were upheld. In 2012, the ECtHR upheld an Article 9 ECHR complaint in the case *Association Les Témoins de Jéhovah v. France,*[7] the French branch of the Jehovah witnesses. The religious society was subject to a tax audit and investigated over donations it had received. The Association refused to provide information relative to tax-exempt donations on the basis of a tax exemption which applied to authorised religious congregations. Eventually, the tax authorities raised an assessment for EUR 45 million against the Association. The Association claimed that the tax assessment amounted to an interference with its right to freedom of religion protected by Article 9 ECHR.

3. Application no. 30260/96.
4. Application no. 17522/90.
5. Application no. 9781/82.
6. Application no. 10358/8.
7. Application no. 8916/05.

The ECtHR found that the tax assessment raised against the Jehovah witnesses association violated the association's right to freedom of religion. It found that a tax assessment is compatible with the ECHR only if it is 'prescribed by law', and the law in question is formulated with sufficient clarity to be foreseeable. The provisions of domestic law which were used by the tax authorities to tax the gifts to the association Les Témoins de Jéhovah were not sufficiently foreseeable, because they were too vague and were not detailed enough, and it found a violation:

> 72. Eu égard à tout ce qui précède, la Cour n'est pas convaincue que la requérante était à même de prévoir à un degré raisonnable les conséquences pouvant résulter de la perception des offrandes et de la présentation de sa comptabilité à l'administration fiscale. Partant, l'ingérence n'était pas prévue par la loi au sens de l'article 9 § 2 de la Convention.
>
> b) Finalité et nécessité de l'ingérence
>
> Eu égard à la conclusion qui précède, la Cour n'estime pas nécessaire de se pencher sur le respect des autres exigences du paragraphe 2 de l'article 9.

The thought process the ECtHR applies in Article 9 ECHR cases is similar to the one it adopts in Article 1 Protocol 1 ECHR. Article 9 ECHR cases tend to refer to Article 1 Protocol 1 ECHR cases extensively. In the 2014 judgment *Christian Religious Organization of Jehovah's witnesses v. Armenia*, the ECtHR applied Article 1 Protocol 1 ECHR considerations.[8] The complaint referred to a refusal to exempt a religious organisation's imports of donated religious literature from taxation, as well as the arbitrary imposition of a grossly inflated customs value on them.

The ECtHR pointed out that freedom of thought, conscience and religion is one of the foundations of a 'democratic society' within the meaning of the Convention. While religious freedom is primarily a matter of individual conscience, it also implies, *inter alia*, freedom to 'manifest [one's] religion'.

Referring to its earlier 'tax' Article 9 ECHR judgment in *Association Les Témoins de Jéhovah v. France*[9] it pointed out that an economic, financial or fiscal measure could, in certain circumstances, constitute an interference with the exercise of rights secured under Article 9 ECHR if that measure were found to have had a real and serious impact on a religious community's ability to pursue its religious activity.

The ECtHR held that it had not been demonstrated that the domestic measure refusing a 20% and 30% VAT on religious publications had such an effect on the applicant organisation as to fundamentally undermine its ability to develop its religious activity. The tax measure did not impact on the right to worship, because the organisation did not produce evidence that it could not afford to pay the tax it was challenging. The individual financial hardship caused by the tax did not infringe freedom to exercise religious beliefs. After pointing out the special nature of the tax sphere where:

> ... the Court's well-established position is that States may be afforded some degree of additional deference and latitude in the exercise of their fiscal functions under

8. Application no. 73601/14.
9. Application no. 8916/05.

> the lawfulness test (see National & Provincial Building Society, Leeds Permanent Building Society and Yorkshire Building Society v. the United Kingdom, 23 October 1997, §§ 75 to 83, Reports of Judgments and Decisions 1997-VII, and OAO Neftyanaya Kompaniya Yukos v. Russia, no. 14902/04, § 559, 20 September 2011).

Taking into account the wide margin of appreciation which the States have in taxation matters, the ECtHR held that the denial of the VAT exemption on the organisation's imports of religious literature did not upset the balance which must be struck between the protection of the applicant organisation's rights and the public interest in securing the payment of taxes.

The 2017 case of *Klein and Others v. Germany*[10] was a case filed by an individual who contested the way German Church Tax worked. In the case of spouses, Church tax was due even if only one of the spouses belonged to the congregation. In addition, it applied on a joint basis. Thus, a person who was married to a member of the Church who was not himself a member of the Church was liable to pay the Church tax just the same. The case was dismissed because it was clear that State legislation gave individuals the possibility of leaving the church opting out of the tax. Church tax did not arise directly from State legislation but derived from a decision taken independently by the Protestant Church of the Land of Thuringia, and the tax measure complained of could not be attributed to the respondent State.

8.3 FREEDOM OF ASSEMBLY AND ASSOCIATION

Cases over freedom of association tend to go hand in hand with cases involving other articles. The case of *Magyar Keresztény Mennonita Egyház and Others v. Hungary*[11] involved a complaint under Article 11 ECHR read in the light of Article 9 ECHR that the de-registration of their church and the discretionary re-registration amounted to violations of their rights to freedom of religion and association. Registration as a church was linked to tax benefits. The ECtHR concluded that, in removing the applicants' church status altogether rather than applying less stringent measures, in establishing a politically tainted re-registration procedure, whose justification is open to doubt as such, and, in treating the applicants differently from the incorporated churches not only in the possibilities of cooperation but also in securing benefits for the purposes of faith-related activities, the authorities neglected their duty of neutrality vis-à-vis the applicant communities. Consequently, despite the margin of appreciation rule, the ECtHR concluded that the impugned measure could not be said to correspond to a 'pressing social need' and found a violation. Interestingly, the ECtHR did not speak of deference and latitude in the exercise of fiscal functions but spoke of powers that had to be used with great caution. The onus of proving a legitimate exercise of the state function fell on the State:

10. Applications nos. 10138/11 and 3 others.
11. Applications nos. 70945/11, 23611/12, 26998/12, 41150/12, 41155/12, 41463/12, 41553/12, 54977/12 and 56581/12.

> 84. The State's power in this field must be used sparingly; exceptions to the rule of freedom of association are to be construed strictly and only convincing and compelling reasons can justify restrictions on that freedom. In this connection, the Court reiterates its position as formulated in the cases of Gorzelik and Others (cited above, §§ 94-95) and Jehovah's Witnesses of Moscow v. Russia (no. 302/02, § 100, 10 June 2010). The burden of proof when it comes to demonstrating the presence of compelling reasons is on the respondent Government (see, mutatis mutandis, Vallianatos and Others v. Greece [GC], nos. 29381/09 and 32684/09, § 85, ECHR 2013). It is therefore for the Government to show in the instant case that it was necessary, in pursuit of the legitimate aims which they relied on, to bar already recognised Churches from maintaining their status with regard to confessional activities, that is, the manifestation of religion ...
>
> 89. The Court therefore considers that, although States have a certain margin of appreciation in this field, this cannot extend to total deference to the national authorities' assessment of religions and religious organisations; the applicable legal solutions adopted in a member State must be in compliance with the Court's case-law and subject to the Court's scrutiny.

The ECtHR proceeded to discuss the matter of positive obligations, applying it in a tax context:

> 90. The Court considers that there is a positive obligation incumbent on the State to put in place a system of recognition which facilitates the acquisition of legal personality by religious communities. This is a valid consideration also in terms of defining the notions of religion and religious activities. In the Court's view, those definitions have direct repercussions on the individual's exercise of the right to freedom of religion, and are capable of restricting the latter if the individual's activity is not recognised as a religious one. According to the position of the United Nations Human Rights Committee (see paragraph 39 above), such definitions cannot be construed to the detriment of non-traditional forms of religion – a view which the Court shares. In this context, it reiterates that the State's duty of neutrality and impartiality, as defined in its case-law, is incompatible with any power on the State's part to assess the legitimacy of religious beliefs (see Metropolitan Church of Bessarabia and Others, cited above, §§ 118 and 123, and Hasan and Chaush, cited above, § 62). However, the present case does not concern the definition of religion as such in Hungarian law. ...

The applicants submitted subsidiary complaints under Article 14 ECHR, read in conjunction with Articles 9 and 11 ECHR, complaining that they had been discriminated against on account of their position as a religious minority. In view of its decision on the Article 11 complaint, the ECtHR did not enter into the merits of this grievance.

8.4 CONCLUSIONS

Cases involving Freedom of thought, conscience and religion, Freedom of assembly and association are curious because they tend to contemplate the most ingenious arguments. An element of imagination is needed to envisage how taxation may interfere with Freedom of thought, conscience and religion, and Freedom of assembly and association. Early cases raised some interesting moral questions, but were dismissed on the grounds that certain freedoms pertain to the forum internum. Later cases pointing out that, in remote circumstances, taxation can constitute an interference with the exercise of rights secured under Articles 9 ECHR and 11 ECHR if that measure is found to have had a real and serious impact on the ability to pursue an activity. The ECtHR's judgments on positive obligations and their careful scrutiny in ensuring effective protection are very well articulated creating a clear jurisprudential line.

CHAPTER 9

Freedom of Expression

ARTICLE 10
Freedom of expression

1. Everyone has the right to freedom of expression. This right shall include freedom to hold opinions and to receive and impart information and ideas without interference by public authority and regardless of frontiers. This Article shall not prevent States from requiring the licensing of broadcasting, television or cinema enterprises.

2. The exercise of these freedoms, since it carries with it duties and responsibilities, may be subject to such formalities, conditions, restrictions or penalties as are prescribed by law and are necessary in a democratic society, in the interests of national security, territorial integrity or public safety, for the prevention of disorder or crime, for the protection of health or morals, for the protection of the reputation or rights of others, for preventing the disclosure of information received in confidence, or for maintaining the authority and impartiality of the judiciary.

9.1 ARTICLE 8 ECHR VERSUS ARTICLE 10 ECHR

Whereas Article 8 ECHR protects data subjects from unnecessary intrusions into their tax data, Article 10 ECHR regulates the legitimate use of such tax data. In a way, Article 8 ECHR protects the data subject, and Article 10 ECHR regulates the Data Processor and the Data Controller. The inference that may be drawn from Article 8 ECHR tax judgments is that, subject to certain, restrictions, States are allowed to publish certain data pertaining to tax defaulters, naming and shaming them. The public has a right to be informed of the fiscal morality of taxpayers implying that, subject to fair comment, investigative journalists have a right to publish tax data pertaining to tax defaulters. Article 10 ECHR lays down the parameters for fair use of tax data, but Article 10 ECHR tax judgments of the ECtHR are not always entirely reconcilable with Article 8 ECHR judgments. While Article 8 ECHR allows certain intrusions, Article 10 ECHR significantly limits the use of data gleaned from such intrusions. Article 10 ECHR judgments risk diluting the core value behind the Article 8 ECHR judgments.

9.2 THE *FRESSOZ AND ROIRE* CASE

The 1999 case of *Fressoz and Roire v. France*[1] must have been the first in a growing list of cases involving the publication of tax data. Fressoz and Rore were satirical journalists who were convicted of defamation. The journalists' case referred to the publication of an article that included a photograph of a person's income tax statement. The journalists argued that their conviction for handling photocopies of tax returns obtained through a breach of professional confidence by an unidentified tax official had infringed their right to freedom of expression. The ECtHR had to determine whether the objective of protecting fiscal confidentiality, which in itself is legitimate, constituted a relevant and sufficient justification for the interference. The ECtHR noted that neither the journalists' account of the events nor their good faith has been called into question. The journalists had acted in accordance with the standards governing their profession. The photograph of the tax statement was intended to corroborate the terms of the article in question. The publication of the tax assessments was thus relevant not only to the subject matter but also to the credibility of the information supplied. Consequently, the ECtHR concluded that:

> 56. In sum, there was not, in the Court's view, a reasonable relationship of proportionality between the legitimate aim pursued by the journalists' conviction and the means deployed to achieve that aim, given the interest a democratic society has in ensuring and preserving freedom of the press. There has therefore been a violation of Article 10 of the Convention.

9.3 THE *EERIKÄINEN* CASE

The naming and shaming of tax dodgers was on the ECtHR's agenda in the 2009 case of *Eerikäinen and Others v. Finland*,[2] a case involving a freelance journalist's publication of an article relating to an individual who had been convicted of five offences of tax fraud and two offences of aggravated fraud. The article was accompanied by a photo of the tax defaulter. Eerikäinen, the journalist, was sued for defamation and ordered to pay damages, so he filed a complaint under Article 10 ECHR of a violation of his right to freedom of expression, on the ground that he had been ordered to pay damages for

1. Application no. 29183/95.
2. Application no. 3514/02.

reporting on pending criminal proceedings which dealt with a matter of general interest. There was no question that the purpose of the article was to contribute to a public discussion, but the question was whether the journalist had gone too far when he communicated the tax defaulter's identity to the public. The defaulter was neither a public figure nor a politician but an ordinary person who was the subject of criminal proceedings. The ECHR found a violation of Article 10 ECHR, because the grounds relied on the defamation case, although relevant, were not sufficient to justify the interference with the applicants' right to freedom of expression, in terms of a 'pressing social need'.

9.4 THE *SATAKUNNAN* CASE

The ECtHR's tax judgment in the case of *Satakunnan Markkinapörssi Oy and Satamedia Oy v. Finland*[3] goes to prove that even limited liability companies benefit from the protection of Article 10 ECHR. In an Article 10 ECHR context, 'everyone' is really meant to mean 'everyone' which is understandable because most publishing undertakings are corporates.

The complaint in the case of *Satakunnan Markkinapörssi Oy and Satamedia Oy v. Finland* referred to the public dissemination of tax data that was in the public domain. Satakunnan Markkinapörssi Oy published an annual magazine that disseminated natural persons' taxable income and assets. Information published was drawn from official public sources and applicants were not the only publishers of tax data. Nonetheless, the Finnish Data Protection authorities stopped Satakunnan Markkinapörssi Oy from continuing to publish their detailed tax publications. The applicants appealed the decision of the Data Protection authorities and filed an appeal, but they lost their appeal and their case was escalated to the ECtHR.

The ECtHR held that there had been an interference with the applicant companies' right to impart information, as guaranteed by Article 10 ECHR, but the ECtHR noted that the right to impart information is subject to the exceptions set out in Article 10 (2) ECHR of the Convention. The ECtHR held that the interference was 'prescribed by law', and it pursued the legitimate aim of protecting the reputation or rights of others, within the meaning of Article 10 (2) ECHR. It found that the interference was necessary in a democratic society because the extent of the published information was excessive. According to the Finnish Authorities, the volume of data published could not be considered as journalism but as processing of personal data, which the applicant companies had no right to do. According to the ECtHR, the publication of a whole database collected for journalistic purposes could not be regarded as journalistic activity. The public interest did not require such publication of personal data to such an extent. Consequently, the claim of breach of freedom of information was dismissed.[4]

3. Application no. 931/13.
4. The applicant's claim under Article 10 was dismissed but its claim under Article 6 (fair hearing) was successful because the ECtHR held that the six-year period within which the case had been decided was unreasonably long.

9.5 THE *MARIAPORI* CASE

In the 2010 case of *Mariapori v. Finland*,[5] Mariapori complained that her right to freedom of expression had been violated because she had been convicted of defamation for statements made in a tax book and in tax fraud proceedings. In the incriminated statements, Mariapori had heavily criticised a particular tax inspector. Mariapori was found guilty of aggravated defamation and sentenced to four months' conditional imprisonment and ordered to pay EUR 5,000 to the tax inspector by way of compensation. The domestic court found that, even though the applicant might have been right about the dysfunctions in the company taxation system, she should not have criticised the civil servants in question in a defamatory manner. As far as the statements she had made during the tax fraud proceedings, the court found them to constitute defamation but not aggravated defamation. Mariapori was ordered to pay in total EUR 4,000 in compensation for mental suffering under both counts. The District Court declared all parts of the case file secret for fifteen years except for the applicable legal provisions and the conclusions.

The ECtHR was clearly perturbed by the fact that Mariapori had been punished with a criminal sentence for defamation in court proceedings:

> 66. In view of the above considerations, as concerns the statements made by the applicant during the court proceedings, the Court finds that, in the context of those proceedings, the tax inspectors could have been reasonably expected to tolerate the statements made by the applicant under oath in her capacity as the defendant's witness (see Nikula v. Finland, cited above, § 51), especially as the applicant was obliged to answer the questions put to her and she could not but give her view of the facts. Viewed against this background and in the absence of exceptional circumstances supporting a different conclusion (see paragraph 62 above), the Court is not persuaded that the national courts, acting within their margin of appreciation, struck a reasonable balance between the interests involved in respect of this part of the case.

The ECtHR proceeded to examine the statements contained in the tax book:

> 67. As to the statements made in the applicant's book, the Court notes that the book could be characterised as a polemical document or pamphlet attempting to contribute to a public debate. The book mainly described the applicant's views about the actions of the tax authorities, including that of tax inspector A. For her statements made in the book the applicant was sentenced to four months' conditional imprisonment and ordered to pay 5,000 euros to tax inspector A. in compensation. Although sentencing is in principle a matter for the national courts, the Court considers that the imposition of a prison sentence for a defamation offence will be compatible with an applicant's right to freedom of expression as guaranteed by Article 10 of the Convention only in exceptional circumstances, notably where other fundamental rights have been seriously impaired, as, for example, in the case of hate speech or incitement to violence ... .

5. Application no. 37751/07.

The ECtHR held that Mariapori's case was a classic case of defamation of an individual in the context of a debate on the actions of the tax authorities which was an important matter of legitimate public interest. The facts in issue presented no justification whatsoever for the imposition of a prison sentence:

> Such a sanction, by its very nature, will inevitably have a chilling effect on public debate. The fact that the applicant's prison sentence was conditional and that she did not in fact serve it does not alter that conclusion. Although the national authorities' interference with the applicant's right to freedom of expression may have been justified by the concern to strike the balance between the various competing interests at stake, the criminal sanction and the accompanying obligation to pay compensation imposed on her by the national courts were manifestly disproportionate in their nature and severity, having regard to the legitimate aim pursued by the applicant's conviction for defamation.

The ECtHR observed that the Parliamentary Assembly of the Council of Europe in its Resolution 1577 (2007) urged those Member States which still provide for prison sentences for defamation, even if they are not actually imposed, to abolish them without delay. Consequently, the ECtHR concluded that the severity of the sanctions imposed went beyond a 'necessary' restriction on the applicant's freedom of expression. Notwithstanding the margin of appreciation afforded to the State in this area, the domestic courts failed to strike a fair balance between the competing interests at stake. The ECtHR found a violation of Article 10 ECHR in respect of the statements made by the complainant during the court proceedings as well as in respect of the statements made in her book.

The financial award was noteworthy by the ECtHR's normal standards. The respondent state was to pay Mariapori EUR 33,390.84 in respect of pecuniary damage, EUR 6,000 in respect of non-pecuniary damage and EUR 10,000 in respect of costs and expenses.

The ECtHR's modern outlook in *Mariapori* may be contrasted with the conclusions reached in the 1989 case of *Barfod v. Denmark*,[6] a case that involved accusations levelled at two tax judges. In the *Barfod* case, the Commission had reached a different conclusion:

> The Court cannot accept this argument. The lay judges exercised judicial functions. The impugned statement was not a criticism of the reasoning in the judgment of 28 January 1981, but rather, as found by the High Court in its judgment of 3 July 1984, a defamatory accusation against the lay judges personally, which was likely to lower them in public esteem and was put forward without any supporting evidence (see paragraph 13 above). In view of these considerations, the political context in which the tax case was fought cannot be regarded as relevant for the question of proportionality.
>
> 36. Having regard to the foregoing, the Court reaches the conclusion that no breach of Article 10 (art. 10) has been established in the circumstances of the present case.

6. Application no. 11508/85.

9.6 THE *LUXLEAKS* CASE

Freedom of speech returned to the ECtHR's agenda in the 2021 case of *Halet v. Luxembourg*,[7] a controversial case that has been referred to the Grand Chamber.

The *Halet* case referred to the Luxleaks scandal. Between 2012 and 2014, several hundred tax opinions and tax declarations prepared by a particular tax planning intermediary were published in various media outlets. These publications drew attention to a practice, over the period from 2002 to 2012, of highly advantageous tax rulings, concluded on behalf of multinational companies and the Luxembourg tax authorities.

An internal investigation by the tax planning intermediary established that the day before his resignation, one of its employees had copied 45,000 pages of confidential documents, including 20,000 pages of tax documents, corresponding to 538 folders of tax rescripts. He had handed these over to a journalist in the summer of 2011, at the latter's request. Eventually, the documents were published and put online by an association of journalists known as the 'International Consortium of Investigative Journalists'. Its authors described this publication as 'Luxleaks'.

Halet and the journalist were identified as the source of the leak and were charged by an investigating judge and committed for trial before the Luxembourg District Court by the investigating court. At first instance, the domestic courts convicted Halet of employee theft (vol domestique), fraudulent access to a system for the processing or automatic transmission of data, betrayal of commercial secrets, breach of professional confidence and laundering and possession (blanchiment-détention). Halet was sentenced to a nine-month prison term, suspended in its entirety, and a fine of EUR 1,000. In addition, he was ordered to pay a symbolic sum of EUR 1 to the tax planning intermediary. On appeal, the domestic courts reduced the prison sentence to six months, suspended in its entirety, and upheld the fine of EUR 1,500.

Halet took his case to the ECtHR complaining that his conviction, following his disclosure to a journalist of sixteen documents emanating from his employer, had amounted to disproportionate interference with his right to freedom of expression.

The ECtHR reflected on the importance of the adjective 'necessary', within the meaning of Article 10 (2) ECHR, implying derogations from the freedom when there was the existence of a 'pressing social need'. The margin of appreciation in determining 'pressing social need' was subject to the ECtHR's supervisory function.

In its case law, the ECtHR has identified certain fundamental principles underlying the assessment of whether an interference with the right to freedom of expression was proportionate. Public interest in the disclosed information, its authenticity, the availability of alternative channels for making the disclosure, the employee's good faith, the damage to the employer and the severity of the penalty are all taken into account. Both the local courts and the ECtHR extensively referred to the non-tax case in *Guja v. Moldova*.[8]

7. Application no. 21884/18.
8. Application no. 14277/04.

While there was no dispute as to whether there had been an 'interference' in the freedom of speech, whether the interference was 'prescribed by law' and pursued a legitimate aim, the point at issue was whether the interference was 'necessary in a democratic society', in particular, whether there was a proportionate relationship between the interference and the aim pursued.

The ECtHR concluded that Halet qualified for whistle-blower protection status, implying that what needed to be examined were the elements of fair balance through the severity of the penalties.

The ECtHR concluded that the national authorities carried out a detailed examination in weighing up the respective interests. Despite the negligible financial damage, the reputation of the tax planning intermediary had been harmed. According to the ECtHR, the domestic courts had taken into consideration, as a mitigating circumstance, the 'disinterested nature of the applicant's actions' imposing only a relatively modest fine that did not have a genuinely chilling effect on the exercise of the applicant's freedom or that of other employees but encouraged due consideration of the legitimacy of the action being envisaged. Considering the Contracting States' margin of appreciation in the sphere, the ECtHR concluded that the domestic courts had struck a fair balance between, on the one hand, the need to protect the rights of the applicant's employer and, on the other, the need to protect the applicant's freedom of expression. Accordingly, the ECtHR did not find a violation of Article 10 ECHR.

9.7 CONCLUSIONS

The contribution the media and individual journalists have made to the 'fair share of taxation debate' has been widely acknowledged and research carried out by media houses has heavily influenced the design of international tax policy. The work of investigative journalists has caused a paradigm shift in perceptions of fiscal morality. The publication of tax data has evolved into an end in itself by serving both as a punitive measure and a powerful tax collection tool. Against this background, it is difficult to reconcile the rationale behind Article 8 ECHR judgments like *L.B. v. Hungary* and *Tiriac v. Romania* allowing the dissemination of sensitive tax data with the rationale of judgments like *Sakutanaan v. Finland* and *Halet v. Luxembourg* punishing disseminators of such tax data. The balanced judgment in *Mariapori* presents a fair compromise between the two positions.

CHAPTER 10

Right to an Effective Remedy

ARTICLE 13
Right to an effective remedy

Everyone whose rights and freedoms as set forth in this Convention are violated shall have an effective remedy before a national authority notwithstanding that the violation has been committed by persons acting in an official capacity.

10.1 'OBSCURE' BUT HIGHLY RELEVANT TO TAX SPHERE

The tax judgments of the ECtHR had the opportunity to explain that Article 13 ECHR guarantees the availability at national level of a remedy to enforce the substance of the rights and freedoms contemplated in the ECHR. Article 13 ECHR is an auxiliary article that requires domestic remedies to deal with the substance of an 'arguable complaint' under the ECHR and to grant an effective remedy. A few tax complaints have cited Article 13 ECHR in conjunction with other articles of the ECHR. The ECtHR's tax judgments have significantly enriched the ECtHR jurisprudence pertinent to an article whose importance is frequently dismissed.

10.2 FOUR IMPORTANT ARTICLE 13 ECHR TAX CASES

Article 13 ECHR was invoked successfully in the case of *Yunusova and Yunusov v. Azerbaijan* (no. 2),[1] a case involving, *inter alia*, a trial for large-scale tax evasion and fraud. Pending the outcome of the trial, the Yunusovs' bank accounts were frozen and their passports were seized, but the domestic legal system did not provide complainants with a judicial mechanism to contest the freezing order and the confiscation of the passports. The Yunusovs filed complaints to the ECHR based on Article 1 of Protocol

1. Application no. 68817/14.

No. 1 ECHR (Property) and Article 2 of Protocol No. 4 ECHR (freedom of movement) and right to an 'effective' domestic remedy within the meaning of Article 13 ECHR.

After the ECtHR declared the applicants' complaints under Article 1 of Protocol No. 1 and Article 2 of Protocol No. 4 arguable, the ECtHR concluded that complainants were entitled to an 'effective' domestic remedy within the meaning of Article 13 ECHR.

Noting that the freezing order and the passport seizure were not liable to any form of judicial review because the domestic legal system did not even contemplate it, the ECtHR found that complaints were not provided with an effective remedy in relation to their complaints under Article 1 of Protocol No. 1 ECHR and Article 2 of Protocol No. 4 ECHR. Accordingly, the ECtHR held that there had been a violation of Article 13 ECHR in conjunction with Article 1 of Protocol No. 1 ECHR and Article 2 of Protocol No. 4 ECHR.

Article 13 ECHR was cited in cases discussed in previous chapters. In the 2021 case of *L.B. v. Hungary*,[2] the complainant had submitted an additional complaint under Article 13 ECHR. L.B. contested that Hungarian domestic law had not provided him with an effective remedy to assert before the domestic courts his complaint concerning the publication of his personal data. The ECtHR explained that Article 13 ECHR does not go so far as to guarantee a remedy allowing a Contracting State's laws as such to be challenged before a national authority on the ground of being contrary to the ECHR. The ECtHR took Article 13 ECHR to mean that it did not require the provision of a remedy to challenge that regime. Consequently, the ECtHR dismissed the Article 13 ECHR complaint as manifestly ill-founded.

The case of *Lindstrand Partners Advokatbyrå AB v. Sweden*[3] incorporated a subsidiary complaint under Article 13 ECHR too. The law firm complained that it did not benefit with an effective remedy contesting coercive measures obtaining access to their privileged data. The ECtHR held that the applicant had an 'arguable complaint' under Article 8 ECHR implying that it was entitled to an effective remedy within the meaning of Article 13 ECHR.

The ECtHR found that, while the coercive measures employed in the case were not directed against the applicant law firm per se, the search in question was carried out on its premises where contents of cupboards, shelves, computers and a safe were examined. It was clear that the search clearly affected the applicant, which had a justified interest in obtaining a review of whether the search complied with its rights under the ECHR, Article 8 especially. The fact that the complainant had been denied legal standing and thus did not have access to any remedy for the examination of its objections to the search implied that complainant had not been allowed an 'effective remedy before a national authority'. Consequently, the ECtHR found a violation of Article 13 ECHR in conjunction with Article 8 ECHR.

Issues relating to the availability of effective remedies played an important in the case of *Riener v. Bulgaria*[4] involving a complaint relating to freedom of movement and an auxiliary complaint under Article 13 ECHR. The applicant complained that her

2. Application no. 36345/16.
3. Application no. 18700/09.
4. Application no. 46343/99.

attempts to reverse the order prohibiting her departure from Bulgaria were arbitrarily refused. The ECtHR observed that Article 13 ECHR requires that the national legal system must make available to the individual concerned the effective possibility of challenging the measure complained of and of having the relevant issues examined with sufficient procedural safeguards and thoroughness by an appropriate domestic forum offering adequate guarantees of independence and impartiality. Bulgarian law provided for avenues for redress, but the courts seemed only to be concerned with the formal lawfulness of the travel ban and the question whether or not the applicant had paid her debt or provided sufficient security. Once satisfied that the tax debt had not been paid, the Bulgarian courts automatically upheld the travel ban. The ECtHR held that a domestic grievance procedure cannot be considered effective within the meaning of Article 13 ECHR, unless it affords scope for proper judicial review. The limited scope of review afforded by Bulgarian law in the applicant's case was not held to satisfy the requirements of Article 13 ECHR with Article 8 and Article 2 of Protocol No. 4 ECHR. Riener had not benefitted from an effective remedy under Bulgarian law. Consequently, the ECHR found a violation of Article 13 ECHR.

The effectiveness of Article 13 ECHR in pre-emptive tax collection proceedings was highlighted in the 2014 case of *East/West Alliance Limited v. Ukraine*,[5] a case involving the confiscation by the tax authorities of valuable assets. The complainants had been denied access to their aircraft fleet for more than ten years, and their strenuous efforts before various administrative, tax, prosecution and judicial authorities to recover their property turned out to be futile. While under the authorities' custody, the aircraft was damaged, vandalised, sold and stolen without anybody being held accountable. The ECtHR held that although, for brief periods, the retention of the aircraft by the authorities complied with some of the principles inherent in Article 1 of Protocol No. 1 ECHR, the concomitant abusive and arbitrary actions of the authorities negated in practice the effectiveness of those safeguards. The ECtHR pointed out that Article 13 ECHR guarantees the availability, at the national level, of a remedy to enforce the right to property. The effect of Article 13 ECHR was described as being to require the provision of a domestic remedy to deal with the substance of an 'arguable complaint' and to grant appropriate relief. The remedy required by Article 13 ECHR must be 'effective' in practice as well as in law:

> 228. The Court has already noted in the present case that the applicant company's strenuous efforts before various authorities to recover its property brought no results for over twelve years (see, in particular, paragraph 216 above). There is nothing to show that it had in practice an opportunity to obtain effective remedies for its complaints, that is to say, remedies which could have prevented the violations from occurring or continuing, or could have afforded the applicant appropriate redress.
>
> 229. The Court concludes, therefore, that there has been a violation of Article 13 of the Convention. It also dismisses the Government's objection regarding the admissibility of the applicant company's complaint under Article 1 of Protocol No. 1 based on the non-exhaustion of domestic remedies, which was previously joined

5. Application no. 19336/04.

to the merits of its complaint under Article 13 of the Convention (see paragraph 148 above).

10.3 CONCLUSIONS

It is interesting to note that even an 'auxiliary and subsidiary' article like Article 13 ECHR has taken pride of place in tax judgments of the ECtHR. Article 13 ECHR is frequently overlooked, but issues arising in tax disputes have raised matters that have involved major Article 13 ECHR considerations too. The judgments in *L.B.*, *Lindstrand* and *Riener* prove the important role Article 13 ECHR can play in tax cases. The problem with many tax dispute resolution mechanisms is their arbitrariness, and the existence of Article 13 ECHR ensures that judicial review occurs on matters of both substance and form.

CHAPTER 11
Prohibition of Discrimination

ARTICLE 14
Prohibition of discrimination

The enjoyment of the rights and freedoms set forth in this Convention shall be secured without discrimination on any ground such as sex, race, colour, language, religion, political or other opinion, national or social origin, association with a national minority, property, birth or other status.

11.1 'THE ENJOYMENT OF THE RIGHTS AND FREEDOMS SET FORTH IN THIS CONVENTION'

In the 1996 case *Magnus Gunnar Gudmundsson v. Iceland*,[1] the European Commission of Human Rights held that according to the established case law of the Commission and the ECtHR, Article 14 ECHR complements the other substantive provisions of the Convention and its Protocols. It has no independent existence, since it has effect solely in relation to the 'rights and freedoms' safeguarded by these provisions. There can be no room for the application of Article 14 ECHR unless the facts of the case fall within the ambit of one or more of the latter. Thus, Article 14 ECHR is considered not to be a 'stand-alone' article but a supplementary article. Article 14 ECHR cannot be invoked on its own and must be invoked in conjunction with one or more Fundamental Human Rights listed in the ECHR.[2]

Article 14 ECHR's feature as a non-stand-alone article was discussed in some of the earliest cases involving complaints of tax discrimination. The fact that Article 14

1. Application no. 23285/94.
2. European Commission, The Prohibition of discrimination for the EU non-discrimination directives – an update (Luxembourg 2011), p. 5.

ECHR cannot be invoked in conjunction with another fundamental freedom protected by the ECHR was taken to mean that if an application fails on the basis of another freedom protected by the ECHR, the Article 14 ECHR complaint dies a natural death. Thus, in the 1979 case *X. v. the Federal Republic of Germany,*[3] a case relating to a turnover tax on notarial acts, the Commission held:

> As the Commission just found that the applicant's expectation that the regulations on fees for notaries would remain unchanged did not constitute a property right within the meaning of Article 1 of Protocol No. 1 a question of discrimination with regard to the rights guaranteed by this Article consequently does not arise.

Most often, complaints regarding discriminatory taxation involve combinations of Article 14 ECHR with Article 1 of the First Protocol ECHR on the right to property. In fact, several cases discussed in Chapter 1 involved complaints based on the right to property read in conjunction with the right to freedom from discrimination. The 1999 Italian case *Galeotti Ottieri della Ciaja v. Italy,*[4] a case involving a challenge to an Italian inheritance case that discriminated against the rich, was filed on discrimination combined with the right to property as was the case in the 1959 cases *X v. Germany,*[5] *AX and BX v. Germany,*[6] the 1971 *X v. UK,*[7] the 1972 case *X v. Ireland,*[8] the 1973 *X v. Austria,*[9] the 1977 case *National Federation of the Self-Employed v. UK,*[10] the 1979 case *ABC&D v. UK,*[11] the 1983 case *X v. France*[12] and many other cases.[13]

Article 14 ECHR has been invoked in conjunction with other rights too. Some cases combined discrimination with the right to a fair hearing under Article 6,[14] while others combined discrimination with the right to respect for private and family life

3. Application no. 8410/78.
4. Application no. 46757/99.
5. Application no. 551/59.
6. Application no. 673/59.
7. Application no. 5168/71.
8. Application no. 5913/72.
9. Application no. 6087/73.
10. Application no. 7995/77.
11. Application no. 8531/79.
12. Application no. 9908/82.
13. *Baudouin Hubaux v. Belgium,* Applications no. 11088/84, *Lindsay v. UK,* no. 11089/84, *Peter Darby v. Sweden,* no. 11581/85, *BA Juby v. UK,* no. 11592/85, *Gunnar Söderberg Byggnads AB v. Sweden,* no. 11692/85, *Hugo Hanzmann v. Austria,* no. 12560/86, *Wasa Liv v. Sweden,* no. 13013/87, *AP v. Austria,* nos. 13580/88, 15464/89, *Antonino Amitrano and 159 others v. Italy,* no. 17154/90, *Catharine Feteris-Geerards v. Netherlands,* no. 21663/93, *Alfred Mika v. Austria,* no. 26560/95, *Pietrantonio Gianquitto v. Italy,* no. 26779/95, *Ianka Riener v. Bulgaria,* no. 28411/95, *Christopher Crossland v. UK,* no. 36120/97, *David Fielding v. UK,* nos. 36940/97 and others, *Kappa Kanzlei und Bürobetriebs GmbH v. Austria,* no. 37416/97.
14. *X v. Germany,* Applications no. 551/59, *AX and BX v. Germany,* no. 673/59, *X v. Belgium,* no. 2145/64, *X & Co., Y, Z v. Germany,* no. 2717/66, *ABC&D v. UK,* no. 8531/79, *X v. France,* no. 9908/82, *Gunnar Söderberg Byggnads AB v. Sweden,* no. 11692/85, *Ernst Körner v. Austria,* no. 20197/92, *Kappa Kanzlei und Bürobetriebs GmbH v. Austria,* no. 37416/97, *Vidacar SA and Opergrup SL v. Spain,* nos. 41601/98 and 41775/98.

under Article 8.[15] Some of the most interesting successful cases involved Article 14 ECHR combined with Article 9 ECHR dealing with Freedom of thought, conscience and religion.[16]

11.2 'WITHOUT DISCRIMINATION ON ANY GROUND'

Judge Zupančič's dissenting opinion in the Grand Chamber judgment in *Burden* discussed below incorporates an excellent analysis of how the concept of discrimination is to be applied in the world of taxation:

> The policies applied to taxation are clearly very important because they give financial incentives to certain choices that people are likely to make ... . In any event, tax policy is an economic policy but it is also a social policy in disguise. For example, progressive taxation is a strongly equalising economic factor undoing many untoward aspects of social stratification ... The mildest proportionality (reasonableness) test is applied to social and economic matters such as the one at hand. Here, the test inquires whether the legislation at issue is rationally related to a legitimate government interest. The question, in other words, is whether not giving tax exemption to the two Burden sisters is rationally related to a legitimate government interest.

According to the Commission, differences in treatment on the basis of suspect grounds such as birth out of wedlock, sex, sexual orientation, race and ethnic origin and nationality must be justified by particularly weighty reasons, but for 'non-suspect grounds' a lower threshold is contemplated. In the words of the Commission, differences in treatment on non-suspect grounds must have an objective and reasonable justification, pursue a legitimate aim and be proportional.[17] The Commission seemed prepared to admit that what is suspect and what is non-suspect evolves over time. Over the past twenty years, views on sexual orientation, birth out of wedlock and transsexualism have changed; all these grounds are now considered to be suspect.[18]

Article 14 ECHR prohibits both direct and indirect discrimination. Indirect discrimination can take a number of forms ranging from apparently neutral regulations that, in practice, are particularly disadvantageous to members of a certain category to measures having a disparate impact on a particular category. Even a failure to take into account existing differences may constitute indirect discrimination.[19]

15. *X v. Ireland*, Applications 5913/72, *AG v. UK*, 24828/94, and *Ianka Riener v. Bulgaria*, 28411/95.
16. Namely the case of *Jehovas Zeugen in Osterreich v. Austria*, Application no. 27540/05, and the case of the *Church of Jesus Christ of Latter-day Saints v. the United Kingdom*, Application no. 7552/09.
17. *Ibid.*, Commission p. 5.
18. *Ibid.*, Commission p. 20.
19. *Ibid.*, Commission p. 23. On this point, *see Thlimennos v. Greece*, Application no. 34369/97, dealing with gypsies, and *Glor v. Switzerland*, Application no. 13444/04, dealing with a diabetes sufferer.

11.3 'SUCH AS SEX, RACE, COLOUR, LANGUAGE, RELIGION, POLITICAL OR OTHER OPINION'

Most of the relevant tax cases deal with discrimination combined with the freedom of worship. 'Religion' is a ground that is specifically mentioned in Article 14 ECHR and the ECtHR delivered interesting tax judgments involving religious minorities.

In 2012, the ECtHR delivered an important tax discrimination judgment in a case involving the Austrian branch of the Jehovah witnesses. In the case of *Jehovas Zeugen in Osterreich v. Austria,*[20] the Jehovah witnesses brought a case against Austria because, unlike other religious societies, it was being made to pay a 14% gift tax on donations. The ECtHR referred to the conditions that must be met in a case of discrimination:

> 32. According to the Court's case-law, a difference in treatment is discriminatory for the purposes of Article 14 of the Convention if it 'has no objective and reasonable justification': that is, if it does not pursue a 'legitimate aim' or if there is not a 'reasonable relationship of proportionality between the means employed and the aim sought to be realised'. The Contracting States enjoy a certain margin of appreciation in assessing whether and to what extent differences in otherwise similar situations justify different treatment (see, among other authorities, Willi v. United Kingdom, no. 36042/97, § 39, ECHR 2002-IV).

The ECtHR found that there had been a violation of Article 14 ECHR taken in conjunction with Article 9 ECHR:

> 37. The Court therefore concludes that section 1(2)(d) of the EA Act, which provides for exemptions from the scope of application of that Act in respect of the employment of aliens for pastoral work as part of a recognised religious society, is discriminatory and that the applicant community was discriminated against on the basis of religion as a result of the application of this provision. There has therefore been a violation of Article 14 taken in conjunction with Article 9 of the Convention.

The ECtHR found a violation of Article 14 ECHR taken in conjunction with Article 1 of the First Protocol too:

> 47. As regards compliance with Article 14, the Court observes that the Government has not given any reason justifying the difference in treatment regarding the liability to inheritance and gift tax between the applicant community and religious communities recognised as religious societies and merely indicated that inheritance and gift tax had ceased to be collected after 31 July 2008.
>
> 48. The Court observes further that the refusal to grant an exemption from inheritance and gift tax was based on the grounds that the applicant community was not a recognised religious society ...
>
> 49. The Court therefore concludes that section 15(1) of the 1955 Act, as applicable at the time, which provided for exemptions from taxation of donations to religious societies recognised by law, was discriminatory and that the applicant community

20. Application no. 27540/05.

> was discriminated against on the basis of religion as a result of the application of this provision. There has therefore been a violation of Article 14 taken in conjunction with Article 1 Protocol No. 1.

In the same year, the ECtHR delivered a very important judgment on discrimination in the case *Association Les Témoins de Jéhovah v. France* involving the French branch of Jehovah witnesses which was subject to a tax audit and investigated over donations received. The Association refused to provide information relative to tax-exempt donations on the basis of a tax exemption which applied to authorised religious congregations. The tax authorities raised an assessment for EUR 45 million against the Association. The association claimed that the tax assessment amounted to an interference with its right to freedom of religion protected by Article 9 ECHR.

The ECtHR found that the tax assessment violated the association's right to freedom of religion. It found that a tax assessment is compatible with the ECHR if it is 'prescribed by law', and the law in question is formulated with sufficient clarity to be foreseeable. The provisions of domestic law which were used by the tax authorities to tax the gifts to the association Les Témoins de Jéhovah were not sufficiently foreseeable because they were too vague and were not detailed enough. The ECtHR adjudicated similar religious issues in *Association des Chevaliers du Lotus D'Or v. France*[21] and the judgment in *Assemblée Chrétienne Des Témoins de Jéhovah d'Anderlecht and Others v. Belgium*[22] involving a denial of a tax objection that lacked a reasonable and objective justification.

In 2014, in the case of the *Church of Jesus Christ of Latter-Day Saints v. the United Kingdom*,[23] the ECtHR decided another case involving an allegation of discrimination based on religion, but the case was rejected on the merits, because discrimination had not been proven. The legislation complained of was found to be neutral:

> 35. In conclusion, insofar as any difference of treatment between religious groups in comparable situations can be said to have been established in relation to tax exemption of places of worship, such difference of treatment had a reasonable and objective justification. In particular, the contested measure pursued a legitimate aim in the public interest and there was a reasonable relationship of proportionality between that aim and the means used to achieve it. The domestic authorities cannot be considered as having exceeded the margin of appreciation available to them in this context, even having due regard to the duties incumbent on the State by virtue of Article 9 of the Convention in relation to its exercise of its regulatory powers in the sphere of religious freedom. It follows that the Court does not find that the applicant Church has suffered discrimination in breach of Article 14 of the Convention, taken in conjunction with Article 9.
>
> 36. In conclusion, and subject to the doubts expressed above, the Court declares the complaint under Article 14 taken in conjunction with Article 9 admissible, but finds no violation.

21. Application no. 50615/07.
22. Application no. 20165/20.
23. Application no. 7552/09.

11.4 'NATIONAL OR SOCIAL ORIGIN, ASSOCIATION WITH A NATIONAL MINORITY, PROPERTY, BIRTH'

Arguably, tax residence has been interpreted as falling within the ECHR meaning of 'national or social origin'. In the 1990 case *Darby v. Sweden*,[24] a case involving a loss of a right to a tax concession following a change in tax residence, the complaint was entertained as a case involving the right to property and freedom from discrimination. Darby was a Finnish doctor of British origin who was considered to be Finnish resident for Double Tax Treaty purpose but was not formally registered as a Swedish permanent resident. Dr Darby complained of an amendment to Swedish law that had the effect of divesting him qua non-resident from the right to claim a church tax exemption. Dr Darby claimed discrimination and the ECtHR unanimously agreed with him:

> 32. It appears first that Dr Darby can claim to have been, as regards his right to an exemption under the Dissenters Tax Act, in a situation similar to that of other non-members of the Church who were formally registered as residents in Sweden.
>
> 33. As regards the aim of this difference in the treatment of residents and non-residents, it is worth noting the following. According to the Government Bill (1951:175) which gave rise to the Dissenters Tax Act, the reason why the right to exemption was reserved for persons formally registered as residents was that the case for reduction could not be argued with the same force in regard to persons who were not so registered as it could in regard to those who were, and that the procedure would be more complicated if the reduction was to apply to non-residents (see paragraph 22 above).
>
> The Government Bill (1978/79:58) containing the tax-law amendments that brought about this complaint did not mention the special situation which the amendments would create for non-residents under the Dissenters Tax Act (see paragraph 20 above). In fact, the Government stated at the hearing before the Court that they did not argue that the distinction in treatment had a legitimate aim.
>
> 34. In view of the above, the measure complained of cannot be seen as having had any legitimate aim under the Convention. Accordingly, there has been a violation of Article 14 of the Convention taken together with Article 1 of Protocol No. 1 (art. 14 + P1-1).

11.5 'ON ANY GROUND... OR OTHER STATUS'

Given that certain tax concessions are linked to marital status, cases based on complaints based on marital status were predictable. The 1984 tax case *Lindsay v. the United Kingdom*[25] analysed a mismatch existing between the tax treatment of married persons and the tax treatment of cohabitees. The complaint was dismissed because the unequal tax treatment was held to fall within the State signatory's wide margin of appreciation:

24. Application no. 11581/85.
25. Application no. 11089/84.

> ... The Commission also finds that the test of proportionality is satisfied in the present case ... the application as it concerns discrimination on the ground of religion does not reveal any difference in treatment between persons married in a religious service and persons married in a civil ceremony ... The Commission considers however that the provisions whereby a married couple is taxed more heavily than unmarried cohabitees cannot be said to interfere with their right to respect for private and family life ... .[26]

The 2002 case of *SA. Dangeville v. France*[27] incorporated a complaint that a French VAT amnesty discriminated against tax compliant taxpayers because it gave tax defaulters an unfair advantage. The French company alleged that discrimination had been compounded by the authorities' failure to take action to refund the sums which the law-abiding taxpayers had paid in error. An independent violation of Article 1 of Protocol No. 1 (the right to property) had already been found, so the allegation of discrimination was set aside:

> 63. The applicant company alleged a violation of Article 14 of the Convention taken in conjunction with Article 1 of Protocol No. 1. Article 14 provides:
>
> ...
>
> 64. The applicant company submitted that by adopting the administrative circular abandoning proceedings against companies that had not paid the VAT, the authorities had been guilty of discrimination by giving those who had defaulted on their tax an advantage over law-abiding taxpayers; that discrimination had been compounded by the authorities' failure to take action to refund the sums which the law-abiding taxpayers had paid in error.
>
> 66. In the light of its finding in paragraphs 61 and 62 above, the Court considers that no separate examination of this complaint is necessary.

The ECtHR's 2006 landmark judgment in *Burden and Burden v. the United Kingdom*[28] is probably the ECtHR's most important tax discrimination case because it is frequently quoted outside of tax circles too. The Burdens alleged that the British Government was discriminating in favour of gay couples. The Burden case involved a challenge brought by two elderly spinster siblings who complained of the severity of inheritance tax. The Burdens found out that because the fair value of the family home was in the region of STG 875,000, the surviving sibling would not be able to afford to

26. The application comprised challenges on the basis of discrimination on grounds of religion and interference with the right to family life. On this point *see Hubaux v. Belgium*, 'Dans la présente affaire, le requérant compare la situation des couples mariés avec celle d'un homme et d'une femme ayant les mêmes revenus mais qui vivent ensemble sans être mariés. Or, sur ce point, la Commission rappelle qu'elle a déjà considéré (voir n° 11089, déc. précitée) que ces deux situations n'étaient pas comparables du fait que, même si dans certains domaines, la notion de "cohabitant" était reconnue, il existait entre un couple marié et un ménage de fait des différences fondamentales notamment quant au statut juridique des personnes mariées et quant aux effets légaux du mariage, ce dernier se caractérisant par un ensemble de droits et obligations non applicable au ménage de fait. En conséquence, la Commission conclut que la situation de couple marié que vivent le requérant et son épouse n'est pas comparable à celle d'un ménage de fait. Sur la base du grief du requérant elle n'aperçoit donc aucune apparence de violation de l'article 14 de la Convention lu en combinaison avec l'article 1 du Protocole additionnel (art. 14 + P1-1).'
27. Application no. 36677/97.
28. Application no. 13378/05.

pay inheritance tax and would be forced to sell her home. The Burdens felt discriminated against because in similar situations to theirs, civil partners (same-sex couples included) were exempt from inheritance tax. The Burdens argued that British Inheritance Tax created a disproportionate burden on them which was unfairly discriminatory. The ECtHR denied their claim of discrimination combined with the right to property. The ECtHR held that it is for the national authorities to assess the aims and means of the taxes they impose and that States enjoy wide margin of appreciation in this field. The ECtHR noted that:

> ... the national authorities are in principle better placed than the international judge to appreciate what is in the public interest on social or economic grounds. The Court will generally respect the legislature's policy choice in this field unless it is 'manifestly without reasonable foundation'.

Laudably, in its application of Article 14 ECHR, the ECHR is very protective of the disabled acknowledging that they benefit from an implied 'status' forming a suspect ground of discrimination. In the 2021 case of *Ryser v. Switzerland*,[29] a case involving a tax charge imposed on persons who do not provide compulsory military service, the ECtHR contrasted the situation of conscientious objectors with those who are unfit to serve finding a violation:

> 61. En conclusion, la Cour est d'avis que la situation du requérant ne se distingue pas suffisamment de l'affaire Glor, précitée, pour arriver à un résultat différent. À la lumière des circonstances de l'espèce, la justification objective de la distinction que les autorités internes ont opérée, notamment entre les personnes inaptes au service et exonérées de la taxe litigieuse et les personnes inaptes au service et néanmoins assujetties à la taxe, n'apparaît pas raisonnable. La Cour note également que le requérant était nettement désavantagé par rapport aux objecteurs de conscience qui, bien qu'aptes au service, pouvaient effectuer un service de remplacement civil et, ainsi, éviter de payer la taxe litigieuse.

The *Ryser* case echoed the conclusion of another case involving swiss military tax, the Chamber judgment in *Glor v. Switzerland*,[30] a case involving a diabetic:

> 96. In conclusion, the Court considers that in the present case the domestic authorities failed to strike a fair balance between the protection of the interests of the community and respect for the Convention rights and freedoms of the applicant, who was not allowed to do his military service, or civilian service instead, but was nevertheless required to pay the exemption tax. It takes into account the particular circumstances of the case, including: the amount payable – which was not a negligible sum for the applicant – and the number of years over which it was charged; the fact that the applicant was willing to do military or civilian service; the lack of provision under Swiss law for forms of service suitable for people in the applicant's situation, and the minor role the tax plays nowadays in terms of preventing or compensating for the avoidance of compulsory national service.

29. Application no. 23040/13.
30. Application no. 13444/04.

11.6 MARGIN OF APPRECIATION

Most of the unsuccessful Article 14 ECHR tax cases floundered on the gates of the margin of appreciation defence, but Chapter 1 explained that the concept of margin of appreciation appears to be subject to special 'Article 14 rules'. The ECtHR's approach to margin appreciation evolved with time, in the *Burden* escalation especially.

The margin of appreciation and discriminatory taxation were discussed at length in the Burden Judgment, but the Chambers took different approaches to it. While the Fourth Chamber largely based its dismissal of the case on the basis of margin of appreciation, the Grand Chamber only mentioned it, dismissing the case principally on the basis of the comparability test. Judge Bratza's concurring opinion brought the divergence under the spotlight.

The more recent judgments of the ECtHR suggest a more balanced application of the margin of appreciation test than the earlier cases. In their dissenting opinion in the Fourth Section Judgment in *Burden*, Judges Garlicki and Bonello had suggested a particular approach to margin of appreciation in discrimination cases:

> We do agree that there must be a wide margin of appreciation offered to the national authorities in tax matters. We further agree that any system of taxation, to be workable, has to use broad categorisations to distinguish between different groups of taxpayers. We would also be prepared to agree that, with regard to tax matters, there may be some kind of presumption that the solutions adopted by the national legislature remain within this margin of appreciation. Such presumption would mean that it is, in principle, the applicant who must demonstrate that the application of the tax legislation in his or her case exceeded the State's margin of appreciation and led to unreasonable und unjustified effects.
>
> However, this 'burden of proof' is not unlimited. In our opinion, once an applicant is able to demonstrate that the way in which the tax legislation was applied created a situation of apparent hardship or injustice, the onus shifts towards the Government, who must then show that there were good reasons for their actions. Furthermore, if our Court decides to accept that such a situation of apparent hardship or injustice remains compatible with the Convention standards, it must give a full explanation as to how it applied the 'margin of appreciation' concept.

Subsequent judgments of the ECtHR appear to have taken the advice of the dissenting judges in *Burden* in their stride. Thus, in the 2016 judgment in the case of *Guberina v. Croatia*,[31] the approach adopted was that suggested by the dissenting judges in *Burden*.

The *Guberina* case involved eligibility to an exemption from Real Property Transfer Tax Act. The exemption applied to citizens who bought their first real property to solve their housing needs. The applicant complained that he was discriminated against because the tax exemption rules failed to distinguish his situation from the general situation falling under the relevant provisions of the tax exemption. The

31. Application no. 23682/13.

taxpayer contended that the exemption framework did not take into account the additional infrastructure required by persons with special needs.

While conceding that, in designing tax policies, state signatories have a wide margin of appreciation, the ECtHR held that in any case, however, irrespective of the scope of the State's margin of appreciation the final decision as to the observance of the Convention's requirements rests with the Court. In addition, it held that, in cases of unequal treatment, the rule of burden of proof is on the State. Once the applicant has shown a difference in treatment, it is for the Government to show that it was justified.

The Court found that Croatia had failed to bring an objective and reasonable justification for its failure to take into account the inequality pertinent to the applicant's situation when making an assessment of his tax obligation. The Court held that there had been a violation of Article 14 (discrimination) in conjunction with Article 1 of Protocol No. 1 (right to property).

The approach taken in *Guberina* was consolidated in the 2019 case of *J.D. and A v. the United Kingdom*,[32] a claim of unequal tax treatment based on disability and gender. The ECtHR held in Article 14 cases that the margin of appreciation test was to be applied in a different way to how it was applied in an Article 1 Protocol 1 context:

> 88. However, as the Court has stressed in the context of Article 14 in conjunction with Article 1 Protocol 1, although the margin of appreciation in the context of general measures of economic or social policy is, in principle, wide, such measures must nevertheless be implemented in a manner that does not violate the prohibition of discrimination as set out in the Convention and complies with the requirement of proportionality (see Fábián, cited above, § 115, with further references). Thus, even a wide margin in the sphere of economic or social policy does not justify the adoption of laws or practices that would violate the prohibition of discrimination. Hence, in that context the Court has limited its acceptance to respect the legislature's policy choice as not 'manifestly without reasonable foundation' to circumstances where an alleged difference in treatment resulted from a transitional measure forming part of a scheme carried out in order to correct an inequality ... .

11.7 CONCLUSIONS

The ECtHR's tax judgments on tax discrimination are humane and considerate with the ECtHR taking the initiative of flexing the margin of appreciation test to ensure the standard of fairness required by the spirit of the ECHR. Predictably, the ECtHR takes a protectionist approach to minorities and the fact that the successful cases were those submitted by minorities does not come as a surprise. When compared to the merits of the tax discrimination cases decided by the CJEU and the European Court of Justice (ECJ), the merits of the tax discrimination cases that have reached the ECtHR were fairly uncomplicated. As yet, the ECtHR has not had the opportunity to determine

32. Applications nos. 32949/17 and 34614/17.

matters involving discrimination caused by State Aid, harmful tax practices, discriminatory approaches to transfer pricing, and preferential tax regimes. Whereas the complexities of international taxation have breached Article 1 of Protocol 1 ECHR, Article 6 and other articles, cases over Article 14 ECHR have dealt with much more mundane matters, at least for the time being.

CHAPTER 12

Limitation on Use of Restrictions on Rights

ARTICLE 18
Limitation on use of restrictions on rights

The restrictions permitted under this Convention to the said rights and freedoms shall not be applied for any purpose other than those for which they have been prescribed.

12.1 PRIDE OF PLACE

When it comes to Article 18 ECHR, the tax judgments of the ECtHR take pride of place. Taxation is one of the Contracting State's mightiest prerogatives, and the zealous exercise of oppressive public prerogatives may be tainted by ulterior motives. Thus, in a tax context, the safeguard offered by Article 18 ECHR becomes extremely important. Not surprisingly, the ECtHR's leading cases on Article 18 ECHR are tax cases and the most interesting cases have originated from interesting jurisdictions.

12.2 FROM RUSSIA AND AZERBAIJAN

The 2016 judgment in the case of *Rasul Jafarov v. Azerbaijan*[1] discussed previously contemplated an Article 18 ECHR complaint. Rasul, a human rights activist, alleged that his arrest and pre-trial detention for a suite of offences that comprised tax fraud had not been justified and had been carried out in bad faith and that his rights had been restricted for purposes other than those prescribed in the ECHR. The ECtHR concluded that the very particular circumstances of the case indicated that the actual purpose of the measures taken against applicant was to silence and punish the applicant for his activities in the area of human rights. In the light of these considerations, the ECtHR

1. Application no. 69981/14.

found that the restriction of the applicant's liberty was imposed for purposes other than bringing him before a competent legal authority on reasonable suspicion of having committed an offence. The ECtHR held that there was sufficient basis for finding a violation of Article 18 of ECHR, taken in conjunction with Article 5 ECHR.

Article 18 ECHR featured in the Yukos suite of cases too. Article 18 ECHR was cited in the case of *OAO Neftyanaya Kompaniya Yukos v. Russia*[2] when the company argued that the circumstances of the tax assessment and enforcement proceedings as well as the allegedly 'political' motivation behind the prosecution of Mr M. Khodorkovskiy and other owners and senior officials of the applicant company showed that the proceedings against it, taken as a whole, were abusive in that the State clearly wanted to destroy the company and to take control of its assets. While explaining that Article 18 ECHR does not have an autonomous role and that a violation can only arise where the right or freedom concerned is subject to restrictions permitted under the ECHR, the ECtHR pointed out that in order to hold a Member State liable under Article 18 ECHR an applicant should be able to furnish the ECtHR with an incontrovertible and direct proof in support of his or her allegations applying a particularly rigid test:

> 665 ... Apart from the findings already made earlier, the Court finds no indication of any further issues or defects in the proceedings against the applicant company which would enable it conclude that there has been a breach of Article 18 of the Convention on account of the applicant company's claim that the State had misused those proceedings with a view to destroying the company and taking control of its assets.
>
> 666. To sum up, the Court finds that there has been no violation of Article 18 of the Convention, taken in conjunction with Article 1 of Protocol No. 1, on account of the alleged disguised expropriation of the company's property and the alleged intentional destruction of the company itself.

Subsequently, similar allegations were made in *Khodorkovskiy and Lebedev v. Russia*[3] where the long list of complaints included a complaint under Article 18 ECHR. Applicants complained about the alleged political motivation for their criminal prosecution and punishment for tax evasion. Complainants referred to Article 18 ECHR read in conjunction with Articles 5, 6, 7 and 8 ECHR. Predictably, the ECtHR referred to its conclusions in the Yukos case with which it shared similar merits. Emphasising that successful cases under Article 18 ECHR were unique rather than rare. The ECtHR emphasised that the ECHR rests on the general assumption that public authorities in the Member States act in good faith. That assumption is rebuttable in theory, but it is difficult to overcome in practice: the applicant alleging that his rights and freedoms were limited for an improper reason must convincingly show that the real aim of the authorities was not the same as that proclaimed (or as can be reasonably inferred from the context). Worryingly, the ECtHR added that it required 'a very exacting standard of proof to such allegations':

2. Application no. 14902/04.
3. Applications nos. 11082/06 and 13772/05.

> 903. However, the Court cannot accept this approach. It considers that even where the appearances speak in favour of the applicant's claim of improper motives, the burden of proof must remain with him or her. It confirms its position in Khodorkovskiy (no. 1) that the applicant alleging bad faith of the authorities must 'convincingly show' that their actions were driven by improper motives. Thus, the standard of proof in such cases is high. Otherwise the Court would have to find violations in every high-profile case where the applicant's status, wealth, reputation, etc. gives rise to a suspicion that the driving force behind his or her prosecution was improper.

The ECtHR added that 'high political status does not grant immunity'. Although the ECtHR was prepared to admit that some political groups or government officials had their own reasons to push for the applicants' prosecution, the fact per se was insufficient for it to conclude that the applicants would not have been convicted otherwise. Elements of 'improper motivation' which may exist in the present case did not make the applicants' prosecution illegitimate 'from the beginning to the end'. Consequently, the ECtHR held that the criminal proceedings at the heart of the present case did not amount to a violation of Article 18 ECHR.

The ECtHR returned to the same matter in the case of *Khodorkovskiy and Lebedev v. Russia* (no. 2),[4] a case relating to a slightly different set of facts. In *Khodorkovskiy and Lebedev v. Russia* (no. 2), the focus of the Article 18 ECHR complaint was specific arrests. Given its previous pronouncements on the matter, the ECtHR dismissed all Article 18 ECHR complaints.

12.3 CONCLUSIONS

Uncharacteristically, Harris, O' Boyle and Warbick were quite critical of the ECtHR's Article 18 ECHR observations in the *Yukos* tax cases:

> The Article 18 cases heard by the Court in recent years (2012-2013) clearly raise issues of considerable concern, their political backdrop and sensitivity being obvious. With the court's approach so heavily dependent on the policy issues noted in this Chapter, a Grand Chamber ruling on Article 18 would be welcome.[5]

The same critical stance was taken in the concurring opinion in *Tchankotadze v. Georgia*[6] recommending a revisitation of the prohibitive standards set by Article 18 ECHR case-law. The standard of proof for Article 18 ECHR violations was found to be prohibitively high, resulting in a practically impossible burden of proof for Article 18 ECHR violations, the concurring opinion suggesting that it would be more consistent with the spirit of Article 18 ECHR to allow a prima facie showing and burden shifting.

One gets a feeling that the Article 18 ECHR component of the *Yukos* judgments went too far creating a prohibitive standard of proof. The ECtHR's strong acceptance of complaints under other articles must have diluted the practical importance of the

4. Applications nos. 51111/07 and 42757/07.
5. David Harris, Michael O'Boyle, Ed Bates and Carla Buckley, *Law of the European Convention on Human Rights* (3rd ed.), Oxford, OUP, p. 861.
Application no. 15256/05.

Article 18 ECHR complaint. Nonetheless, the Article 18 ECHR dicta are bound to return to haunt taxpayers. Interferences to human rights caused by improperly motivated tax policies are extremely dangerous and should be outlawed under the lawfulness criteria pervading the ECHR.

CHAPTER 13

Admissibility Criteria

ARTICLE 35
Admissibility criteria

1. The Court may only deal with the matter after all domestic remedies have been exhausted, according to the generally recognised rules of international law, and within a period of four months from the date on which the final decision was taken.

2. The Court shall not deal with any application submitted under Article 34 that

(a) is anonymous; or

(b) is substantially the same as a matter that has already been examined by the Court or has already been submitted to another procedure of international investigation or settlement and contains no relevant new information.

3. The Court shall declare inadmissible any individual application submitted under Article 34 if it considers that:

(a) the application is incompatible with the provisions of the Convention or the Protocols thereto, manifestly ill-founded, or an abuse of the right of individual application; or

(b) the applicant has not suffered a significant disadvantage, unless respect for human rights as defined in the Convention and the Protocols thereto requires an examination of the application on the merits.

4. The Court shall reject any application which it considers inadmissible under this Article. It may do so at any stage of the proceedings.

13.1 THE STRONG-WALL

Those of us who submitted and had to evaluate tax complaints to the ECHR are all too familiar with the importance of Article 35 ECHR. At times one forms the opinion that, in the tax sphere, Article 35 ECHR has been construed as a prohibitive threshold. Under the single-judge system, some extremely interesting tax complaints have been dismissed on the basis of Article 35 ECHR. The death-knell of many dignified tax complaints has been signalled in a telegraphic one-page letter from the ECtHR[1] containing a brief reference to Article 35 ECHR.

Tax cases are, by their very nature, complex and the body of case law relating to Article 1 of Protocol 1 ECHR has created a very tight admissibility filter. In the absence of detailed motivated decisions, it is impossible to tell why so many tax complaints are floundering in the dark shallow waters of Article 35 ECHR, but some of the published admissibility decisions are indicative of the general direction of travel.

13.2 EXHAUSTION OF DOMESTIC REMEDIES, THE JUDGMENT IN *ATEV V. BULGARIA*[2]

The feasibility of tax complaints has been significantly curtailed by the ECtHR's approach towards domestic remedies. There have been instances when the ECtHR was prepared to treat, stretched 'last ditch' remedies contained in generic national laws as an alternative remedy to a human rights complaint.

The dangerous precedent set in the 2014 case of *Atev v. Bulgaria*[3] is worrying because it tends to reverse inroads made in the *Bulves*[4] line of judgments dealing with the right to recover credit for input VAT. The merits of the case in *Atev* were very similar to those in the *Bulves* line of cases; Bulgaria had declined to grant credit for input VAT because of defaults caused by third-party suppliers.

In the *Atev* case, the ECtHR acknowledged common denominators with *Bulves*, but dismissed the complaint as manifestly ill-founded because of non-exhaustion of domestic remedies. The ECtHR concluded that, instead of proceeding against the State with a human rights complaint, Atev should have sued his supplier in tort:

> 36. The Court further notes that in contrast to the case of Bulves AD, where albeit with some delay, the applicant company's supplier had paid the VAT due on the chain of supplies and for that reason the refusal to allow the applicant company to deduct the input VAT was not justified by any indication of negative repercussions on the State budget (see Bulves AD, cited above, §§ 67-68), in the present case the absence of the supplier's accounting records objectively impeded a proper verification of these circumstances. In this regard the interference with the applicant

1. For a critique of this practice, *see* the separate opinion of Judge Albuquerque in *Centre for Legal Resources on Behalf of Valentin Câmpeanu v. Romania*, Application no. 47848/08.
2. Application no. 39689/05.
3. Application no. 39689/05.
4. Baker described this case as a case similar to *Bulves* which reached 'different conclusion'. Philip Baker, 'Some Recent Decision of the European Court of Human Rights in Taxation Matters', European Taxation (February/March 2015) p. 109.

> company's interests in the case of Bulves AD was entirely attributable to the authorities' automatic approach and not to the supplier's conduct. In contrast to the case of Bulves AD in the case at hand the actions of the authorities pursued the public interest of maintaining fiscal stability and securing the collection of taxes, which is inherent in any taxation system. The Court considers that in so far as the interference with the applicant's rights in the present case was triggered by the supplier's failure to maintain diligently his accounting records and resulted in a similarly automatic approach of the authorities towards the applicant, this situation was further balanced by the possibility of the applicant to seek and obtain compensation from his supplier within the framework of civil proceedings for damages. For the Court, and having in mind the wide margin of appreciation given to States in the area of taxation matters, that suffices for the conclusion that in the case at hand, a fair balance was struck between the protection of the applicant's rights and the demands of the general interest.

Unfortunately, the approach in *Atev* was confirmed in the more recent case of *Alojzy Formela v. Poland*,[5] a judgment that merits further analysis for its particularly *pro auctoritate* approach. Formela's case was another case involving a claim for credit for input VAT; his claim had been rejected because it turned out that his supplier was not validly registered for VAT. The ECtHR articulated the reasons which distinguished the merits in Formela with the merits in Bulves:

> 98. Moreover, the Court finds that, unlike in the case of 'Bulves' AD, the domestic authorities undertook a thorough review of the relevant circumstances, free from arbitrariness, which resulted in a finding that there had been a failure on the part of the applicant to meet relevant statutory requirements for entitlement to VAT deduction.

It went on to analyse the availability of domestic remedies. Although there was no question that Formela had complied with his own statutory VAT obligations, the ECtHR noted that the legal issue which was at the core of the case was whether the application of clearly established rules of Polish VAT law on the applicant imposed an excessive burden on him. The fact that Formela could have sued his supplier in damages but failed to do so was fatal:

> 124. The Court observes, nevertheless, that the situation was balanced by the existence of a remedy within the framework of civil proceedings for damages, as invoked by the Government, allowing the applicant to seek and obtain compensation from his supplier (see paragraphs 80–83 above). In the Atev case, in view of the wide margin of appreciation given to States in the area of taxation matters, that sufficed for the conclusion that a fair balance had been struck between the protection of the applicant's rights and the demands of the general interest (see, Atev, cited above, § 36 and in contrast with Euromak, cited above, § 48).
>
> 125. In view of all the above considerations, the Court finds that the complaint in respect of the applicant's transactions with K. is manifestly ill-founded and must be rejected in accordance with Article 35 §§ 3 (a) and 4 of the Convention.

The view that an action in tort may serve as an effective domestic remedy to the exclusion of the right to pursue an individual complaint to the ECtHR has major

5. Application no. 31651/08.

ramifications. The existence of the availability of an action in tort could be used to exclude several human rights complaints imaginable. Even the victim of torture could have his complaint dismissed on the grounds that he should have sued his torturers in tort before resorting to the ECtHR.

Judgments in the *Atev* line are undesirable because they create unnecessary filters and lengthy procedures which exercise a chilling effect. The need for fiscal stability does not justify the creation of situations where persons acting in good faith are denied what is due to them by law. The *Formela* and *Atev* cases may be contrasted with the 2019 case in *Alexandru-Mihai Pop and Others v. Romania*[6] when the right to claim a tax refund had been lost because complainants had not used an ad hoc administrative procedure and the case of *Düriye Karalar v. Turkey*[7] when the applicant had not respected a peremptory term. 'Stop-gap' actions in damages based on generic remedies in tort can never serve as a substitute for a human rights complaint.

13.3 'SUBSTANTIALLY THE SAME AS A MATTER THAT HAS ALREADY BEEN EXAMINED BY THE COURT'

Over the past sixty years, the ECtHR's vast body of tax case law has determined a multitude of issues with some judgments being couched in generic terms. Sweeping statements contained in the judgments in *Wasa Omsesidigit, Kaira, Huitson, Plaisier B.V, Ferrazzini* and *Cacciato* may have led the premature death of important cases. Some unpublished complaints relating to tax treaty rights and right to recover input VAT must have fallen victim to dicta contained in judgments where the ECtHR expressed its lack of appetite to cause tremors in the tax sphere.

13.4 'MANIFESTLY ILL-FOUNDED ... NOT SUFFERED A SIGNIFICANT DISADVANTAGE'

The ECtHR uses the term 'manifestly ill-founded' quite liberally, and previous chapters have described how some respectable complaints have been dismissed as manifestly ill-founded. In a tax context, the words 'did not suffer a significant disadvantage' lend themselves to very dangerous situations too. The particularities of taxation combined with some inflexible dicta from the ECtHR create a restrictive environment for tax complaints.

13.5 CONCLUSIONS

Judgments on margin of appreciation are extremely restrictive and have led to a dismissal of a significant percentage of tax complaints. Interpreting Article 35 ECHR in the way it has been interpreted in *Atev* and *Formela* risks creating further restrictions risking the exclusion of most, if not all, tax cases with a property element. The ECHR

6. Applications nos. 54494/11, 67699/11 and 21251/12.
7. Application no. 1964/07.

is not there only to protect persons who find themselves in the extremely desperate situations which Khodorkovsky, Lebedev, Yanusov and Rasul found themselves in but is meant to protect citizens from less egregious incursions into their human rights, persons like Euromak Meta Doo who were simply suing for a tax credit they were legally entitled too. In this context, the 2022 decision in *Krayeva* is encouraging. Krayeva's predicament was due to an error committed by a third party because she was held liable to pay a disproportionate penalty only because she relied on an incorrect invoice provided by a supplier. Although, presumably, Krayeva could have acted in tort, the ECtHR felt that it had to strike down the punitive measure in question because it went beyond what was strictly necessary.

CHAPTER 14

Freedom of Movement

ARTICLE 2 OF PROTOCOL 4
Freedom of movement

1. Everyone lawfully within the territory of a State shall, within that territory, have the right to liberty of movement and freedom to choose his residence.

2. Everyone shall be free to leave any country, including his own.

3. No restrictions shall be placed on the exercise of these rights other than such as are in accordance with law and are necessary in a democratic society in the interests of national security or public safety, for the maintenance of ordre public, for the prevention of crime, for the protection of health or morals, or for the protection of the rights and freedoms of others.

4. The rights set forth in paragraph 1 may also be subject, in particular areas, to restrictions imposed in accordance with law and justified by the public interest in a democratic society.

14.1 THE LEADING CASE *RIENER V. BULGARIA*

In the tax sphere there is a great deal of awareness of the fact that taxation can interfere with freedom of movement. Unlike the ECtHR, the CJEU has been kept busy with tax cases involving freedom of movement complaints.[1] Arguably, the Treaty on the Functioning of the European Union provides more effective means of redress relating

1. Including especially Case C-9/02, *Hughes de Lasteyrie du Saillant v. Ministère de l'Économie, des Finances et de l'Industrie*, when the ECJ considered a French exit tax on unrealised income as a hindrance to the free movement of capital. The fact that a taxpayer was subjected to a disadvantageous tax treatment solely on the grounds that he decided to avail himself of a right vested in him by the EU Treaty was held to incompatible with EU law on the grounds that it discriminated between those individuals who chose to retain their residence in France and those individuals who decided to transfer their residence to another EU Member State.

to tax measures restricting freedom of movement but the role of the ECHR cannot be overlooked, especially in movements from States that are not EU Member States.

The ECtHR's leading case on the matter is the 2006 case of *Riener v. Bulgaria*[2] referring to facts in issue that occurred before Bulgaria joined the EU. Mrs Riener had dual nationality, Austrian and Bulgarian and was the director of an Austrian Company which was registered as a trader on the Bulgarian Trade Register. Mrs Riener's company was heavily indebted to the Bulgarian tax authorities, and the Bulgarian Authorities banned Mrs Riener from leaving the country until she settled all her tax debts. Thus, Riener became a tax hostage of the Republic of Bulgaria and was unable to join her family in Austria. She tried to contest the executive act relating to her impediment of departure from Bulgaria in terms of Bulgarian law, but she lost her case at first and second instance. Riener submitted a complaint under Article 2 of Protocol 4 ECHR read in conjunction with Article 13 ECHR. The ECtHR upheld her complaints on both counts.

The ECtHR observed that Article 2 of Protocol No. 4 guarantees to any person a right to liberty of movement, including the right to leave any country for such other country of the person's choice to which he or she may be admitted. Any measure restricting that right must be lawful, pursue one of the legitimate aims and strike a fair balance between the public interest and the individual's rights. The ECtHR proceeded to stress-test Riener's travel ban against the parameters set forth by the ECHR.

Clearly, the prohibition against the applicant leaving Bulgaria constituted an interference by a public authority with her right to leave the country, as guaranteed by Article 2 § 2 of Protocol No. 4 to the Convention.

The Bulgarian courts had established that Riener owed Bulgaria a significant amount in taxes implying that travel ban had legal basis in Bulgarian law and that it pursued a legitimate aim, the collection of taxes. The crux of the matter was whether the travel ban was proportional. The fact that the travel ban had been retained in force for a lengthy period of time was deemed to be abusive:

> 126. Contrary to the respondent Government's assertion, the periodic 'confirmations' of the travel ban were not based on analysis of the applicant's attitude, on information about her resources or any concrete indication that the chances for recovery would be jeopardised if she were allowed to leave the country. The fact that the applicant had a family abroad was not taken into consideration. Neither the administrative decisions related to the travel ban, nor the courts' judgments upholding them contained any proportionality analysis, either before or after the entry into force of Protocol No. 4 to the Convention in respect of Bulgaria (see paragraphs 17, 19, 23, 28, 34, 36, 37 and 39-44 above).
>
> 127 ... The only grounds on which the travel ban could be lifted were payment, submission of sufficient security (apparently understood as security covering the full amount) or, as it happened in the event, extinction of the debt by prescription (see paragraphs 36, 37, 39 and 57-66 above). In these circumstances the travel ban was in reality an automatic measure of indefinite duration. The yearly 'confirmations' were merely information notes certifying that the applicant had not paid,

2. Application no. 46343/99.

with the automatic consequence of the travel ban remaining in place, without examination of its justification and proportionality (see paragraph 41 above).

The ECtHR concluded that the travel ban's lack proportionality, its lack of clarity in the relevant law and practice and the fact that the travel ban was maintained over a lengthy period implied that the Bulgarian travel ban breached Article 2 of Protocol 4 ECHR.

14.2 THE PROGENY OF *RIENER*

More recently, issues pertinent to Article 2 of Protocol 4 ECHR were raised in the case of *Yunusova and Yunusov v. Azerbaijan* (no. 2)[3] a case involving, *inter alia*, a trial for large-scale tax investigation. Pending the outcome of the trial, Yunusovs' passports were seized, implying that the Yunusovs could not leave the country. The Yunusovs filed an application that comprised a complaint under Article 2 of Protocol No. 4 ECHR, and their complaint was upheld:

> 162. The Court observes that there was no formal decision taken by the authorities to impose a travel ban on the applicants. At the same time, they were de facto unable to leave the country as a result of the seizure of their passports. In this connection, the Court reiterates that a measure by means of which an individual is dispossessed of an identity document such as, for example, a passport, amounts to an interference with the exercise of liberty of movement (see Napijalo v. Croatia, no. 66485/01, § 69, 13 November 2003, with further references). However, the Court notes that it has already found under Article 8 that the search and seizure of various documents, including the applicants' passports, did not pursue a 'legitimate aim'. In these circumstances, the Court finds that there is no need to examine separately the applicants' complaint under Article 2 of Protocol No. 4 to the Convention (compare Penchevi v. Bulgaria, no. 77818/12, § 77, 10 February 2015).

14.3 CONCLUSIONS

Unlike the CJEU, the ECtHR has not been called to determine whether the right of freedom of movement applies to persons who are not physical persons. Interesting cases involving corporations could arise in the sphere of exit taxation. Nonetheless, it is important to keep in mind that the Conventional right to freedom of movement safeguards the right of the person wanting to move and not the movement of his property. In the 1985 tax case of *S. v. Sweden*,[4] the Commission had ruled that the right to take property out of a country without restriction is not a right embodied in the right to leave the country.

---

3. Application no. 68817/14.
4. Application no. 10653/83.

CHAPTER 15

Non Bis in Idem

ARTICLE 4 OF PROTOCOL 7
Right not to be tried or punished twice

1. No one shall be liable to be tried or punished again in criminal proceedings under the jurisdiction of the same State for an offence for which he has already been finally acquitted or convicted in accordance with the law and penal procedure of that State.

2. The provisions of the preceding paragraph shall not prevent the reopening of the case in accordance with the law and penal procedure of the State concerned, if there is evidence of new or newly discovered facts, or if there has been a fundamental defect in the previous proceedings, which could affect the outcome of the case.

3. No derogation from this Article shall be made under Article 15 of the Convention.

15.1 TREMORS FROM THE HARD-CORE OF PUBLIC PREROGATIVES

Tax judgments of the ECtHR relating to the *Non Bis in Idem* principle have sent shock waves across the legal systems of the Contracting States. Liberal interpretations that may have come as an answer to the inflexibility of the *Ferrazzini* dictum led to a radical approach towards the legal treatment of tax administrative penalties. The fact that the ECtHR has characterised most tax administrative penalties as criminal charges within the meaning of Article 6 ECHR implies that tax administrative penalties are treated as 'criminal charges' for the purposes of all the articles of the ECHR, including especially Article 4 of Protocol 7 ECHR on *Non Bis in Idem*.

The re-characterisation of tax penalties into criminal charges implies that Contracting States are severely constrained with respect to design of their tax administrative penalty regimes. Article 4 of Protocol 7 ECHR creates tight parameters governing multiple criminal charges, tax penalties re-characterised as criminal charges included, for the same default. In practice, this means that, in most cases, a person who has been punished with a tax administrative penalty for a default should not be independently prosecuted criminally for the same default. The fact that such a radical change had to originate from the hard-core of public prerogatives is ironic.

15.2 BREAKTHROUGH

The turning point came from the periphery of tax law, customs law. Although the issue of *Non Bis in Idem* in tax matters had been anticipated in a 1999 case,[1] the real breakthrough came in 2009 in the case of *Ruotsalainen v. Finland*. The merits of the Ruotsalainen case were quite simple explaining why its outcome resonated.

While driving his pickup van across the Finnish Border, Jukka Ruotsalainen was stopped by the border police who discovered that Ruotsalainen was carrying diesel oil without paying the correct amount of additional tax. The Finnish customs authorities punished Ruotsalainen for his omission inflicting an administrative penalty of EUR 121 via a summary penal order. Ruotsalainen did not contest the imposition of the penal fine and paid it. Subsequently, in separate proceedings, the Vehicle Administration inflicted a second penalty for the same default, a fuel fee debit of EUR 15,137. Thus, Ruotsalainen had been punished twice for the same wrongdoing, first with a penal order and subsequently with an administrative penalty. Ruotsalainen complained to the ECtHR of a violation of Article 4 of Protocol No. 7 ECHR dealing with *Non Bis In Idem* and, to the surprise of many, the ECtHR upheld his complaint:

> '44. As noted above, first, the applicant was fined in summary penal order proceedings because he had used more leniently taxed fuel than diesel oil in the tank of his vehicle, which constituted petty tax fraud. The proceedings were "criminal" according to the Finnish legal classification. Those proceedings were "criminal" also for the purposes of Article 4 of Protocol No. 7 and consequently the applicant was "finally acquitted or convicted in accordance with the law and penal procedure of [the] State". The guarantee of Article 4 of Protocol No. 7 comes into play where a new set of proceedings is instituted after the previous acquittal or conviction has acquired the force of res judicata. In this case, the applicant did not appeal against the summary penal order, which therefore became res judicata.'
>
> '45 ... It may therefore be concluded that the fuel fee debit was imposed by a rule whose purpose was not only compensatory but also deterrent and punitive. The Court considers that this establishes the criminal nature of the offence.'
>
> '47. In the light of the above considerations the Court concludes that the nature of the offence was such as to bring the issuing of the fuel fee debit on 17 September 2001 within the ambit of "penal procedure" for the purposes of Article 4 of Protocol No. 7 ...

1. *Ponsetti and Chesnel v. France.*

> 57. The foregoing considerations are sufficient to enable the Court to conclude that there has accordingly been a violation of Article 4 of Protocol No. 7 to the Convention.'

At this stage the implications of the landmark customs judgment had not been properly appreciated. In essence, the ECtHR's decision in *Ruotsalainen v. Finland* had established that a person who, because of an act or omission is punished with a tax surcharge may not, subsequently, be tried and punished again criminally for the same act or omission. To determine whether a tax surcharge is to be treated as a 'criminal charge' within the meaning of the ECHR the ECtHR used Article 6 tools which included the Engel criteria.[2]

The moment of reckoning came in 2014, the case of *Lucky Dev v. Sweden*,[3] a VAT case. The Swedish tax authorities had investigated Ms Dev for tax reporting defaults, concluding that she had not declared all her supplies properly. The tax authorities raised a tax assessment against Ms Dev, and the assessment incorporated a significant element of tax surcharges. Subsequently, the competent authorities instituted criminal proceedings against Ms Dev for the defaults previously punished with the tax surcharges. In criminal proceedings, Ms Dev was convicted of aggravated bookkeeping but acquitted of the tax offence. Ms Dev was given a suspended sentence and ordered to perform 160 hours community service. Ms Dev complained of a breach of the *Non Bis in Idem* principle taking her case to the ECtHR. Based on the logic of the *Ruotsalainen* case, the ECtHR found a violation:

> 63. Accordingly, the present case concerns two parallel and separate sets of proceedings of which the tax proceedings commenced on 1 June 2004 and were finalised on 20 October 2009 and the criminal proceedings were initiated on 5 August 2005 and became final on 8 January 2009. The two proceedings were thus pending concurrently for almost three and a half years. This duplication of proceedings did not involve a breach of Article 4 of Protocol No. 7. However, the tax proceedings were not terminated and the tax surcharges were not quashed after the criminal proceedings had become final but continued for a further nine and a half months until 20 October 2009. Therefore, the applicant was tried 'again' for an offence for which she had already been finally acquitted.
>
> 64. For these reasons, there has been a violation of Article 4 of Protocol No. 7 to the Convention.

The same legal principle was tested in a case involving a relative of Lucky Dev and clear jurisprudential line was created. Cases started flooding in and in 2015, uncharacteristically, the ECtHR upheld a considerable number of tax complaints.[4]

Notable judgments include the case of *Glantz v. Finland*[5] involving a Finish taxpayer who failed to comply with Finnish Tax law and was held liable to a penalty

---

2. *Engel v. Netherlands*: the legal classification of the offence under national law, the very nature of the offence and the degree of severity of the penalty that the person concerned risks incurring.
3. Application no. 7356/10.
4. Including *Shibendra Dev v. Sweden*, no. 7362/10, *Häkkä v. Finland*, no. 758/11, *Nykänen v. Finland*, no. 11828/11, *Pirttimäki v. Finland*, no. 35232/11, *Österlund v. Finland*, no. 53197/13, *Kiiveri v. Finland*, no. 53753/12, among others.
5. Application no. 37394/11.

contemplated in the Finnish criminal code system and a tax surcharge. The ECtHR concluded that the tax surcharge was essentially a criminal penalty within the meaning of the ECHR and that a taxpayer could be punished twice for the same offence. The ECtHR found a violation of Article 4 of Protocol No. 7. Similar rules were articulated in the case of *Nykänen v. Finland*[6] creating a *jurisprudence costante*. The 2015 case of *Rinas v. Finland*[7] was particularly interesting because in *Rinas* criminal proceedings were initiated after tax surcharge proceedings had been exhausted. The 2015 case of *Kiiveri v. Finland*[8] must be singled out too because Kiiveri had not exhausted all national remedies. Kiiveri was served with an assessment to additional tax that he did not contest. After the assessment to additional tax became final and conclusive, criminal proceedings were instituted against him. The ECtHR found that the institution of criminal proceedings violated the *non bis in idem* principle. The same conclusion was reached in the 2015 case of *Österlund v. Finland*,[9] another case involving the institution of criminal proceedings after the conclusion of administrative tax proceedings. Predictably, the ECtHR found a violation of the *non bis in idem* principle.

15.3 TOO GOOD TO BE TRUE

The 2014 and 2015 judgments caused tremors across the administrative punitive regimes of the Contracting State, and there were rumours that the ECtHR had gone too far with its revolutionary 'una via' course. The message arrived to the Grand Chamber of the ECtHR which, in its surprise 2016 Grand Chamber judgment in *A. and B. v. Norway*,[10] reviewed its approach to the matter. The facts of the *A. and B.* case were quasi-identical to those in the Finnish and Swedish cases discussed above but, to a certain extent, the ECtHR had a change of heart. In its ninety-eight-page judgment, the ECtHR dismissed a complaint whose merits were quite similar to those of the successful Scandinavian cases discussed above.

The ECtHR listed a number of judgments when the imposition by different authorities of different sanctions concerning the same conduct was accepted by the ECtHR as being to some extent permissible under Article 4 of Protocol No. 7, a conclusion that had been based on the premise that the combination of sanctions in those cases ought to be considered as a whole, making it artificial to view the matter as one of duplication of proceedings leading the applicant to being 'tried or punished again ... for an offence for which he has already been finally ... convicted' in breach of Article 4 of Protocol No. 7.

The ECtHR pointed out that even its recent judgments in *Glantz*, *Nykänen*, and *Lucky Dev* could be read as a reaffirmation that parallel proceedings were not excluded in relation to the imposition of tax penalties in administrative proceedings and prosecution, conviction and sentencing for tax fraud in criminal proceedings, but

6. Application no. 11828/11.
7. Application no. 17039/13.
8. Application no. 53753/12.
9. Application no. 53197/13.
10. Applications nos. 24130/11 and 29758/11.

found a violation only because the test of 'a sufficiently close connection ..., in substance and in time' had not been satisfied in the particular circumstances under consideration. The ECtHR zoomed into the conclusions in *Nykänen* where what led to the acceptance of the complaint was that the criminal and the administrative sanctions had been imposed by different authorities without the proceedings being in any way connected: both sets of proceedings followed their own separate course and became final independently of each other. Furthermore, neither of the sanctions had been taken into consideration by the other court or authority in determining the severity of the sanction, nor was there any other interaction between the relevant authorities. Under the Finnish system, the tax penalties had been imposed following an examination of an applicant's conduct and his liability under the relevant tax legislation, which was independent from the assessments made in the criminal proceedings.

Arguments raised by intervening parties heavily influenced the outcome of the judgment, and the CJEU's Advocate General's opinion in the *Hans Åkeberg Fransson* case[11] added fuel to the fire. In the *Fransson* case, the imposition of penalties under both administrative law and criminal law in respect of the same offence was described as a widespread practice in the EU Member States, especially in fields such as taxation. Even the fact that six Contracting Parties to Protocol No. 7 had intervened in the case was noted by the ECtHR:

> 123. It cannot be the effect of Article 4 of Protocol No. 7 that the Contracting States are prohibited from organising their legal systems so as to provide for the imposition of a standard administrative penalty on wrongfully unpaid tax (albeit a penalty qualifying as 'criminal' for the purposes of the Convention's fair-trial guarantees) also in those more serious cases where it may be appropriate to prosecute the offender for an additional element present in the non-payment, such as fraudulent conduct, which is not addressed in the 'administrative' tax-recovery procedure. The object of Article 4 of Protocol No. 7 is to prevent the injustice of a person's being prosecuted or punished twice for the same criminalised conduct. It does not, however, outlaw legal systems which take an 'integrated' approach to the social wrongdoing in question, and in particular an approach involving parallel stages of legal response to the wrongdoing by different authorities and for different purposes ... .

The ECtHR's judgment is characterised by a certain uneasiness on the part of the ECtHR. After articulating what may be described as the essential requisites of duplication proceedings, the Grand Chamber did admit that:

> 130. On the basis of the foregoing review of the Court's case-law, it is evident that, in relation to matters subject to repression under both criminal and administrative law, the surest manner of ensuring compliance with Article 4 of Protocol No. 7 is the provision, at some appropriate stage, of a single-track procedure enabling the parallel strands of legal regulation of the activity concerned to be brought together, so that the different needs of society in responding to the offence can be addressed within the framework of a single process. Nonetheless, as explained above (see notably paragraphs 111 and 117-120), Article 4 of Protocol No. 7 does not exclude the conduct of dual proceedings, even to their term, provided that certain

11. C-617/10.

> conditions are fulfilled. In particular, for the Court to be satisfied that there is no duplication of trial or punishment (bis) as proscribed by Article 4 of Protocol No. 7, the respondent State must demonstrate convincingly that the dual proceedings in question have been 'sufficiently closely connected in substance and in time'. In other words, it must be shown that they have been combined in an integrated manner so as to form a coherent whole. This implies not only that the purposes pursued and the means used to achieve them should in essence be complementary and linked in time, but also that the possible consequences of organising the legal treatment of the conduct concerned in such a manner should be proportionate and foreseeable for the persons affected.

Nonetheless, the conclusion was that the Grand Chamber did not find a violation, tweaking its jurisprudence in the process. The Grand Chamber pointed out that the material factors for determining whether there is a sufficiently close connection in substance include:

- whether the different proceedings pursue complementary purposes and thus address, not only in abstracto but also in concreto, different aspects of the social misconduct involved;
- whether the duality of proceedings concerned is a foreseeable consequence, both in law and in practice, of the same impugned conduct (*idem*);
- whether the relevant sets of proceedings are conducted in such a manner as to avoid as far as possible any duplication in the collection as well as the assessment of the evidence, notably through adequate interaction between the various competent authorities to bring about that the establishment of facts in one set is also used in the other set;
- and, above all, whether the sanction imposed in the proceedings which become final first is taken into account in those which become final last, so as to prevent that the individual concerned is in the end made to bear an excessive burden, this latter risk being least likely to be present where there is in place an offsetting mechanism designed to ensure that the overall amount of any penalties imposed is proportionate. Consequently, the Grand Chamber reached the following conclusion:

> 146. In these circumstances, as a first conclusion, the Court has no cause to call into doubt either the reasons why the Norwegian legislature opted to regulate the socially undesirable conduct of non-payment of taxes in an integrated dual (administrative/criminal) process or the reasons why the competent Norwegian authorities chose, in the first applicant's case, to deal separately with the more serious and socially reprehensible aspect of fraud in a criminal procedure rather than in the ordinary administrative procedure.
> Secondly, the conduct of dual proceedings, with the possibility of different cumulated penalties, was foreseeable for the applicant who must have known from the outset that criminal prosecution as well as the imposition of tax penalties was possible, or even likely, on the facts of the case (see paragraphs 13 and 16 above).
> Thirdly, it seems clear that, as held by the Supreme Court, the criminal proceedings and the administrative proceedings were conducted in parallel and were interconnected (see paragraph 29 above). The establishment of

> facts made in one set was used in the other set and, as regards the proportionality of the overall punishment inflicted, the sentence imposed in the criminal trial had regard to the tax penalty (see paragraph 17 above).
> 154. Against this background, it cannot be said that either of the applicants was 'tried or punished again ... for an offence for which he had already been finally ... convicted' in breach of Article 4 of Protocol No. 7. The Court accordingly finds no violation of this provision in the present case in respect of either of the two applicants.

The Grand Chamber judgment in *A. and B. v. Norway* came as a cold shower to those of us who had grown accustomed to using Article 4 of Article 7 ECHR in domestic cases.

The Grand Chamber judgment in *A. and B.* was heavily criticised. The dissenting opinion of Judge Pinto de Albuquerque was strongly worded:

> This policy may turn into a never-ending, vindictive story of two or more sets of proceedings progressively or successively conducted against the same defendant for the same facts, with the prospect of the defendant even being castigated, in a retaliatory fashion, for exercising his or her legitimate procedural rights, and especially his or her appeal rights.

Criticism came from the academic world too. Understandably, Bruno Peeters was worried by the different approaches used by the ECtHR and ECJ lamenting an element of uncertainty:

> ... The ECtHR emphasizes exclusively the degree of integration of the two procedures. When the two procedures are 'sufficiently closely connected in substance and in time', there is only a single, coherent procedure, and so the bis-condition is not met. The EUCJ, on the other hand, assumes the existence of two procedures. It does not demonstrate that the two procedure are one given their close connection ... Therefore the EUCJ does not entirely follow the same track as the ECtHR. As indicated in the press release of 20 March 2018, the Court admits that the ne bis in idem principle may be limited for the purpose of protecting the financial interests of the EU and the financial markets thereof. Only the future will make clear whether these divergent approaches of the ne bis in idem principle by EUCJ and the ECtHR shall lead to undesired different applications thereof in concreto.[12]

15.4 FIFTY SHADES OF *NON BIS IN IDEM*

It turned out that the future after *A. and B. v. Norway* was not as dismal as we had feared, it was worse. The subsequent case law was as negative as our initial reading of *A. and B. v. Norway* suggested, because after *A. and B.*, the ECtHR upheld some *Non Bis In Idem* tax cases, but did not in similar cases, showing the fifty shades of an erratic jurisprudence as demonstrated in Judge Albuquerque's separate opinion in *Mihalache*

12. Bruno Peeters, 'The Ne Bis in Idem Rule: Do the EUCJ and the ECtHR Follow the Same Track?', EC Tax Review, Volume 4 (2018) pp. 182–185.

v. Romania.[13] As Judge Albuquerque pointed out, judgments in the vein of *A. and B. v. Norway* and its progeny seem to be designed to maximise State repression, even when the prosecution is at fault for having failed to conduct a thorough investigation. Such a repressive strategy was the result of the Grand Chamber's acritical and precipitate absorption of the Luxembourg case law in the Romanian case.

A. and B. v. Norway did not stop the strong line of judgments condemning the imposition of administrative penalties and criminal penalties. After *A. and B.*, most of the known *Non Bis in Idem* tax complaints were upheld.

In the 2017 judgment in *Johannesson and Other v. Iceland*[14] the Court found a violation, because it transpired that the state signatory had responded to applicants' under-declaration of income via parallel administrative and criminal proceedings. Integration between the two sets of proceedings was absent:

> 55. Having regard to the above circumstances, in particular the limited overlap in time and the largely independent collection and assessment of evidence, the Court cannot find that there was a sufficiently close connection in substance and in time between the tax proceedings and the criminal proceedings in the case for them to be compatible with the bis criterion in Article 4 of Protocol No. 7.

In the 2019 tax case of *Bjarni Ármannsson v. Iceland*[15] the Court again found a violation, applying the interpretative principles in *A. and B.* as a non-prohibitive threshold:

> ... the Court considers that the sanctions already imposed in the tax proceedings were sufficiently taken into account in the sentencing in the criminal proceedings ...
>
> 58. Consequently, the applicant was tried and punished for the same or substantially the same conduct by different authorities in two different sets of proceedings which lacked the required connection. There has therefore been a violation of Article 4 of Protocol No. 7 to the Convention.

The ECtHR upheld another *Non Bis in Idem* complaint in the 2019 case of *Ragnar Thorisson v. Iceland:*[16]

> 50. Having regard to the above circumstances, in particular the lack of overlap in time and the largely independent collection and assessment of evidence, the Court cannot find that there was a sufficiently close connection in substance and in time between the tax proceedings and the criminal proceedings in the case for them to be compatible with the bis criterion in Article 4 of Protocol No. 7.
>
> 51. Consequently, the applicant was tried and punished for the same or substantially the same conduct by different authorities in two different sets of proceedings which lacked the required connection. For these reasons, there has been a violation of Article 4 of Protocol No. 7 to the Convention.

13. Application no. 54012/10.
14. Application no. 22007/11.
15. Application no. 72098/14.
16. Application no. 52623/14.

The ECtHR delivered yet another favourable judgment in the 2021 case of *Milošević v. Croatia*:[17]

> 42. The foregoing reinforces the Court's conclusion that, notwithstanding their foreseeability, the two sets of proceedings had not been sufficiently linked in substance, as required under the Court's case-law, to be considered to form part of an integral scheme of sanctions under Croatian law, as in force at the material time, for illegal use of specially-taxed heating oil as fuel. On the contrary, having been punished twice for the same conduct, the applicant had in the Court's view suffered disproportionate prejudice resulting from the duplication of proceedings and penalties, which did not form a coherent and proportionate whole in his case (see, mutatis mutandis, A and B v. Norway, cited above, §§ 112, 130 and 147).

Similarly, in 2021, the ECtHR determined another *Non Bis In Idem* case favourably in the case of *Bragi Guðmundur Kristjánsson v. Iceland*:[18]

> 77. The Court thus finds that the dual proceedings against the applicant were neither sufficiently connected in substance nor in time as to avoid a duplication of the proceedings. Consequently, the applicant was tried and punished for the same or substantially the same conduct by different authorities in two different sets of proceedings that lacked the required connection. There has therefore been a violation of Article 4 of Protocol No. 7 to the Convention.

The 2018 case of *Matthildur Ingvarsdottir v. Iceland*[19] represents one of the cases when the ECtHR dismissed a complaint on the basis of *A. and B.* In the *Matthildur* tax case, the question put to the ECtHR was whether the imposition of tax surcharges was criminal in nature, whether the criminal offence for which the applicant was prosecuted and convicted was the same as that for which the tax surcharges were imposed (idem), whether there was a final decision and whether there was duplication of the proceedings (bis). Although the ECtHR accepted that the dual proceedings pursued a complementary purpose in addressing the issue of taxpayers' failure to comply with the legal requirements relating to the filing of tax returns, the ECtHR did not find a violation because:

> 64. On the facts before it, the Court finds no indication that the applicant suffered any disproportionate prejudice or injustice as a result of the impugned integrated legal response to her failure to declare income and pay taxes. Consequently, having regard to the circumstances of the case, in particular the overlap in time and cooperation between the tax authorities and the police and prosecution authorities in the collection and assessment of evidence, the Court finds that, while different sanctions were imposed by two different authorities, there was nevertheless a sufficiently close connection, both in substance and in time, for them to be compatible with the bis criterion in Article 4 of Protocol No. 7.
>
> 65. For the reasons set out above, this complaint is manifestly ill-founded and must be rejected pursuant to Article 35 §§ 3 (a) and 4 of the Convention.

17. Application no. 12022/16.
18. Application no. 12951/18.
19. Application no. 22779/14.

A *Non Bis In Idem* complaint was dismissed in one of the *Yukos* cases, the 2020 case of *Khodorkovskiy and Lebedev v. Russia* (no. 2),[20] but the dismissal was purely based on factual grounds and, for the purposes of the grander scheme of things, is inconsequential.

Khodorkovskiy and Lebedev argued that at their second trial they had been tried for a second time for the same offence. Both trials had concerned the activities related to the sale of the oil extracted by the Yukos production entities to Yukos trading companies. In their view, the tax evasion charges in the first set of criminal proceedings against them were based on an assessment of concrete factual circumstances and were inextricably linked in time and space to the charges brought against them in the second set of criminal proceedings. They further argued that their convictions were mutually exclusive and incompatible. In the applicants' view, they could not have been convicted of misappropriation of oil and money laundering and, at the same time, of tax evasion in respect of the amounts that they had allegedly obtained unlawfully as a result of such misappropriation and laundering. Their complaint was dismissed on the merits:

> 614. The Court therefore concludes that the applicants were not prosecuted or convicted in the second set of criminal proceedings on the basis of facts that were substantially the same as those that were the subject of their final conviction in the first set of criminal proceedings.
>
> 615. As regards the aspect of the applicants' complaint about their convictions being mutually exclusive and incompatible, in so far as they may be understood to complain about the nature of the charges brought against them in the second set of criminal proceedings, the Court has examined this grievance under Article 7 of the Convention (see paragraphs 568-587 above).
>
> 616. It follows that this part of the application is manifestly ill-founded and must be rejected in accordance with Article 35 §§ 3 and 4 of the Convention.

15.5 CONCLUSIONS

On 5 May 2022, the CJEU delivered a judgment on *Non Bis in Idem* in its VAT case C-570/20. The CJEU concluded that that *Non Bis In Idem* rules guaranteed by Article 50 of the Charter, read in conjunction with Article 52 (1) thereof, must be interpreted as meaning that:

- it does not preclude a situation whereby the limitation of the duplication of proceedings and penalties of a criminal nature in the event of fraudulent concealment or omissions from a return relating to VAT provided for by national legislation to the most serious cases is based only on settled case-law interpreting restrictively the legal provisions laying down the conditions for the application of that duplication, provided that it is reasonably foreseeable, at the time when the offence is committed, that that offence is liable to be the subject of a duplication of proceedings and penalties of a criminal nature, but

20. Applications nos. 51111/07 and 42757/07.

- it precludes national legislation which does not ensure, in cases of the combination of a financial penalty and a custodial sentence, by means of clear and precise rules, where necessary as interpreted by the national courts, that all of the penalties imposed do not exceed the seriousness of the offence identified.

The CJEU judgment highlights the need for a coordinated approach in the *Non Bis In Idem* sphere. Roller coaster judgments are not the best way to tackle a sensitive area which is at the very core of the ECHR. The current situation is crying out for common rules to conclusively determine the elements of *Non Bis in Idem* in situations involving administrative penalties. In a time when the coordinated approach is earmarked as the preferred options for anti-avoidance measures, a common coordinated framework is the approach to tackle mismatches in the *Non Bis In Idem* area too. Amendments to the Charter could offer a solution.

As Paulo de Albuquerque and Hyun-Soo Lim put it recently, in an article dealing with the consequences of Brexit on human rights protection in the UK:

> The cautionary tale of cross-fertilization between the ECtHR and the CJEU is that it is a double-edged sword. Cross-fertilization can just as easily lead to a 'vicious cycle' of troublesome jurisprudence multiplied through mutual encouragement. For instance, in *Hans Akeberg Fransson*, the Grand Chamber of the CJEU had held that the principle of ne bis in idem obligated States not to impose an administrative proceeding against an individual who already faced criminal charges (*Erledigungsprinzip*, or 'exhaustion-of-procedure principle'). Three years later, in *A and B v. Norway*, the European Court of Human Rights ruled differently, holding that duplicate proceedings are permissible if the penalties were proportionate and the proceedings were coordinated (*Anrechnungsprinzip*, or 'accounting principle'). *A and B* thus represented a regression of the protection against double jeopardy. What is noteworthy is that the ECJ then followed this approach in *Luca Menci*, concluding that deviation from ne bis in idem is permissible if it 'pursues an objective of general interest ..., contains rules ensuring coordination which limits to what is strictly necessary the additional disadvantage [for the defendant] ..., [and] provides for rules making it possible to ensure that the severity of all of the penalties imposed is limited to what is strictly necessary'.[21]

21. *See* Paulo Albuquerque and Hyun-Soo Lim, 'The Cross-Fertilisation Between the Court of Justice of the European Union and the European Court of Human Rights: Reframing the Discussion on Brexit', European Human Rights Law Review, Issue 6 (2018) pp. 567–577.

CHAPTER 16

Right to Free Elections

ARTICLE 3 PROTOCOL 1
Right to free elections

The High Contracting Parties undertake to hold free elections at reasonable intervals by secret ballot, under conditions which will ensure the free expression of the opinion of the people in the choice of the legislature.

16.1 ELECTORAL SANCTIONS FOR TAX FRAUD

The tax judgments of the ECtHR are quite eclectic, and their diversity is fascinating. Even the article on free election was caught within the net of its tax judgments. In some countries, convictions for economic crimes bring with them punitive interdictions from exercising civil rights. In some countries, a conviction for tax fraud brings with it a punitive revocation of the voting right and the matter was examined in the 2003 case of *M.D.U. v. Italy*.[1]

The *M.D.U.* case involved a tax offender who had been convicted to three years imprisonment and interdicted from exercising public functions (interdizione dai pubblici uffici) for two years. M.D.U. filed an application to the ECtHR complaining under Article 3 of Protocol no. 1. The ECtHR dismissed the complaint as manifestly ill-founded on the grounds that the interdiction measure was foreseeable, predictable and imposed for a limited time:

> Elle relève ensuite qu'en l'espèce l'application de la peine accessoire était prévue par le droit interne, à savoir par l'article 6 de la loi no 516 de 1982.
>
> Au vue de ce qui précède et ayant égard notamment au fait que la mesure litigieuse avait une durée limitée, la Cour considère que rien dans l'arrêt de la Cour de cassation ne donne à croire que l'application de la peine accessoire ou le

1. Application no. 58540/00.

> non-octroi immédiat d'une remise de peine étaient contraires à la législation italienne, arbitraires ou disproportionnés, ou qu'ils contrecarraient 'la libre expression de l'opinion du peuple sur le choix du corps législatif' (voir, mutatis mutandis, Mathieu-Mohin et Clerfayt c. Belgique, arrêt précité, p. 25, § 57).
>
> Il s'ensuit que ce grief doit être rejeté comme manifestement mal fondé, en application de l'article 35 §§ 3 et 4 de la Convention.

16.2 CONCLUSIONS

The conclusions that may be drawn from this unusual judgment is that punitive measures imposed on tax defaulters may include revocation of voting rights too. Nonetheless, the regulatory framework governing the revocation of voting rights must meet a 'lawfulness' test which, presumably, is the same as that contemplated under Article 1 of Protocol 1 ECHR and Article 7 ECHR. Interestingly, the judgment in *M.D.U.* allowed the revocation of the voting right because it was a temporary measure. Had the interdiction been a perpetual one, the ECtHR could have reached a different conclusion suggesting an implied proportionality test.

Epilogue

TAXATION AND STATE OPPRESSION

The history of the ECtHR has demonstrated that, in the past sixty years, Contracting States have used taxation to oppress their citizens. The conclusions of certain cases are unequivocal. The power to tax has been used to harass citizens and, in isolated instances involving corporations, has been used to destroy too. Contracting States have been quite creative in finding ways how to use taxation to breach the fundamental human rights of their citizens, the fact that violations were reported under so many articles is a cause for concern. The ECHR has a major role to play in protecting taxpayers from State Oppression, and the ECtHR acts as a gatekeeper.

Would Edberg be surprised to learn that, over the years, some Scandinavian tax policies have gone too far? Would Tiegen be intrigued by French cases establishing the extent of the power of judicial review in tax matters? Would Azara be surprised to learn of Italian cases relating to abuse of the principle of subsidiarity? What would Maxwell-Fyfe have to say of some cases originating from Russia and Azerbaijan relating to the treatment of political dissidents? Was the ECHR intended to cover the type of abuses lamented in the jurisprudence of the ECtHR?

Regardless of what the drafters of the ECHR originally intended, the fact remains that the case law of the ECtHR has evolved to such an extent that the subject of taxation has earned itself a firm foothold in the ECtHR's jurisprudence. Data relating to the submission of tax cases is not readily available because most admissibility decisions are not published, but cases uploaded on the ECtHR's database suggest that the number of tax cases submitted has increased exponentially. The indications are that even the number of successful tax complaints has increased. The ECtHR is not always shying away from its supervisory function delivering some strong judgments.

TAXATION AT THE GRAND CHAMBER

Statistics speak for themselves. In the summer of 2022, out of twenty-two cases[1] pending before the Grand Chamber, three of the cases were tax cases.[2] The fact that the Grand Chamber thought that it was fit to hear cases over taxation and the right to a fair hearing, taxation and freedom of expression and taxation and the right to privacy is very telling. The Grand Chamber's interest in tax matters is unprecedented and shows promise because Grand Chamber pronouncements tend to resonate in the Contracting States. Tax cases are raising complex issues that influence the development of the tax policy of the Contracting States and supranational guidance is needed. Cases involving taxation and the right to property have disappointed[3] and judgments involving the *Non Bis In Idem* have been confusing.[4] The Grand Chamber is getting actively involved in tax matters, and we await the outcome of the cases in Hallet and L.B. with bathed breath. How will L.B. and Hallet balance Article 8 ECHR with Article 10 ECHR? To what extent does the ECHR allow the dissemination of stolen tax data when the dissemination of such data is in the public interest? To what extent may whistle-blowers and journalists invoke the protection of the ECHR?

INTERNATIONAL TAXATION AT THE ECtHR

Since Maxwell-Fyfe's time, the tax landscape has evolved significantly. The global economy has changed; wealth has become more mobile, and the types of cases submitted to the ECtHR have changed accordingly. Whereas the older cases dealt with simple legislative frameworks such as Poll Taxes,[5] Church Taxes[6] and Inheritance Taxes,[7] the more recent cases reflect the reality of a globalised economy. Recent cases have tackled issues revolving around some of the most complex tax rules including international tax avoidance using letter-box companies, transfer pricing, tax treaty shopping and the diversion of profits to low-tax jurisdictions.[8] Meanwhile, the tools used by tax inspectors have evolved too. Databases of tax data, automation and artificial intelligence created technologies which were unthinkable in Maxwell-Fyfe's time and concerns relating to data integrity are warranted. Major alliances between Contracting States have been forged through tax treaties providing for exchange of information and mutual assistance and tax evasion and, arguably, tax avoidance have

1. https://echr.coe.int/Pages/home.aspx?p = hearings/gcpending&c = .
2. *Vegotex International S.A. v. Belgium* (no. 49812/09) decided on 3 November 2022 7 July 2021, *L.B. v. Hungary* (no. 36345/16), the Court held a hearing in this case on 3 November 2021 and *Halet v. Luxembourg* (no. 21884/18), the Court held a hearing in this case on 2 February 2022.
3. Robert Attard, 'Not a Pleasure to the Eye: The ECtHR's Judgment in P. Plaisier B.V. Against the Netherlands', EC Tax Review, Volume 27, Issue 3 (2018) pp. 177–179.
4. Robert Attard, 'The ECtHR's Recent Tax Judgments on the Non Bis in Idem Rule', EC Tax Review, Volume 26, Issue 6 (2017) pp. 335–338.
5. *Benham v. the United Kingdom*, Application no. 19380/92.
6. *Iglesia Bautista 'El Salvador' and José Aquilino Ortega Moratilla v. Spain*, Application no. 17522/90.
7. *Galeotti Ottieri della Ciaja v. Italy*, Application no. 46757/99.
8. *Khodorkovskiy and Lebedev v. Russia*, Applications nos. 11082/06 and 13772/05.

been demonised by the international press. Digitalisation has changed the rules of engagement and the tax landscape with and judgments of the ECtHR have already begin to delve into some of the most challenging areas.

TRANSFER PRICING AT THE ECtHR

Transfer pricing, one of the most complex areas of international taxation was mentioned in *OAO Neftyanaya Kompaniya Yukos v. Russia,*[9] *Khodorkovskiy and Lebedev v. Russia,*[10] *Khodorkovskiy and Lebedev v. Russia* (no. 2)[11] and *Nazarev and Others v. Bulgaria.*[12]

The *Yukos* and *Khodorkovskiy* cases shared similar merits and involved transfer pricing transactions undertaken within a multinational group of companies; some cases involved 'domestic' transfer pricing with the diversion of profits to low-tax districts and others contemplated international transfer pricing arrangements involving the diversion of profits to low-tax foreign jurisdictions.

In the case of *OAO Neftyanaya Kompaniya Yukos v. Russia,*[13] the multinational group had sold its goods from its production division to its marketing companies. The goods were sold at lowered prices to entities registered in a low taxation region situated in Russia. The ECtHR held that the findings of the domestic courts that the applicant company's tax arrangements were unlawful at the time when the company had used them were neither arbitrary nor manifestly unreasonable. In addition, the legal basis of the transfer pricing methodology was found to be sufficiently accessible, precise and foreseeable. Russian transfer pricing case law allowed the tax authorities to re-characterise and cancel activities that did not meet the requisite good faith test: a test which the company had failed.

In reply to the complainants' assertion that the good faith doctrine contemplated in the Russian Tax Code was too vague, the ECtHR pointed out that:

> ... in any system of law, including criminal law, there is an inevitable element of judicial interpretation and there will always be a need for elucidation of doubtful points and for adaptation to changing circumstances. In order to avoid excessive rigidity, many laws are inevitably couched in terms which, to a greater or lesser extent, are vague and whose interpretation and application are questions of practice ... On the facts, it would be impossible to expect from a statutory provision to describe in detail all possible ways in which a given taxpayer could abuse a legal system and defraud the tax authorities. At the same time, the applicable legal norms made it quite clear that, if uncovered, a taxpayer faced the risk of tax reassessment of its actual economic activity in the light of the relevant findings of the competent authorities. And this is precisely what happened to the applicant company in the case at hand.

9. Application no. 14902/04.
10. Applications nos. 11082/06 and 13772/05.
11. Applications nos. 51111/07 and 42757/07.
12. Applications nos. 26553/05, 25912/09 and 40107/09.
13. Application no. 14902/04.

Having regard to the margin of appreciation enjoyed by the State in the tax sphere and the fact that the applicant company was a large business holding resources which could draw from the expertise of professional auditors and consultants, the ECtHR found that there existed a sufficiently clear legal basis for finding the applicant company liable in the tax assessments. The inference that may be drawn from the Yukos Judgment seems to be that, in so far as the qualitative requirements of transfer pricing legislation are concerned, the ECtHR concedes contracting states a particularly wide margin of tolerance. Vague transfer pricing rules would be tolerated because multinational groups addressed by such complex rules are expected to equip themselves with the resources to navigate through the complexities of the relative rules.

The case of *Khodorkovskiy and Lebedev v. Russia*[14] was even more interesting because, unlike the *Yukos* case which involved the use of low-taxed companies registered in regions within Russia itself, the *Khodorkovskiy and Lebedev* case involved low-taxed companies registered outside Russia. At the time of the case, Russian law did not contemplate detailed international transfer pricing rules because Russia was not a signatory to the OECD Convention on Transfer Pricing. There was no general reporting obligation on commercial organisations to disclose the extent to which they were making use of transfer pricing to divert profits. There was not even an obligation to produce consolidated accounts. Nonetheless, the proceedings against the complainants were largely based on international transfer pricing principles. Consequently, the applicants argued that their conviction for tax irregularities was totally unpredictable and arbitrary. Referring to Russian case law on the matter, the ECtHR disagreed. Despite flaws in the domestic proceedings, decisions reached by the domestic courts based on generic anti-avoidance rules providing for a substance-over-form approach were not found to be arbitrary or manifestly unreasonable. Once more, the ECtHR took a hesitant approach to the subject of transfer pricing allowing judicial creativity to plug loopholes in legislation.

The subject of transfer pricing was discussed once more in the case of *Khodorkovskiy and Lebedev v. Russia* (no. 2).[15] Complainants argued that they had not been given the opportunity to defend their transfer pricing methodology in tax proceedings because they had been denied the right to produce certain evidence. Considering the voluminous documentary evidence presented to the court by the prosecution, the ECtHR considered that the complainants' attempts to adduce the documents in question and to obtain disclosure of evidence were not vexatious, were sufficiently reasoned, relevant to the subject matter of the accusation, and could arguably have strengthened the position of their defence. In refusing the motions to produce evidence, the trial court confined itself to stating that it found 'no legal grounds for granting' them. The ECtHR found that such a formulaic statement could not be considered a reasoned decision. Accordingly, the ECtHR found a breach of Articles 6 (1) and 3 (d) ECHR.

14. Applications nos. 11082/06 and 13772/05.
15. Applications nos. 51111/07 and 42757/07.

DOUBLE TAX TREATIES AT THE ECtHR

Rights conferred on tax subjects by Double Tax Treaties were the subject of a number of cases with one of the earliest cases being that of *Hanzmann v. Austria.*[16] The *Hanzmann* case involved a discrimination claim. In essence, Hanzmann complained of the different tax treatment of residents compared to non-residents. Hanzmann contested that, under the Austrian German Tax Treaty, residents were liable to tax on their worldwide income, but non-residents were liable to tax only locally sourced income. The matter was further complicated by the fact that a domestic tax deduction was available only to non-residents. Hanzmann's case was dismissed on the basis of the margin of appreciation allowance. Interestingly, the Commission referred to the fact that the difference in tax treatment was justified even by the fact that investigating the income generated by residents is easier than investigating the income of non-residents.

The case of *Miailhe v. France (no. 2)*[17] involved a tax investigation under Article 26 of the Franco-Philippine Tax Convention. The double-tier judicial control over the whole tax investigation process led to a dismissal of Miailhe's complaint under Article 6 ECHR.

The case *Arnaud and Others v. France*[18] involved the Double Tax Treaty between France and Monaco. Arnaud alleged that the exit tax rules contemplated in the Treaty were discriminatory because the rules applicable to emigrations to Monaco were not found in other Tax Treaties. The case was dismissed because the challenged provisions were held to be necessary to combat tax avoidance and that the case failed the comparability test:

> En l'espèce, la Cour observe que l'imposition prévue par l'Avenant du 26 mai 2003 à la convention franco-monégasque du 25 juin 1969 et par la loi du 14 mars 2005 autorisant l'approbation de celle-ci, s'applique de manière uniforme aux personnes placées dans une situation analogue et clairement identifiées par ces textes, à savoir les Français ayant transporté leur domicile ou leur résidence à Monaco à compter du 1er janvier 1989. La Cour ne partage pas le point de vue des requérants selon lequel les intéressés sont dans une situation analogue aux autres Français de l'étranger. En effet, elle observe qu'en matière de conventions fiscales internationales bilatérales, les règles définies par les États sont le fruit d'une négociation qui dépend à la fois des relations diplomatiques existant entre eux et de leurs régimes d'imposition nationaux respectifs. À cet égard, les Français de l'étranger ne peuvent être considérés comme formant une catégorie uniforme dont les membres se trouveraient dans une situation analogue. Au contraire, la Cour estime qu'il convient de les distinguer selon le pays où ils ont élu domicile.
>
> 44. Compte tenu de ces éléments, la Cour considère qu'il n'y a pas lieu d'examiner le caractère objectif et raisonnable des motifs avancés par le Gouvernement pour justifier la mesure litigieuse. Néanmoins, elle rappelle ses conclusions relatives au grief tiré de l'article 1 du Protocole no 1 pris isolément et observe que l'imposition des Français résidant à Monaco à l'ISF avec effet rétroactif au 1er janvier 2002, pour les besoins de la lutte contre l'évasion fiscale, ne saurait passer pour

16. Application no. 12560/86.
17. Application no. 18978/91.
18. Applications nos. 36918/11, 36963/11, 36967/11, 36969/11, 36969/11, 36970/11 and 36971/11.

disproportionnée au regard du but visé au sens de l'article 14 de la Convention (Di Belmonte (no 2), précitée).

The case of *Eirik Lindkvist v. Denmark*[19] involved a more complex cross-border matter, a form of mutual agreement procedure. At the request of Lindkvist, the Danish tax authorities wrote to the Swiss tax authorities and invited them to initiate negotiations pursuant to the Danish-Swiss Double Taxation Treaty concerning the applicant's tax liability. The Swiss authorities claimed that the applicant should be considered resident in Switzerland and thus liable to pay taxes in Switzerland. The Danish Tax Administration asked the Swiss authorities to produce further documentation and information, but the Swiss replied with a request to reconsider the question of the applicant's liability to pay taxes in Denmark. At that point in time, the Danes abruptly closed the case.

Lindkvist complained that the process followed by Denmark in reaching its conclusions had breached his right to a fair hearing. Like Miailhe, Lindkvist complained of the length of time taken to resolve the issue. The Strasbourg organs reflected on the particular nature of the cross-border issue. The Commission held that the Danish authorities could not be blamed for the delays in sorting out the matter. Although Lindkvist was entitled to use all the remedies available to him under Danish law, he had undoubtedly prolonged the proceedings. An element of delay was due to the complex negotiations between the Danish and Swiss tax authorities, which were conducted at the applicant's request. Having regard to the complexities of the case, the Commission concluded that there had not been disproportionate or wrongful interference with the applicant's possessions.

Mutual Assistance was at the heart of the complaint in the case of *G.S.B. v. Switzerland*,[20] a case involving the Swiss Double Tax Treaty with the US and other arrangements relating to administrative mutual assistance to the US. The case referred to the conflict between the Bank UBS and the US tax authorities. The ECtHR held that the measure that was complained of was conducive to protecting the country's economic well-being accepting the Government's argument that the US tax authorities' allegations against Swiss banks were liable to jeopardise the very survival of UBS SA, a major player in the Swiss economy employing a large number of persons, which explained Switzerland's interest in finding an effective legal solution in cooperation with the US. Thus, the ECtHR found that the impugned measure pursued a legitimate aim within the meaning of Article 8 (2) ECHR. With reference to its observations on the pursuit of a legitimate aim, the ECtHR accepted that Switzerland had an important interest in acceding to the American request for administrative mutual assistance so that the US could track down any assets concealed in Switzerland. The US Agreement had averted a major conflict with the United States of America.

Lastly, the ECtHR observed that the applicant benefited from certain procedural safeguards against the transfer of his data to the US tax authorities. The applicant had been given several effective and real procedural safeguards at his disposal to challenge

19. Application no. 25737/94.
20. Application no. 28601/11.

the surrender of his bank details, thereby protecting him against arbitrary implementation of the agreements concluded by Switzerland and the United States of America. Thus, the ECtHR concluded that:

> 97. Having regard to all the circumstances of the case, and particularly in the light of the non-personal nature of the data disclosed, it was not unreasonable for Switzerland to prioritise the general interest of an effective and satisfactory settlement with the United States of America over the private interest of the applicant. That being the case, Switzerland did not overstep its margin of appreciation.
>
> 98. It follows that there was no violation of Article 8 of the Convention.

The case of *Othymia investments BV v. the Netherlands*[21] involved a request for information under Article 4 of the Mutual Assistance Directive[22] and Article 28 of the Double Tax Treaty between Spain and the Netherlands. Othymia BV complained under Article 13 ECHR taken alone and in conjunction with Article 8 ECHR because the investigation and the transfer of the resulting information to the Spanish tax authorities constituted an unwarranted interference with its privacy rights. Othymia BV argued that it had not had access to an effective remedy because:

(a) The Administrative Jurisdiction Division of the Council of State had dismissed the applicant company's appeal for lack of pecuniary damage, thus applying a restriction not recognised in Netherlands domestic law.
(b) The Deputy Minister of Finance had authorised the transfer of tax information concerning the applicant company without prior notification, arbitrarily citing 'urgent reasons' and denying the applicant company access to relevant documents, thus undermining the applicant company's position in the subsequent proceedings.
(c) The Administrative Jurisdiction Division had disregarded the applicant company's interest in protecting the privacy of its personal data.

Othymia Bv contended that the Double Tax Treaty, which, in its view, took precedence over the Mutual Assistance Directive, did not empower the Deputy Minister to provide the company's tax information to the Spanish tax authorities without prior notification. The Company contended that Article 28 of the Treaty did not authorise the Netherlands tax authorities to make investigations, but only to exchange information which they had 'in proper order at their disposal'. In Othymia's opinion, the transfer of its tax information to the Spanish tax authorities without its prior knowledge was not 'in accordance with the law' because the bilateral arrangement in place did not admit of the investigation by which this information was obtained. The ECtHR disagreed:

21. Application no. 75292/10.
22. Council Directive 77/799/EEC of 19 December 1977 concerning mutual assistance by the competent authorities of the Member States in the field of direct taxation.

> 39. The Court notes at the outset that the applicant company can derive no comfort from Article 28 of the 1971 Convention between the Government of the Kingdom of the Netherlands and the Government of the State of Spain for the avoidance of double taxation with respect to taxes on income and on capital (see paragraph 20 above). In becoming a Member State of the European Communities, Spain committed itself to the entire acquis communautaire, including Council Directive 77/799/EEC (see paragraphs 18 and 19 above). The parties to the pertinent international instrument, the 1985 Accession Treaty, include all States then Member States of the European Community including the Netherlands. Whether or not it be correct that Article 28 of the 1971 bilateral treaty opposes investigations by the respondent Party for the purpose of providing information to the Spanish tax authorities as the applicant company argues, the Court therefore finds, consistently with Article 30 § 3 of the Vienna Convention on the Law of Treaties, that that provision is superseded by Council Directive 77/799/EEC.

The ECtHR added that it did not doubt that the aim of ensuring that taxes are paid is a legitimate one for the purposes of Article 8 (2) ECtHR because its earlier case law[23] had established that the economic well-being of the country is a legitimate aim. The ECtHR went on to make an interesting observation:

> In the Court's opinion, this is so even though the taxes concerned be due to Spain, the economies of the European Union Member States forming a unified whole.

Referring to judgments of CJEU on the matter, the ECtHR held that it cannot be a requirement of Article 8 ECHR that prior notice of lawful tax investigations or exchanges of tax-related information be given to all persons potentially implicated. Consequently, the ECtHR found that Othymia BV had no 'arguable claim' under Article 8.

The judgment in *Robert Huitson v. the United Kingdom*[24] involved domestic provisions aimed at Double Tax Treaty abuse. Huitson contended that the anti-abuse provisions violated Article 1 of Protocol 1 ECHR. The ECtHR pointed out that when framing and implementing policies in the area of taxation, contracting states enjoy a wide margin of appreciation, and the ECtHR is expected to respect the legislature's assessment in such matters unless it is devoid of reasonable foundation. It transpired that the applicant had entered into what the domestic courts described as a marketed and wholly artificial tax avoidance scheme with the effect that the general rule that United Kingdom taxpayers should pay United Kingdom income tax on the profits of their trade or profession was contravened. By the time the challenged legislation, with its retrospective amendments, was enacted, there were about 2,500 taxpayers exploiting similar arrangements, and the amount of income tax at stake for the respondent Government had risen to GBP 100 million. The ECtHR concluded that:

> 30. The Court notes that in the present case the object of the legislative amendments in issue was to prevent the DTA tax relief provisions from being misused for a purpose different from their originally intended use, that is relieving tax payers from double taxation. The Court considers that it is a legitimate and important aim

23. Including especially *Rousk v. Sweden*, Application no. 27183/04.
24. Application no. 50131/12.

> of public policy in fiscal affairs that a DTA should do no more than relieve double taxation and should not be permitted to become an instrument by which persons residing in the United Kingdom avoid, or substantially reduce, the income tax that they would ordinarily pay on their income. Moreover, it is in the general interest of the community to prevent taxpayers resident in the United Kingdom from exploiting the DTA in a way which would enable them to substantially reduce their income tax and secure a competitive advantage over those who chose not to use such a scheme.

The case was dismissed as manifestly ill-founded.

SHELL COMPANIES AT THE ECtHR

The use of shell companies for tax avoidance purposes was discussed in a few cases. One of the earliest cases was that of *Thommy Forsström v. Sweden*,[25] a case that involved a tax appeal contemplating tax surcharges (skattetillägg). The Swedish tax authorities had alleged that the applicant had evaded declaring his income from business according to his true earnings, that he had carried out shell company transactions and that he had not declared the real value of certain stocks which he had sold. The applicant complained under Article 6 (1) ECHR of the length of the tax proceedings. The issue was settled amicably.

The case of *Khodorkovskiy and Lebedev v. Russia*[26] contemplated the analysis of a tax optimisation technique involving switching the tax burden from the applicant company and its production and service units to letter-box companies in domestic tax havens in Russia. The Letter-Box companies had no assets, employees or operations of their own, were nominally owned and managed by third parties and, in reality, were set up and run by the applicant company itself. In essence, the applicant company's oil-producing subsidiaries sold the extracted oil to the letter-box companies at a fraction of the market price. The letter-box companies, acting in cascade, then sold the oil either abroad, this time at market price or to the applicant company's refineries and subsequently re-bought it at a reduced price and re-sold it at the market price. Thus, the letter-box companies accumulated most of the applicant company's profits. Since they were registered in domestic low-tax areas, they enabled the applicant company to pay substantially lower taxes in respect of these profits. Subsequently, the letter-box companies transferred the accumulated profits unilaterally to the applicant company as gifts. The domestic courts had found that the tax-minimisation technique applied by the company was unlawful involving the fraudulent registration of trading entities by the applicant company in the name of third persons and its corresponding failure to declare to the tax authorities its true relation to these companies The ECtHR concluded that tax authorities may have had access to scattered pieces of information about the functioning of separate parts of the arrangement, located across the country, but, given

25. Application no. 62174/00.
26. Applications nos. 11082/06 and 13772/05.

the scale and fraudulent character of the arrangement, they certainly could not have been aware of the arrangement in its entirety. The whole arrangement was believed to be intended to evade the general requirements of the Tax Code expecting taxpayers to trade at arm's length.

The ECtHR held that the concept of 'sham transaction' was known in Russian law applying the 'substance-over-form' rule, invalidating a transaction as 'sham'. The ECtHR emphasised that such an approach exists in many European countries and that the Court does not see anything unreasonable or unusual in it. Turning to the practical application of the 'substance-over-form' theory, the Court noted that despite the formal domiciliation of the trading companies in Lesnoy, all business activities which generated profit were in fact carried out in Moscow. The trading companies presented themselves as real companies having assets and personnel in the low-tax zone; however, as was established in the domestic proceedings and later confirmed by the Court in the Yukos case all of the trading companies had virtually no assets or personnel in the low-tax centre and had enjoyed no operational independence whatsoever from the Moscow headquarters. Thus, the trading companies claimed tax cuts as if they were really operating in the low-tax zone, but in reality, they were merely registered there for form's sake, and all the operations were conducted in Moscow. The complainants had not informed the tax authorities about their true relation to the trading companies. The Yukos structure was found to be deliberately opaque. The trading companies were registered in the names of third persons not formally connected to Yukos or its managers and had been managed by fictional directors. Benefits of the trading companies were returned to Yukos indirectly, through a special fund which received 'gifts' from the trading companies. The ECtHR found that such a coordinated reorganisation implied that it was done in order to render it more difficult for the authorities to scrutinise the business operations of those companies, to trace their assets and their affiliation with other companies and persons. In sum, by organising its sales in this way the applicants evaded application of the provisions of the Tax Code which permitted recalculation of taxes on the basis of 'market prices' in the relations between affiliated companies. Consequently, the ECtHR concluded that:

> 811. The Court is not called upon to develop a comprehensive legal theory explaining the differences between legitimate tax-minimisation techniques and tax evasion. Similarly, it is impossible to set an exhaustive list of criteria for defining a particular operation or a company as 'sham'. However, the cumulative effect of the elements discussed was sufficient to demonstrate that the operations of the trading companies were likely to be 'sham', that the reporting based thereon did not reflect the realities of the business operations, and that the applicants therefore 'knowingly' submitted 'false data' in order to reduce the overall tax burden of the company. Such inferences of fact were not 'arbitrary or manifestly unreasonable' … .
>
> 820. In sum, the Court cannot find that the authorities' attitude towards such practices amounted to a conscious toleration. It could not, therefore, absolve the applicants from criminal liability for tax evasion.

THE FUNDAMENTAL HUMAN RIGHTS OF THE TAX EVADER AND TAX AVOIDER

The title of this heading is meant to provoke thought. The judgments of the ECtHR lay down minimum standards of taxpayer protection, and this chapter will attempt to list the minimum rights that may be claimed by defaulters and alleged defaulters.

Article 1 of Protocol 1 ECHR prescribes that laws forming the basis of an action against a taxpayer must meet minimum qualitative criteria. The underlying tax law must respect the principle of lawfulness; it must be foreseeable and predictable.[27] Nonetheless, in view of the complexity of tax law, the ECtHR would permit judge-made laws supplementing lacunae in statutory law. Judicial law-making is allowed.[28] Furthermore, the requirement of foreseeability would still be met if the taxpayer needs to take appropriate legal advice to assess the implications of the law.[29]

Tax penalties must be proportionate and must not create an individual excessive burden.[30] Proportionality is calculated by reference to the tax in dispute but also with reference to other criteria. The core value of proportionality entails that the diligence and behaviour of the taxpayer must be taken into consideration.[31] Within certain limits, retrospective measures are allowed, in the field of tax avoidance legislation especially.[32] Even vicarious, joint and several liability is permitted.[33]

Predictably, tax offences may result in interferences with the right to liberty. Nonetheless, conviction and pre-trial detention must follow procedures prescribed by law. Pre-trial detention of tax offenders is permitted too, but pre-trial detention must be subject to effective and speedy judicial review.[34] Continuous detention must be justified by compelling reasons outweighing the presumption of liberty.[35] For there to be an arrest, the respondent State must prove that there was a reasonable suspicion of the commission a tax offence.[36]

Tax proceedings are, in principle, not subject to the right to a fair hearing,[37] but tax proceedings contemplating a punitive element must follow the requirements of the criminal head of Article 6 ECHR[38] contemplating the right of access to court, equality of arms and the right to silence. Tax proceedings determining penalties must be held in public by an independent and impartial tribunal. Persons charged with punitive measures equivalent to a criminal charge are presumed innocent until proved guilty according to law. In addition, the subject of the criminal charge would need to be informed promptly of the nature of accusation, be given time to prepare his defence, to

27. *Shchokin v. Ukraine,* Applications nos. 23759/03 and 37943/06.
28. *Khodorkovskiy and Lebedev v. Russia,* Application no. 5829/04.
29. *Heinrich Josef Bley v. Germany,* Application no. 68475/10.
30. *Mamidakis v. Greece,* Application no. 35533/04.
31. *Krayeva v. Ukraine,* Application no. 72858/13.
32. *Huitson v. the United Kingdom,* Application no. 50131/12.
33. *Busuttil v. Malta,* Application no. 48431/18.
34. *Mooren v. Germany,* Application no. 11364/03.
35. *Khodorkovskiy and Lebedev v. Russia,* Application no. 5829/04.
36. *Rasul Jafarov v. Azerbaijan,* Application no. 69981/14.
37. *Ferrazzini v. Italy,* Application no. 44759/98.
38. *Bendenoun v. France,* Application no. 12547/86.

engage a lawyer, if he has not had the necessary financial means to free legal aid and free assistance of an interpreter and to examine witnesses.[39] Tax procedures must be settled within a reasonable time, and the ECtHR has been intolerant of delays.

Of course, if the taxpayer is charged in 'pure' criminal proceedings, there is no question that Article 6 ECHR would apply under its criminal head. Furthermore, the additional guarantees of Article 7 ECHR would apply too.[40]

Data pertaining to tax evaders and avoiders is liable to interference, but intrusions into tax data must fulfil a lawfulness requirement and must meet a proportionality test. In any case, effective judicial control of intrusions into tax data both *ex ante* and posteriori is required.[41] The ECHR does not prohibit mutual assistance and exchange of information between tax authorities.[42] The naming and shaming of tax offenders are not prohibited but, once more, the value of proportionality must be respected.[43]

TAXATION IN TIMES OF EMERGENCY AND WAR

We are living in times of emergency and war. The financial demands created by the COVID epidemic and the Ukrainian War call for austerity measures that will influence the development of the tax policies of the Contracting States. Inevitably, Contracting States are expected to adopt tax measures that, in other times, would have been described with the politically incorrect term of 'War Taxes'. Regrettably, the judgments of the ECtHR in this area tend to be quite *pro auctoritate* with the judgment in Plaisier B.V.[44] creating a dangerous precedent. The ECtHR has taken the view that State Margin of Appreciation in designing tax measures intended to meet obligations assumed under EU law without delay, in circumstances aggravated by a financial and economic crisis of a magnitude seen in wartime is particularly wide. In this respect, the conclusions reached by the ECtHR in the non-tax case *Mamatas and Others v. Greece,*[45] a case relating to the Greek Financial Crisis are very indicative of the ECtHR's forma mentis. The ECtHR would be expected to be extremely tolerant.

THE ECHR AND THE BEPS PROJECT

The disputes raised in the *Yukos* cases and other 'international tax cases' discussed above were essentially cases that, *inter alia*, involved the artificial reduction of taxable income and the shifting of profits to low-tax centres in which little or no economic activity was performed. Thus, unwittingly, the ECtHR has already had the opportunity

39. Article 6 (3) ECHR.
40. *Prigală v. Moldova,* Application no. 36763/06.
41. *Brazzi v. Italy,* Application no. 57278/11.
42. *Othymia Investments BV v. the Netherlands,* Application no. 75292/10.
43. *L.B. v. Hungary,* Application no. 36345/16.
44. *Plaisier B.V. v. the Netherlands,* Application no. 46184/16.
45. Applications nos. 63066/14, 64297/14 and 66106/14.

to determine matters relating to the phenomenon of base erosion and profit shifting and there already exists a small body of case law that anticipates what may lie in store.

The OECD's 15-point Base Erosion and Profit Shifting (BEPS) Action Plan[46] promised to revolutionise the international tax rules in almost a hundred years allocating taxing rights to the jurisdiction where the economic activities are carried out and where value is created. Some of the BEPS measures, including the EU's measures especially, impact on taxpayers' rights and need to be carefully examined from a human rights perspective.

The BEPS Action Plan contemplates a framework for compulsory spontaneous information exchange in respect of rulings related to preferential regimes, Unilateral advance pricing arrangements or other cross-border unilateral rulings in respect of transfer pricing, Rulings providing for a downward adjustment of taxable profits, Permanent establishment rulings and Related party conduit rulings. Judgments of the ECtHR did not object to exchanges of information analogous to those that are being contemplated.[47]

Similarly, the Action Plan's emphasis on using a substantial activity requirement to assess preferential regimes and taxing rights in general is an issue which, in the light of the 'international tax judgments' discussed above, would find the full support of the ECtHR.[48] Disclosure obligations on taxpayer and promoter are another kettle of fish raising concerns relating to the *nemo tenetur se ipse accusare* principle.[49] Similarly, penalties for non-compliance especially when described as having a dissuasive function lend themselves to scrutiny under Article 1 of Protocol 1 ECHR attracting the procedural guarantees of Article 6 ECHR.

The Action Plan's bid to make dispute resolution mechanisms more effective by strengthening and enhancing Mutual Agreement Procedure would find the full support of the ECtHR. Similarly, the OECD's efforts to introduce minimum standards providing for timeliness, access and implementation are in line with ECtHR pronouncements on Article 6 ECHR.

Each action point must be individually stress-tested against the minimum standards set by the ECtHR. Action 1 addressing the risk of international tax avoidance in a digital economy would involve the introduction of anti-avoidance measures that would be expected to fall within the margin of appreciation of contracting states. The same applies to Action 2 aimed at neutralising the effects of hybrid mismatch arrangements and the phenomenon of stateless income. The judgment in *Huitson*[50] makes it clear that Contracting States have a wide margin of appreciation in designing international tax avoidance rules.

Action 3 involving the design of effective rules on controlled foreign companies (CFC) rules to address the risk that taxpayers with a controlling interest in a foreign low-taxed subsidiary can shift income to it and avoid taxation must not only be

46. For a summary of the Action Plan, *see* https://www.europarl.europa.eu/RegData/etudes/BRIE/2019/642258/EPRS_BRI(2019)642258_EN.pdf accessed in July 2022.
47. *Othymia Investments BV v. the Netherlands*, Application no. 75292/10.
48. *Khodorkovskiy v. Russia*, Application no. 5829/04.
49. *J.B. v. Switzerland*, Application no. 31827/96.
50. *Ibid.*

considered under Article 1 of Protocol 1 ECHR. Although the ECtHR's approach in *Bley* allows rules contemplating the complexities of CFC legislation, the imputation of chargeable income to parents requires judicial oversight, more so when the imputation contemplates the imposition of punitive measures.

The complexities envisaged in Action 4 contemplating limiting base erosion via interest deductions would be allowed by the line of judgments in *Bley*,[51] but the rationale behind Action 4 implies a covert revocation of an existing possession consisting in a right to a tax deduction giving rise to concerns under Article 1 of Protocol 1 ECHR. Nonetheless, the ECtHR would not be expected to treat the partial revocation of a tax advantage as an unjustified interference because of the margin of appreciation rules, international commitments undertaken by Contracting States and latitude allowed to Contracting State in design their anti-tax avoidance rules.

Action 5 promised to counter harmful tax practices via automatic exchanges of information that have already been allowed by the ECtHR in the *GSB* case. Similarly, Action 6 preventing double tax treaty abuse and treaty shopping resulting in double non-taxation has already been allowed in the *Huitson* case. Anti-abuse rules contemplating 'limitations-on-benefits' clauses and 'principle purpose tests' would likewise fall within the wide margin of appreciation accorded to Contracting States; the judgment in *Huitson* was clear enough in this respect.

Action 7 aimed at preventing the artificial avoidance of permanent establishment status does not raise any concerns. The same applies to Actions 8, 9 and 10 that seek to ensure that transfer pricing outcomes are in line with value creation. The suite of *Yukos* cases discussed above found nothing objectionable in transfer pricing rules per se. Conversely, Action 11 contemplating methodologies to collect and analyse data and Action 12 requiring taxpayers to disclose their aggressive tax planning arrangements give rise to some legitimate concerns. Article 8 ECHR requires effective judicial control regulating the collection and processing of data. Requiring taxpayers and their intermediaries to disclose aggressive tax planning arrangements creates issues from the point of the view of the right to freedom from self-incrimination.

Action 13 setting a minimum standard regarding transfer pricing documentation does not give rise to any issues, and Action 14 promising to make dispute resolution mechanisms is fully in line with Article 6 ECHR. A minimum standard ensuring resolution of disputes within an average timeframe of twenty-four months should actually be welcome. The guidelines in *Scordino* suggest that a twenty-four-month deadline to adjudicate over a complex issue should be acceptable.

The ECtHR would probably not intervene on Action 15 contemplating a multilateral instrument to modify bilateral tax treaties to swiftly implement tax treaty measures developed in BEPS actions. The EU's zealous response to the BEPS Action Plan and the EU's Directives and proposed Directives implementing the BEPS Action Plan raises the same issues raised by the Action Plan itself.

Council Directive (EU) 2018/822 of 25 May 2018 amending Directive 2011/16/EU, known as DAC 6, needs to be considered carefully. DAC 6 binds tax

51. *Ibid.*

planning intermediaries[52] and, at times,[53] even the relevant taxpayers themselves to disclose information to the competent authorities when such information may clearly be self-incriminating. Concerns under Article 6 ECHR on the principle of *nemo tenetur se detergere* are fully justified.

Another dangerous trait of EU directives implementing the BEPS Action Plan is the ingrained element of retrospectivity, an element that was present in DAC 6 and versions of the Anti-Avoidance Directive (ATAD).[54] Sadly, the ECtHR has been too permissive on the matter and EU Directives implementing BEPS seem to stretch the limits of the ECtHR's permissiveness.

The ATAD's aims are fully in line with the public interest exceptions and other exceptions contemplated in the ECHR, but there is a general feeling that some measures went a bit too far. Concerns relating to the effect of rules on interest deductibility[55] on existing possessions and CFC Rules[56] have been tackled above. Exit taxation[57] is unlikely to give rise to concerns under Article 2 of Protocol 4 ECHR because in the case of *S. v. Sweden*, the Commission had ruled that the right to take property out of a country without restriction is not a right embodied in the right to leave the country. The General Anti-Avoidance Rule[58] is aligned to the core values of the ECHR sitting

52. Defined as meaning any person that designs, markets, organises or makes available for implementation or manages the implementation of a reportable cross-border arrangement. It also means any person that, having regard to the relevant facts and circumstances and based on available information and the relevant expertise and understanding required to provide such services, knows or could be reasonably expected to know that they have undertaken to provide, directly or by means of other persons, aid, assistance or advice with respect to designing, marketing, organising, making available for implementation or managing the implementation of a reportable cross-border arrangement. Any person shall have the right to provide evidence that such person did not know and could not reasonably be expected to know that that person was involved in a reportable cross-border arrangement. For this purpose, that person may refer to all relevant facts and circumstances as well as available information and their relevant expertise and understanding. In order to be an intermediary, a person shall meet at least one of the following additional conditions:
    (a) be resident for tax purposes in a Member State;
    (b) have a permanent establishment in a Member State through which the services with respect to the arrangement are provided;
    (c) be incorporated in, or governed by the laws of, a Member State;
    (d) be registered with a professional association related to legal, taxation or consultancy services in a Member State.
53. In the circumstances contemplated in Article 8ab (6) of DAC 6 laying down that each Member State shall take the necessary measures to require that, where there is no intermediary or the intermediary notifies the relevant taxpayer or another intermediary of the application of a waiver under paragraph 5, the obligation to file information on a reportable cross-border arrangement lie with the other notified intermediary, or, if there is no such intermediary, with the relevant taxpayer.
54. Council Directive (EU) 2016/1164 of 12 July 2016 laying down rules against tax avoidance practices that directly affect the functioning of the internal market.
55. Article 4 ATAD 1.
56. Article 7 ATAD 1.
57. Contemplated in Article 5 ATAD 1.
58. Article 6 ATAD 1.

comfortably within State Margin of Appreciation. Transposition Rules contemplated in ATAD 1 are a typical example of the practical dangers posed by retrospective tax law.[59]

In conclusion, the authors endorse most[60] of the points raised by the European Parliament's FISC[61] Committee in its Report entitled Assessment of Recent Anti-tax Avoidance and Evasion measures (ATAD & DAC 6):

> Compliance with taxpayers' fundamental rights, as enshrined in the Charter also raise concerns. The most 'problematic' rights in this case are the fundamental rights of privacy (Article 7, Charter), the protection of personal data (Article 8, Charter), together with the right against self-incrimination ...
>
> The retroactivity of DAC 6, that is, the introduction of the look back period (reporting of cross-border arrangements if the first step of the arrangement was implemented between 25 June 2018 and 1 July 2020) raises several concerns. The first one pertains to the practical difficulties associated with the obligation to report before the directive has been implemented into national law.[62]

The complexities of ATAD 2[63] on tax avoidance involving hybrid mismatches give rise to concerns from the standpoint of the lawfulness requirement. Although the aim of the Directive is perfectly aligned with the ECHR, the complexity of the rules gives rise to concerns under the *Cantoni* principles. The general feeling, even among the experts, is that the rules are overwhelmingly complex and difficult to understand. The same concern applies equally to Proposal for a Council Directive on ensuring a global minimum level of taxation for multinational groups in the Union. The complex nature of the law has been acknowledged at the European Commission's Hybrid meeting of the Platform for good tax governance, aggressive tax planning and Double taxation held on 8 December 2021.[64] Although, based on the argument in Bley, it is highly unlikely that the ECtHR will ever strike down any ATAD 2 and Pillar Two Directive measures on the basis of the principles established in *Shchokin*[65] and *Cantoni*,[66] the severity of penalties for non-compliance should eventually factor in for the complexity of the rules. The judgment in *Krayeva*[67] is clear in this respect.

Lastly, the Proposal for a Council directive laying down rules to prevent the misuse of shell entities for tax purposes and amending Directive 2011/16/EU brings to

59. Article 11 ATAD 1.
60. Subject to the point on freedom of movement made above.
61. 'FISC was set up to assist the ECON Committee on tax-related matters and particularly the fight against tax fraud, tax evasion and tax avoidance, as well as financial transparency for taxation purposes', https://www.europarl.europa.eu/committees/en/fisc/about#: ~ :text = FISC%20wa s%20set%20up%20to,financial%20transparency%20for%20taxation%20purposes.
62. https://www.europarl.europa.eu/RegData/etudes/STUD/2022/703353/IPOL_STU(2022)7033 53_EN.pdf viewed in July 2022.
63. Council Directive (EU) 2017/952 of 29 May 2017 amending Directive (EU) 2016/1164 as regards hybrid mismatches with third countries.
64. *See* https://taxation-customs.ec.europa.eu/system/files/2022-01/211208%20Platform%20Mee ting%20Summary%20Record.pdf viewed in July 2022.
65. *Shchokin v. Ukraine*, Applications nos. 23759/03 and 37943/06.
66. *Cantoni v. France*, Application no. 17862/91.
67. *Krayeva v. Ukraine*, Application no. 72858/13.

mind the very same type of tax structures discussed in the *Yukos* cases and, in a way, the proposal creates norms that have already been stress-tested under the ECHR. Nonetheless, rules in Article 9 on the Rebuttal of the Presumption of Shell Status should incorporate more detailed 'Article 6 ECHR-type' standards governing the process to be followed in the rebuttal process. Regrettably, even this proposal may be criticised for its latent retrospectivity.

DU BIST NICHTS, DEIN VOLK IST ALLES[68]

Had the drafters of the ECHR been thoroughly familiar with the tax policies of Nazi Germany, Fascist Italy, and Stalinist Russia, they would have found more time to discuss how taxation could interfere with human rights. Recent research carried out by the European Association of Tax Law Professors[69] proves that there exists a strong link between state oppression and taxation. Similarly, recent economic research shows 'that bad tax policy was instrumental in bringing about the rise of the Nazi Party in 1933'.[70] Experience has shown that the power to tax must be carefully scrutinised, and the ECtHR should reconsider its reluctance to intervene on the tax policies of the Contracting States.

Lessons learnt from recent history seem to solicit the ECtHR to reconsider its approach towards its Margin of Appreciation doctrine, especially in times when Contracting Stares are becoming more radicalised by fiscal pressures, emergency and war.

Procedures leading to the imposition of sanctions require tight judicial controls. Diverting from the jurisprudential rule developed in *Bendenoun* would lead to situations where the imposition of tax penalties would not be subject to judicial intervention. The fact that totalitarian regimes disliked court scrutiny in administrative procedures is very telling. Speaking of the Soviet military administration in East Germany in his monograph 'The Dialectical Relationship between Taxation and the Political Balance of Power', Peter Essers made the following observation:

> Tax rules were established, interpreted and applied by the tax administration; legislative and executive powers were not separated. Legal protection against tax assessments was available through administrative channels, but not through court appeals. Tax advisers were hindered in various ways, beginning with the Steuversabotageerlass (tax evasion decree) … .[71]

---

68. You are nothing, your nation is everything.
69. Peter Essers (ed.), 'History and Taxation', EATLP International Tax Series Volume 20, IBFD 2022.
70. Linette Lopez, 1930s Germany Shows Us That Bad Tax Policy Can Magnify Washington's Worst Problem by 1,000 viewed at https://www.businessinsider.com/bad-tax-policy-led-german-radicalization-and-rise-of-the-nazi-party-2017-12 in July 2022.
71. Peter Essers, 'General Report on History and Taxation: The Dialectical Relationship Between Taxation and the Political Balance of Power', in Essers, Peter (ed.), *History and Taxation: The Dialectical Relationship Between Taxation and the Political Balance of Power*, Amsterdam, IBFD, 2022, pp. 3–38.

The ECtHR is called to ensure that history does not repeat itself. Article 6 ECHR exists to exclude sinister situations such as those described by Essers, and declaring Article 6 ECHR inapplicable is tantamount to opening doors to a totalitarian tax regime. If the ECtHR is to remain relevant in key areas, its hesitant approach to matters of tax policy should be seriously reconsidered.

Table of Cases

Church of Jesus Christ of Latter-day Saint v. the United Kingdom, no. 7552/09, 4 March 2014, 139, 141
Atev v. Bulgaria, no. 39689/05, 18 March 2014, 154-156
Glantz v. Finland, no. 37394/11, 20 May 2014, 165
Häkkä v. Finland, no. 758/11, 20 May 2014, 165
Nykänen v. Finland, no. 11828/11, 20 May 2014, 165, 166
Pirttimäki v. Finland, no. 35232/11, 20 May 2014, 165
Azienda Agricola Silverfunghi s.a.s. and Others v. Italy, nos. 48357/07, 52677/07, 52677/07, 52687/07 and 52701/07, 24 June 2014, 11, 17
Hämäläinen v. Finland (Grand Chamber), no. 37359/09, 16 July 2014, 11
Shibendra Dev v. Sweden, no. 7362/10, 21 October 2014, 165
Melo Tadeu v. Portugal, no. 27785/10, 23 October 2014, 87
Lucky Dev v. Sweden, no. 7356/10, 27 November 2014, 165
Huitson v. the United Kingdom, no. 50131/12, 13 January 2015, 6, 29, 184, 187
Arnaud and Others v. France, nos. 36918/11 and 5 others, 15 January 2015, 9, 30, 181
Rinas v. Finland, no. 17039/13, 27 January 2015, 67, 166
Robert Huitson v. the United Kingdom, no. 50131/12, 5 February 2015, 6, 29, 184, 187
Kiiveri v. Finland, no. 53753/12, 10 February 2015, 68, 165, 166
Österlund v. Finland, no. 53197/13, 10 February 2015, 68, 165, 166
Penchevi v. Bulgaria, no. 77818/12, 10 February 2015, 161
Dimitrovi v. Bulgaria, no. 12655/09, 3 March 2015, 25
Morice v. France, no. 29369/10, 23 April 2015, 82
Maurice Marcellin Marie Van Weerelt v. the Netherlands, no. 784/14, 16 June 2015, 78
Othymia Investments BV v. the Netherlands, no. 75292/10, 16 June 2015, 102, 108, 183, 188, 189
M.N. and Others v. San Marino, no. 28005/12, 7 July 2015, 102, 103, 109
Da Silva Carvalho Rico v. Portugal, no. 13341/14, 1 September 2015, 21
Brito Ferrinho Bexiga Villa-Nova v. Portugal, no. 69436/10, 1 December 2015, 102, 109
G.S.B. v. Switzerland, no. 28601/11, 22 December 2015, 109, 182
Rasul Jafarov v. Azerbaijan, no. 69981/14, 17 March 2016, 55, 149, 187
Guberina v. Croatia, no. 23682/13, 22 March 2016, 11, 145
Société Oxygène Plus v. France, no. 76959/11, 17 May 2016, 96
Arnaud and Others v. France, nos. 36918/11, 36963/11, 36969/11, 36970/11 and 36971/11, 12 July 2016, 9, 30, 181
Mamatas and Others v. Greece, nos. 63066/14 and 2 others, 21 July 2016, 21, 188
Žaja v. Croatia, no. 37462/09, 4 October 2016, 68
A and B v. Norway (Grand Chamber), nos. 24130/11 and 29758/11, 15 November 2016, 25, 166
Polimerkonteyner, TOV v. Ukraine, no. 23620/05, 24 November 2016, 25
Lindstrand Partners Advokatbyrå AB v. Sweden, no. 18700/09, 20 December 2016, 101-103, 109, 134
Maharramov v. Azerbaijan, no. 5046/07, 30 March 2017, 27
Lopac and Others v. Croatia, nos. 7834/12, 43801/13, 19327/14 and 63535/16, 26 April 2017, 15, 99
Chap Ltd v. Armenia, no. 15485/09, 4 May 2017, 68, 70

Index

E

F

G

H

I

J

L

www.ingramcontent.com/pod-product-compliance
Ingram Content Group UK Ltd.
Pitfield, Milton Keynes, MK11 3LW, UK
UKHW020811290926
15470UKWH00003B/1091

9 789403 518961